# OUR RUNAWAY SOCIETY

## HOW TO RESTORE BALANCE IN LIFE

## THE RESCUE OF CORE VALUES AND THE POWER OF POSITIVE CHANGE

Author:
Rafael Augusto Carreras

Copyright © May 16, 2016 - 1130706
by Carreras Interiors Ltd. / Rafael Augusto Carreras
Canadian Intellectual Property Office – An Agency of Industry
Canada – http://cipo.gc.ca
Office de la propriété intellectuelle du Canada – Un organism
d'industrie Canada – http://opic.gc.ca

1$^{st}$ Edition – June 2017 / Revised March 2018
Editorial: Dr. John McAllister
Cover Design & Illustration: Kristian Lehner
Author Photo: Cornelia Bujara

Issued in print, electronic and digital formats.
Paperback:  ISBN  978-0-9952562-2-4
Hard Cover:  ISBN  978-0-9951739-9-6


For reference visit:  http://www.collectionscanada.gc.ca/ciss-ssci/app/index.php?lang=eng

Publisher:
Carreras, Rafael Augusto. "Our Runaway Society". Self-Published via Createspace, Charleston, 2018
www.createspace.com

Printed and bound in the United States
First printing: June 2017
10 9 8 7 6 5 4 3 2 1

# IMPORTANT MESSAGE

An Algerian theologian and philosopher of the 4th century, Augustine of Hippo (known as Saint Augustine), once wrote:

"Men go abroad to wonder at the height of the mountains, at the huge waves of the sea, at the long courses of the rivers, at the vast compasses of the ocean, at the circular motion of the stars, and they pass by themselves without wondering."

# THE RUNAWAY TRILOGY

## Our Runaway Society

## Our Runaway Globe

## Our Runaway Rights

===========================================

# TABLE OF CONTENTS

## DEDICATIONS

Happiness is difficult to achieve and even more complex to retain. It is said that real happiness is in the enjoyment, not in the having. Regardless, it is a fact that the less we need and the more we give, the happier we tend to be. Since true happiness is in the quality of our thoughts, I tried my best to write this book with sincere thoughts and the finest intentions at heart. I dedicate this to my family and to three very distinct groups of people outside the boundaries of family and friends.

## To My Family

~To my wife Cornelia. She is an extraordinary woman, and I am very lucky that destiny made her cross my path. Cornelia has always made me feel and be a better person by her side. We first met 24 years ago and we fell in love immediately. We have been lucky to share, ever since, our first sip of coffee of the day, the first morning sunshine, and our best moments for all these years. My wish is to grow old and healthy along with Cornelia. I deeply value Cornelia's love, understanding, sweetness, and kindness – the qualities that define Cornelia as the wonderful human being she is – by my side!

~To my daughter Tania, who has always been in my heart since I first laid eyes on her and who has given me the strength and initial motivation to write this book. She is intelligent and a quick thinker. Today, she is a woman of strong convictions and spirit, but at the same time, she is fragile like the wings of a sweet, colorful, beautiful dragonfly. I hope this book guides her to enjoy a more balanced, stable, and happy future, which she deserves! I also want to reiterate that I will always be there for her.... always!

~To my son Erick, who has been a real fighter in his relentless need for self-improvement and who has challenged life head-on since the day he was born with a ventricular septal defect, which he defeated through an amazing will for survival, strength, tenacity, and relentless balance in his daily activities, studies, meal selection, and overall healthy style of living.

I have full confidence he will grow to be a productive man in our society. In fact, at 24 years of age, he has already started. I am very proud of him. At his young age, he stands out for being observant, intuitive, empathetic, and intelligent. He is kind and has a big heart. He is also an excellent, motivated, and creative writer.

~To my mom, dad, and brothers who, as a team, taught me the sense of self-esteem, responsibility, hard work, commitment, integrity, tenacity, ethics, and, above all, respect and honesty to myself, to others, and to all my surroundings. This includes not just my local community but our overall environment as well.

## To Two Groups of People:

I. To those people afraid of living life to its fullest, afraid of living in harmony with their surroundings and at peace with themselves. To those people who lack self-esteem, who lack a sense of belonging, who are lost within their own confusion, loneliness, or darkness. To those who live in two or more dimensions or in the confines of their own limited boundaries and are afraid to step beyond into a loving and real, down-to-earth life.

To those people that lack self-esteem, self-control, and self-respect, or an exaggerated self-esteem and cocky or ignorant attitude. I consider all the above a capital sin that compounds an unfit world filled with disrespect, arrogance, and selfishness. An aggrandized and inflated self-esteem can transcend the barriers of logic, common sense, ethics, and decency. It can be an absolute aberration and a contradiction to seeking a stable and healthy self-esteem, self-control, and self-respect in the search for happiness. Yes, unfortunately some people cannot get over themselves or control themselves; this alone will bring them frustration and unhappiness with time.

2. To those people who have tried and stumbled but are eager to try and live again. To those willing to dare once more, refocus, change their attitudes and energy towards improving their present for a better future. To those individuals who, regardless of past negative experiences, are willing and eager to challenge destiny once more and hopefully take off without fear, willing to fly to higher altitudes of self-esteem, self-composure, and self-respect in their relentless pursuit of self-improvement, excellence, and, above all, happiness!

We all need to keep in mind that in life it is not a matter of whether you fall or not; it is a matter of how, when, and with what attitude you get up and try again! The comeback attitude is what really counts, not whether you have failed at any given moment.

For examples of this group of people, refer to **Appendix 3**.

## Special Appreciations to three individuals:

1st In memory of my first editor, Dona Sturmanis, who did the initial edition with enthusiasm and good will.

Life works in mysterious ways. I would have never imagined her last edited work would be my first published book.

Unfortunately, Dona passed away on the night of March 7, 2016, the night after she finished the first edit of this book and sent it to me for my review. Refer to her last message regarding this book, quoted below.

==============
*On Mar 6, 2016, at 6:52 PM, Dona Sturmanis <donasturmanis@yahoo.com> wrote:*
*Please see attached book #1 that I have edited after your edits. Look it over one last time, send it back and I will format it for CreateSpace.*
*Dona*

*Dona Sturmanis*
*WRITER+EDITOR+PRESENTER*
*778.214.6318*
*donasturmanis@yahoo.com*
*Impeccable with words.*
==============
The Kelowna Daily Courier published the following:

"Kelowna writer Dona Sturmanis dies after long battle with cancer ". Posted: Wednesday, March 9, 2016

**2<sup>nd</sup>** To Dr. John McAllister who kindly took on and finished what was earlier started by Dona Sturmanis in this first book. He is punctual, detail-oriented, and a professional editor with always a positive approach.

**3<sup>rd</sup>** To the design artist, Mr. Kristian Lehner, who, at his young age, came up with an attractive and intriguing cover design after just having a brief conversation with him of what I specifically had in my mind and wanted to achieve with the cover. He provided his own artistic design with great creativity after the exact description of my vision. I wish him a long and successful artistic career.

# PREAMBLE

## Peace and Happiness

Every human being has the right to enjoy peace of mind and be happy. But what are peace and happiness?

There are literally hundreds of definitions of peace and happiness. To my mind, they all depict the states of satisfaction, joy, contentment, prosperity, optimism, and serenity that any individual can attain. Happiness itself is a combination of euphoria and overall good feelings blended with positive and satisfying emotions, exhilaration, great pride, and valuable appreciation for oneself and one's personal achievements within one's surroundings. The senses of freedom and gratitude contribute to a deeper degree of happiness, offering a sense of joy, jubilation, peace of mind, and an exceptional and delightful existence. Put simply, peace and happiness are sensations of well-being in yourself and with your surroundings.

Through research and my own personal experience, I can confirm that most individuals who value money and capital assets are less likely to be content and fulfilled with their success and achievements than those who value other goals in life. Years will go by, and when they turn their heads, look back and really evaluate their life footprints, comfortably set in the midst of their financial success, many will doubt the choices they made to get to where they are and regret the cost they paid to get there. If given a second chance, will they take the same pathway again? Twenty-nine out of thirty-five successful acquaintances I asked answered with a strong and convincing "No."

Personally, I would change many decisions that I thought at the time were the right ones, valuing success and achievements, but not realizing the excessive cost I was going to pay for them in the future. When I die, I am leaving all that financial success and material abundance behind. Sadly, I am also leaving this world with some memories I do not really feel proud of. I am also missing the good memories I never made because of working too hard. I would definitely choose differently. I do not understand and vehemently reject the desire some people have of trying to be the richest skeletons in the cemetery, but they now have to live with this with whatever life they have left.

The pursuit of peace and happiness is a real challenge that, throughout human history, everybody strives to attain. However, very few, if any, have been able to achieve long-lasting happiness before their last breath on earth. Achieving peace and happiness depends on your own expectations, interpretations, goals, surroundings, and, above all, your values and attitude. Regrettably, peace and happiness for some people (or cultures) are totally beyond their control. Their surroundings absorb them fully and can restrict them almost as strongly and as far as their own extinction. In these situations, there is almost nothing they can do about it! Their possibilities for peace and happiness are extremely limited. For example, it is profoundly different to have been born in Switzerland vs. Bangladesh, or North Korea vs. South Korea, or Malawi vs. Brazil.

They say that peace and happiness are a choice! Are they

really? Are they a choice for everyone? I highly doubt it, but hey, there is a lot you can try to do to get close to peace and happiness and even perhaps attain them. No doubt in my mind! Some say that happiness cannot be achieved! American author Alan Lightman once wrote, "The tragedy of this world is that no one is happy, whether stuck in a time of pain or joy." I partly agree with him, if we evaluate people's lives over time, over their short existence here on earth. But I also disagree, because part of me believes that happiness comes and goes many times throughout people's lives. There are always ups and downs, so it is impossible to try and achieve peace and happiness all the time.

The real challenge is to achieve peace and happiness and retain them as long as possible and, when derailed, get back on track again as best and fast as you can. Yes, when circumstances change, the degree or the existence of peace and happiness may vary or even disappear. If that happens, we need to stand up straight and strive to achieve that degree of peace and happiness we were comfortable with again and again, and even try to go beyond and improve it, if possible.

My absolute conviction is that all human beings deserve to have peace and happiness, and that it is usually within their means to achieve. All should try to live in harmony with their surroundings, and above all, strive to achieve a safe level of self-esteem, respect for oneself, and self-discipline and control, which will ultimately assist in attaining peace and happiness. If this is not successfully achieved, how can we then live in harmony with our surroundings, and how can we respect others? If we fail in these matters, everything will unfortunately crumble.

## Immigration to Canada

I immigrated to Canada from a beautiful country called Mexico. I graduated from the Universidad Iberoamericana (a private university) in economics and then went to study for my master's degree in the United States and England. I obtained the degree of Master of Business Administration (MBA). This was a combined MBA program between Notre Dame University (South Bend, Indiana) and London Graduate School of Business (London, Great Britain). When finished, I went back to Mexico and worked in corporate banking in the Mexican banking system for a few years. I worked on several syndicate loans between banks from Mexico, Canada, and the United States. A few years later, I was offered a position as the administrative director of a state-owned organization called Pronósticos para la Asistencia Pública. I worked there for about two years before being accepted and coming to Canada as an immigrant under the Independent Category (based on educational and professional background, point scale, language abilities, clean criminal record, good health, and potential to succeed).

At the time, Mexico had suffered a very strong monetary devaluation, and all the savings of an average person (including mine) had disappeared overnight into the pockets of "others." With corruption rampant, the economy was unstable. At the time, the levels of traffic and air pollution were off the charts in Mexico City, where I was born and brought up.

I was in the early stages of my professional career and made a decision to look for better opportunities for my future family and myself. With pain in my heart and deep sadness, I left my native country and came to Canada with high dreams and expectations. After an initial exploratory trip to the city of

Calgary (Alberta) in the middle of winter (February, 1987), I decided to start my new life in Vancouver instead. Why?

I only lasted three days in Calgary, because one morning, while walking towards a Rotarian meeting at 7:30 am, still wearing my Mexican shoes, I experienced in my right toe one of the worst cramps I have ever had. With the wind factor that morning, the temperature had dropped to -41 degrees Celsius. It did not matter how physically fit I was at the time and that I had never experienced a cramp in my life. At that moment, I had to limp to the closest building to protect myself from the wind and cold, because I thought the cramp was forcing the toe to pierce my shoe. I sat down on the floor of the lobby of the closest building and started rubbing my foot, waiting for the cramp to ease off and the pain to disappear. While I was doing that, I realized that I only had "cactus juice" in my blood at the time, so I ventured to Vancouver, where winters are more benign and where I ultimately got established. I never looked back.

When I arrived in Canada and got established in Vancouver with my devalued pesos, and after exchanging them into Canadian dollars, I had barely enough to survive for three to four months at the cost of living at the time in a beautiful city like Vancouver. From 12.50 pesos per one USD, the peso had fallen to 75 per one USD after several consecutive devaluations. This had a strong impact on any other foreign currency when you sold your devalued pesos, with a corresponding proportionate impact in relation to the Canadian dollar.

What were the main attractions for me in this unique country known worldwide as the Big White North?

- Beautiful cities with modern buildings and wonderful, friendly people.
- An environmentally oriented country.
- Lower tax rates than other countries.
- An impeccable and envious international reputation.
- The use of two official languages.
- People's respect and admiration for their flag as well as their national anthem (...oh yes, and for hockey, football and baseball!).
- The maple leaf, regarded as a symbol of peace, trust, friendship, and harmonious international relationships.
- The neutral political ground where Canada was positioned in the international arena.
- A stronger economy with more capital-intensive industries per capita compared to other countries.
- Open doors to immigration on an equal and fair basis.
- A highly-educated workforce.
- Strong financial stability.
- Low or almost nonexistent levels of corruption.
- The magnificent international reputation of the Royal Canadian Mounted Police (RCMP).
- A diversified economy with vast natural resources across our huge country.

In summary, Canada was one of the three best countries in the world to live in at the time. However, many of the previous positive aspects that attracted me to come to Canada have been, if not disappearing, diminishing steadily in the past 29 years, a process now accentuated under Prime Minister Justin Trudeau.

As an immigrant and citizen of Canada, I have a responsibility to raise my concerns in a positive way, which I will try to achieve with this book, and two more to come in the Runaway Trilogy (Our Runaway Society, Our Runaway Globe, and Our Runaway Rights).

Among a few factors that make me uncomfortable as a Canadian citizen and that have motivated me to write this book are the following nineteen (19) points:

- The overall level of political corruption has risen beyond acceptable levels.

- Our economy has not diversified at the rate it should have for an "industrialized country".

- The growth of the country is still heavily focused on the exploitation of natural resources.

- The abuse and misuse of our natural resources is taking place, in many instances, with absolute disregard for our environment.

- Qualified immigrant workers struggle to find good opportunities because of local barriers in each province (especially in BC), resulting in overprotection of many careers and industries, while promoting the inefficient and the lazy.

- A less diversified economy has caused growth potential to slow down while other countries are getting stronger.

- Canada is among the three worst contributors of carbon dioxide, which is harming the ozone layer, and practically nothing has been done to date despite our commitments to the international community and our global needs.

- Our international competitiveness has decelerated and is being surpassed by countries such as China, India, Brazil, and many others. Canada is screaming for industrial diversification and expansion. As a capital-intensive country, we have the ability, the knowledge, and the economic means to do this. Our attitude of apathy and conformity needs changing to a more dynamic, progressive, and entrepreneurial spirit and attitude.

- Income inequality has increased. Government should pay more attention to this and implement proper policies to avoid noticeable inequalities.

- Municipal waste per capita in this country is among the three highest in the world.

- The average Canadian takes things for granted, such as uninterrupted electricity, easy access to food in supermarkets, our beautiful natural environment, our medical system, our liberty and our right to free speech, our right to public service, and many more social benefits. Encouraging Canadians to travel abroad will open their eyes and understanding as to how much better we have it here in Canada. This will help them not take things for granted while appreciating and cherishing what we have.

- The reputation of the Royal Canadian Mounted Police (RCMP) is still highly regarded by the average

Canadian, but it is definitely not what it used to be. Many officers have used excessive force and abusive attitude in situations where they should not have, and have gotten away with it. Proper investigations by police and third parties should immediately be performed to evaluate each incident in question and not take so long to reach a decision to desensitize the public who never really forgets.

The RCMP has such a strong and sometimes uncontrollable feeling of power that, in 2013, Officer James Forcillo shot an 18-year old nine times in a streetcar. The young man, Sammy Yatim, was holding a knife but was alone and scared inside the streetcar and was not an imminent threat. He was surrounded by at least 10 or more armed RCMP officers, all of whom were at a safe distance of at least 30 feet away from him. It was not until three years later that Mr. Forcillo was found guilty of attempted murder.

Having said the above, I strongly believe the great majority of RCMP officers across Canada are people of integrity, trustful, devoted to their responsibilities, and totally dedicated to their work with efficiency and pride. There are always one or two rotten apples in every tree, and that is understandable and undeniable.

• The levels of courtesy, friendliness, and respect are not what they used to be. More emphasis should be given to these in the schooling system, and parents should be encouraged to practice them at home.

- The international reputation of Canadians as peacekeepers has disappeared. Many countries consider Canadians the new enemies. Our international reputation has drastically changed, but not for the better. We have been sucked into wars by the US and Great Britain that we would have never been involved in, if it were not for our strong political ties with these two countries. In my opinion, we should respect the Commonwealth for now, but aim towards an independent Canada for the well-being of future generations. This will provide us with more independent decision-making and the willpower to act according to our best interests, instead of following other countries' leads. Fortunately, since PM Trudeau took power, Canada has been labelled "a progressive country" where multiculturalism is strong and diversity and inclusion might bring a stronger future. As of January, of 2018, the open-door policy for new immigrants, asylum seekers and refugees, is still strong. This is being acknowledged around the world. European countries see this with skepticism, while developing countries applaud it. Our differences will make us stronger (says PM Trudeau), but it can certainly hurt a country if mismanaged. Time will tell!

- Many provinces have monopolies that restrict free trade and competition. For example, in British Columbia, we have only one insurance company for automobiles – ICBC (Insurance Company of British Columbia). No competition has been allowed in for the past twenty-nine years. Is this a free and fair competitive market like the one we are supposed to live in? This needs to change to allow a free competitive market, which will ultimately increase the quality of services and ensure fair and reasonable costs for the end user.

- We have too many over-privileged, overrated, and overprotected professional services that are essential for average citizens but cost them an arm and a leg. A good example is the dental industry in Canada, where the average cost of a crown is about 1,200 CAD, when its equivalent in Mexico, for example, is about 400 CAD, with the same or better quality of work and service. The average cost of an implant in Canada is about 4,200 CAD compared to about 1,400 CAD in other countries, again for the same or better quality of work, service, and warranty.

- The concept of responsibility and accountability is running thin in Canada, and getting thinner as the years go by due to loopholes in the system, weak laws, dicey politicians, immoral defense lawyers and judges who fail to apply the fair hand of the law against the obvious perpetrators, leaving the victims living in despair for the rest of their lives. Obviously, I am not saying all are like that. It is the minority but the number is without a doubt, continuously on the rise.

- Our manufacturing capacity has not been developed, as it should have been. We mainly export natural resources that we later import as finished products. This has a negative impact on gross national product, causes inflation, and inhibits future growth.

I want to provide just a few quick examples of points eighteen and nineteen just listed so that the reader can start understanding my frustration, and therefore, part of my motivation in writing this first book of The Runaway Trilogy.

## Example 1

Paul Russell from The National Post wrote on Mar 22, 2012: "A slap on the wrist for a rapist and a coward". Graham James raped two boys, likely over 100 times and got a sentence of only 24 months in prison. The two-year sentence will never compensate for the suffering and trauma these two boys experienced, who will endure the pain and resentment for the rest of their lives.

Graeme Hamilton from The National Post reported on June 22, 2016 that Christine Mequish is "among the most dangerous women in the country, a convicted killer with a record that includes 25 violent crimes since 1984." She has been acknowledged publicly as a dangerous offender and the Quebec Court Judge David Bouchard, gave her a sentence of two years and three months in addition to time served. The reason for the light sentence is blamed on the fact that she is an aboriginal and a member of the Atikamekw First Nation. Many believe that a non-aboriginal would have most likely received life in prison.

On March 30, 2017, Farrah Merali of CBC News posted that Samuel Alec had a blood alcohol level almost three times over the legal limit several hours after the car accident he caused while driving. He instantly killed three innocent people in the car crash. He was heavily intoxicated and therefore, impaired to drive.  He was sentenced to only eight years and four months in prison. His defense team was pushing for only four years behind bars. Alec truly felt sorry and apologized to the victim's families and the court system, but the community found the sentence extremely lenient with only two years and eight months per each life he took using his car as a weapon.

On Feb 04, 2003, CBC News Canada wrote: "Bahadur Singh Bhalru from 23, and Sukhvir Singh Khosa, 20, were handed conditional sentences of two years to be served at home, so they can continue to work and go to school". They killed a pedestrian in the streets of Vancouver while racing their cars for fun and challenge. In this case, the victim and his family seemed to have been deprived of justice and considered irrelevant, while apparently "praising" the perpetrators.

Judges turn their back on appropriate punishment in relation to the severity and seriousness of the crime. The Canadian justice system itself, seems to let it go with ease and with a serious lack of consideration and responsibility to its law-abiding citizens. The above brief examples were randomly selected over time to show how the legal system has not been modified and seems far from changing.

Example 2

This is in relation to the eternal battle of the Canada-U.S. softwood lumber dispute. Since President Donald Trump got into power, there has been a continued threat to our softwood trade from the United States. Unfortunately, BC Premier Christy Clark, is fighting "tête-à-téte" against President Trump instead of taking advantage of this golden opportunity to promote in Canada, with tax incentives to private companies, the opportunity to diversify the economy and create new jobs. This would help the Canadian economy to be less dependent on the United States. Instead, Ms. Clark decided to strike back, and in my view, fomenting an unproductive trade-war. Justine Hunter, from The Globe and Mail (April 29, 2017), wrote: "Former international trade minister David Emerson, who was appointed in February to represent the province in Washington, said in an interview he was not consulted on Ms. Clark's bid to block shipments of thermal coal in a tit-for-tat measure in response to the new punitive softwood lumber tariffs imposed on Canada's softwood exports to the United

States. "Ms. Clark vowed at the time to act unilaterally if Ottawa did not agree", says Hunter.

In my mind, this shows the narrow and obtuse retaliation attitude against Goliath, who can crush our economy (not just in BC) if so desired. Politicians in Canada seem not to fully understand that the less dependent we are and the more we diversify, the stronger we get. Yes, with a more industrially diversified country in every industry and the less dependent we are in exploiting our natural resources, Canada will compete better and get stronger. This will end up creating more jobs for locals and for the increasing immigrant population.

Unfortunately, there are economic ties "under-the-table" too strong for some politician to circumvent. But they need to start somewhere, and in the last thirty years, they have done close to nothing. Our 34 per cent share of the softwood lumber in the United States is known to be high and unsustainable. The Trump administration is still trying to bring it down to 22 per cent, says Hunter. We have been debating this since the Obama administration, and to date, we have not picked up the potential 12 per cent loss of trade with alternative new foreign markets or by diversifying our manufacturing industries increasing our own internal demand for our own softwood lumber. After the Second World War, Japan was destroyed and in 40 years they re-built their economy by diversifying their industries while importing more natural resources from many parts of the world. The same thing happened to Germany, and for many years now, Germany's economy has held the European Union tightly together.

Why can't we do the same as a country sitting on some of the most bounteous natural resources on planet Earth?

It is very important that readers understand and open their

minds to a wider vision to acknowledge that we are no longer the Canada we used to be. If we all do not try in our own way to do something positive and constructive about this, we are going to steadily lose the things we have treasured and that have made us proud of our country. We need to voice our thoughts peacefully and positively regarding our freedom, social security, civic conduct, and our country's potential for a stable future and consistent economic growth. Regrettably, similar things are happening in the United States.

Readers might advise me to go back to where I came from if I am not happy here. Guess what? I am not just happy but delighted I am here. I love this country more than many of the people who had the good fortune to be born here, but who are incapable of comparing and realizing that we are losing our competitive edge along with the strength and international image we used to have. Unfortunately, the majority take things for granted. But where I come from – and after all that I have seen in my trips around the world – I will never take things for granted. That would be a sin.

It is very well known that many Americans have been using our flag when traveling in countries where they are not well thought of or accepted. Unfortunately, nowadays Canadians are not always welcome in countries like Iraq, Afghanistan, Syria, and others. That makes me worry and even sad, because I now have more maple syrup in my blood stream than cactus juice—the reason I raise my voice in defence of this great nation of ours. And yes, the percentage of cactus juice that I still have (and always will) continues to crystalize in cold winter weather, but I love it.

Canada is where I have lived for the past 30 years. Here is

where I have been self-employed since I arrived, where my children were born and raised, where I met my lovely wife, where my friends live, where I have developed my professional career while working hard, creating business opportunities, diversifying business activities, contributing to the creation of new job opportunities, manufacturing new product lines, providing a variety of business services, subcontracting companies, importing new products to Canada, paying taxes, and, overall, making my contribution to the economic growth of this wonderful and magnificent country.

## Laissez Faire, Laissez passer vs. Freedom of Choice

In my understanding, the concept of "laissez faire, laissez passer," besides just being passive, is the idea of leaving economic activity and development to market forces acting freely without any control from government policies. The forces of the market run free without the guidance and intrusion of government restrictions or controls. This attitude can be extremely risky (e.g. the repercussions of the 2008 financial crisis in the United States), but taking action according to our personal needs and preferences can go a long way in our favour. To take advantage of our freedom of choice is extremely valuable and beneficial.

The same phenomenon is happening with the traditional social values that are not being followed and respected by new generations of immigrants and some North American citizens themselves (Canada, United States and Mexico). Nowadays, the attitude that "anything goes" prevails in our societies, but guess what—this is wrong and needs fixing through proper social guidance or self-restraint!

I still have my Mexican citizenship, but as an immigrant to Canada 30 years ago and as a Canadian citizen for 27 years, I have experienced social and economic events in a more down-to-earth, deeper, and clearer manner than the average North American by far. I have had the valuable opportunity to work in other countries around the world, with people of totally different backgrounds, ways of thinking, ways of conducting business, and with traditions utterly different from those of the average Canadian, US citizen, or Mexican. Throughout the years, this has thoroughly enriched my own background, understanding, perspective, overall schooling, and general culture, which in conjunction with my unique upbringing, traditions, educational background, and continued research in social, economic, and environmental matters, has allowed me to understand and master areas misunderstood or neglected by the average North American.

Because of my direct personal and professional experience in several foreign countries, and my life efforts to stay current with worldwide news, I have definitely earned the right, parallel to my duties and responsibilities as a Canadian and Mexican citizen, to do my best to bring to the attention of all people living in North America (immigrants, asylum seekers, refugees, or native to the land) that we need to do something to improve our daily lives and ways of doing things to keep Canada, the United States, and Mexico as top examples for other countries to follow and admire.

Freedom of choice allows us an infinite array of alternatives to select from. For example, there is the freedom of choosing where we want to live, who we want to live with, who we want to surround ourselves with, the freedom of our own religion (or lack thereof), our own thoughts, and our own dreams. We, and only we, choose the group or subgroup we want to belong to. However, what is good for my group and me may not be good for other individuals or groups, and vice versa. We have to acknowledge and respect that.

We require accepting others the way they are, but we need to strive, work hard, and even sometimes make sacrifices to maintain the minimum standards of a civilized nation with social rules and regulations that should be applied to, and followed by, everybody in our society, regardless of the group, subgroup, or religion they choose to affiliate with. This does not impact people's rights to be themselves and to be different. Let us be very clear. I am not talking about a totalitarian and oppressive society. I am talking about basic respect. If you decide you want purple and green hair, go for it. If you decide to have a bull's ring hanging on your nose, then go for it. But if you are covered with lice that can infest others, you should be stopped; you should respect others' health and well-being. If you decide to put your feet on a coffee table in public (e.g. at Starbucks), then, again, you should be stopped. People need to respect others' rights as well and not just do whatever they please. Respect for others should not affect anyone's ability to be creative, dynamic, original, or unusual.

If, within these three strong North American nations, there are groups of people who are not following minimum civic standards, then it is our obligation, duty, right, and responsibility to do something about this in a peaceful and intelligent, but decisive, manner. Otherwise, we are betraying the same principles our ancestors worked hard for, fought for, and, in some cases, even gave their lives for. It is very easy to remain quiet and passive, while sitting down watching TV or stuck at the computer screen, but it takes guts, strong will, determination, and a big heart to speak our minds and thoughts out loud and try to do something. We cannot hide and live quietly and cowardly when it is within our reach to make an effort and do something. It is our choice, so let us choose the right thing to do. Otherwise, our problems are just going to get completely out of control.

My grandfather used to tell me, "Rafael, remember always that by realizing something is wrong and remaining passive and quiet, you are being more of an aggressor than the perpetrators themselves. Instead, arm yourself with courage and do something about it." As the years went by and I grew to understand things better, I realized he was telling me to avoid being "passive-aggressive."

We owe what we have and who we are to all those that built this great nation, so let's kick into gear and do something to keep it afloat in good standing and with a decent and fine international reputation. Do it for yourself, for your children and for your children's children.

The above is of extreme importance if we want to live in a healthy, peaceful, and happy society. Remember, we are all searching desperately (consciously or unconsciously) for peace and happiness. Respect for minimum civic standards and guidelines of education are fundamental to achieve peace, pleasure, and happiness, whether people want to abide by them or not, and will help provide a stable foundation for societies to expand and flourish. Just as a house needs a concrete foundation to withstand time, any group of people needs minimum behavioral and civic guidelines to keep peace and harmony within themselves. Complex, modern societies like ours need them even more. We all need to follow a specific set of civic virtues accepted and imposed by the society we live in, period!

This is extremely important in countries like Canada, where the Liberal party and PM Trudeau have launched an open-door policy to increase the number of immigration by over 350,000 per year from of 2018 to 2020. We also need to add the refugees and asylum seekers accepted by Canada. All these people tend to have different background and many, quite different civic virtues or values, which need to be taken into consideration by the Canadian government during their hopefully, smooth integration process.

## Civic Virtue

According to Merriam-Webster, civic virtue is "a morally good behaviors or character, a good and moral quality. It is the standard of righteous behavior in relationship to a citizen's involvement in society."

To my mind, civic virtue is all those accumulated habits that have been cultivated and acknowledged as important for the proper interaction of people within a civilized community or society. It is the behavioral attitude among people that conforms to the principles and specific laws of a society.

Another interesting approach to the concept of civic virtue is found in Encyclopedia Britannica:

> Civic virtues, in political philosophy, [are] personal qualities associated with the effective functioning of the civil and political order, or the preservation of its values

and principles. Attempts to define civic virtue vary, as different political systems organize public life around alternative visions of the public good and the demands of citizens commensurate with this good. Understanding civic virtue has become increasingly urgent as scholars seek to identify the causes of declining levels of civic engagement and the virtues that will reverse this trend.

Most discussions of civic virtue center on the obligation of citizens to participate in society by performing the minimally necessary activities in support of the society and state, such as paying taxes. Political theorists agree that the total sum of a person's well-being is not solely attributable to his or her own talents, but is a product of social cooperation, or civic virtue. People generally do not feel motivated to get involved in their communities. There are various reasons for this, but I believe the fundamental one is that they think they cannot make a difference; they are just one person, one lonely voice. Well, they are wrong. One single voice can move mountains, if determined and persistent.

Peaceful, happier, and healthier societies seem to be those where civic virtue is clearly defined and followed willingly by its members. However, every person and every society achieves happiness differently. Each individual, on a personal basis, living even within the same community, seeks peace and happiness in a different way and to a different level or depth. We all have our own tastes and preferences. We all have our own levels of comfort or, for that matter, our own levels of discomfort. It is our choice to make and nobody else's.

Some examples of happy and peaceful communities are those that make an effort to:

- Decrease their crime rates.
- Reduce graffiti and general vandalism.
- Repair potholes and broken sidewalks.
- Provide more greenery and parks.
- Clean their backyards, back alleys, and back lanes.
- Encourage more open and friendly communication.
- Strive for less pollution and overall environmental Contamination.
- Foster more citizen engagement and pride.
- Discourage apathy and disrespectful attitudes.
- Encourage greater awareness of what is happening in their community.

In the Journal of Public Deliberation (Volume 7, Issue 1, Article 9, 2011), Chris Barker and Brian Martin write about "Participation: The Happiness Connection":

> Participation in decision-making has the potential to contribute to greater happiness. To explore this connection, we examine three areas: the family, the workplace and politics. In each of these areas, happiness research suggests that greater participation should increase happiness, most directly through the channels of personal relationships and helping others. There is some empirical research suggesting that participation contributes to happiness. It is useful to consider the connections between the three areas. In particular, examination of participation-happiness, connections within families and workplaces can provide some insights for promoting a stronger connection at the level of politics.

My own research confirms this. The more conscientiously

people practice their civic virtues, the closer they are knitted or bound together, resulting in fewer confrontations, healthier relationships, more respect between each other, and better harmony among their members. These are the things that will bring more peace, pleasure and happiness into any society.

What is interesting in this world is that we all tend to have different conditions and perceptions of our surroundings and therefore of the best methods of achieving the degree of well-being which we would interpret as being peaceful and happy. Not everybody can agree or will agree with this book's approach or its efforts to help people achieve peace and happiness. Why? Precisely because of the above. We are all different, and we will achieve success, peace, and happiness differently and at dissimilar levels within our own perceptions, needs, and preferences.

However, there is a spectrum of characteristics that every human being has and that makes each person unique. Among the most relevant are people's capacity to reason, their levels of logic and intelligence, along with their ability to apply common sense and emotional maturity.

# INTRODUCTION

As human beings, we all have different strengths and weaknesses and distinctive thoughts and actions. We have divergent feelings, goals, understandings, and behaviors.

We all have very different ways of being as individuals and absolutely dissimilar ways of adapting comfortably while trying to be happy in our specific surroundings. We all see and interpret things distinctively based on our personal views, surroundings, circumstances, perspectives, thoughts, feelings, reasoning, and overall experiences. It is a very complex process.

At the same time, we all possess a combination of positive traits and negative traits. In this book, I will focus on both ends of this bell curve: that is, on positive human traits and on negative ones.

## Who Is Wrong and Who Is Right?

There is never a simple answer. In fact, there is no correct or wrong answer either, because everything depends on who we are, where we live, what it is that we do, our own personalities and ways of being, our attitudes, our specific surroundings, our limitations, and our overall needs in any given space and time. It also depends on whether you see the world through rose-tinted glasses or not.

Does this leave the door open to the possibility that everybody could be right? That political correctness applies to everything? That anything goes in this day and age, regardless of what others might think? That we have the right to do as we please? Absolutely not!

As social beings, we all need to follow certain minimum civic virtues, standards, and values. However, many seem to be neglected nowadays, and this situation is getting worse as time goes by. We will go into more detail on the civic virtues and values later in this book. The subject is important to bring to the table and try to do something about it.

My goal is to write three consecutive books to enlighten the perspectives and points of view of others in their efforts to improve themselves, their communities, and our environment. While teaming up with others, we can all do something about our surroundings and our environment, but only if we choose the actions (or reactions) appropriate to our specific situation and to our vision of where we see ourselves five, ten, or twenty years from now. We need to seed today to reap the benefits in the future, but only we ourselves can do this.

Nobody is going to do it for us. We are not alone in this world, but in the matter of survival and self-improvement, we are pretty much dependent on our own dreams, vision, efforts, and sacrifices. My main reasons for writing this first book are summarized in the following sections.

## Bleak future for North America's stability

The future of Canada as a nation does not look as healthy, strong, and promising as it did when I first immigrated to this great country on September 1, 1987. For example, the younger generations want to have more fun with less work and are focused on immediate enjoyment as their main goal.

That worries me, and I believe some things need to change.

Many people do not care anymore what others think about them. Self-respect, self-control, and self-esteem have been declining at alarming rates. In general, the sloppy dress code, the loud and uneducated expressions (on and off cellular phones), the rude and vulgar behaviors in public, and excessive self-indulgence leading to obesity are rampant. To the great majority of the population, even the excess tattooing is also questionable. But we dare not say anything, because it is the "right" of people who practice these apparently bad habits to do as they wish, regardless of whether they invade somebody else's private space and dampen our well-being, our peace, and our own rights to a better quality, peaceful, educated, dignified, and proud life. The same things are happening in the US, Mexico, and many other parts of the world. We are not alone. But I am now Canadian-Mexican, and that is the reason I care about Canada first.

Canada, the United States, and Mexico have their separate problems and issues. They are quite different from each other, but they also follow and fight for the same values and goals as independent nations.

In Mexico, it is imperative to consider the problem of open corruption at all levels and the detrimental role of the drug cartels, street assaults, murders, and kidnapping, which are damaging and terrorizing the country.  Unfortunately, the cartels are doing a very lucrative business, thanks to the demand for drugs in the US and Canada. In the United States, we also need to acknowledge the big financial scams carried out by financial institutions in the past to the detriment of their own people, when hundreds of thousands across the country lost their savings and their homes in economic crises such as the one that took place in 2008.

The United States is known to send soldiers to war who do not even know the war's real purpose. The US and its allies always seem to have economic interests beyond and above the protection of the liberty and rights of the people whose country they sometimes invade. They also invade countries under the banner of antiterrorism in search of "weapons of mass destruction." Look at Iraq's invasion by George W. Bush, where he found nothing, but left behind thousands of dead US soldiers, and many more innocent civilians killed as a result of "friendly fire," or "mistakes," or "military duty."

In regard to the above, a friend of mine once asked me: "Why don't the concepts of war crimes and mass murder apply to George W. Bush?" This is a very good question for which, to date, I still do not have a clear answer.

These three countries constitute what is known as North America, and I worry about them. Canada, the United States, and Mexico, the "Three Amigos," really need to help each other and play their cards better against the European, Asian, Southeast Asian, and South American market blocks. Unfortunately, as of February of 2018, the Trump administration keeps threatening the dissolution of the Free Trade Agreement between these three countries.

Regardless, urgently need to rescue principles such as self-esteem, self-control, and self-respect, along with respect for others. We need to start taking more responsibility for our actions, restore minimum levels of civic virtues, and improve our values and principles. We are in urgent need of acknowledging that all our natural resources are limited and that our environment, flora, and fauna, need protection <u>now</u>, for the benefit of future generations as well as ourselves. It is critical and imperative to protect these vital natural assets with proper planning and management, and by putting aside the relentless and desperate need for growth and profits as well as the narrow view of a country's or company's bottom line.

## Dwindling and decline of our values, principles, and ethical behaviors

Attitudes, in the shape of the principles and values of the average person in Canada (and in the US and Mexico) have changed, but not for the better. Contrary to what many people think or want to believe, they are going steadily downhill.

Respect for self and others has weakened and diminished; efforts to instill a good education in children at home have become too lax, careless, and indifferent; our school system is not as strong and responsible as it used to be; the concept and attitude of "anything goes" has reached a crescendo in the daily and social life of the average citizen.

People dress very casually and sometimes even sloppily for important meetings, eat publicly without manners, and answer their cell phones regardless of where they are and what they are doing, showing absolute disrespect to others. They continually invade other people's space. They text and drive without caring, while pedestrians constantly challenge vehicles with a daring attitude and without seeming to care for their own safety. These and more examples will be dealt with in this book as we go along.

Even though these things are happening to a greater or lesser extent in many different parts of the world, it is important to emphasize that the average North American, and specifically the average Canadian (regardless of whether he or she is an immigrant or not), have been adopting a lifestyle and civic behaviors which are below the standard that we used to have. I do not think this is healthy. It is detrimental to all our lives, and this is why I am putting my ideas and observations in writing in the hope of making a difference, at least in some families. The lack of interest in traditional behaviors, values, and principles is allowing the average citizen to become sloppy, disrespectful, and careless towards themselves and others. But there is always hope, because "where there is a will, there is a way." The solutions are at our fingertips, but first we need to accept our problems first. To search for proper medium-term and long-term solutions requires adopting the right attitude.

We are in urgent need of salvaging and restructuring basic concepts such as education, responsibility, consideration, integrity, decency, honesty, appreciation, self-esteem, and self-control. I hope my books will assist in some way to enable us to "get into gear" for a more responsible future regardless of our individual backgrounds. But to do it, we must change our mindset! We all need to remember what Albert Einstein once said:

> "We can't solve problems by using the same kind of thinking we used when we created them."

**Changing our attitudes towards "C'est la vie" and "Laissez faire, laissez passer"**

We need to work and commit ourselves to do the best we can on a daily basis for the benefit of ourselves and, above all, for future generations. We need to put aside our selfishness and our need for immediate indulgence and rewards, a need which seems to be excessive, especially in our younger generations. I would despise myself if I were in a position to do something about this but decided not to do anything at all due to a passive attitude, which is sometimes more aggressive than taking action.

I feel a strong motivation and responsibility to raise my voice, to create public awareness, and to make a statement with the power of free speech in honor of those thousands of Canadian soldiers who sacrificed their lives to build a great nation and to provide future generations with peace, security and better opportunities. All those Canadians for whom their word, their honor, and a firm handshake still had a strong value and meaning.

Regrettably, the younger generations are now taking for granted their comfortable and enviable way of life compared to that of over 95 per cent of the rest of the world. We cannot let down all the soldiers that made this country unique and a great place to work and live, nor all those people that dedicated their lives to make Canada a great country such as:

- Those who helped build the railroad joining east and west.

- Those who fought for universal healthcare in Canada. It

was not easy to set up, but many people were brave and strong enough to do it for us.

- Those who built our hydroelectric power plants and built a complex electrical system all across our nation.

- Those who helped establish our own country with so little bloodshed compared to many other countries. Yes, unfortunately, we are still part of the Commonwealth, but that is not the end of the world, for now.

It is of utmost importance to respect our flag, feel proud of who we are, and accept our weaknesses and deficiencies, so that we can work hard and focus to overcome them. Yes, and keep on playing the great sports of hockey and curling!

Our traditional ways of life need to be acknowledged, cherished, and preserved, but, above all, we need to keep setting standards and being an example to other countries, not just in the peacekeeping and financial worlds, but in the preservation of our environment and ecosystem. It is in the hands of all of us to do something about it on a daily and weekly basis. It is not just the responsibility of the government to take care of it! We are all responsible for the environment and our ecosystem, and make no mistake about it.

It is very easy to complain about our surroundings, but what are we personally doing to improve them? The average person is a big complainer, but they need to change their attitude and provide real, positive alternatives and solutions. It is very easy to grumble, disagree, moan, oppose, and criticize. It is not easy to provide answers and well-thought-out, viable solutions, which is the reason I will do my best in this book (and the following two) to dig deeper into these subjects.

When we discuss current problems with people and then ask, "What have you done about it?" typical responses can be:

- "What can I do?" (They often answer with a question!).

- "Forget it, I can't do anything about it!" (Already they feel overwhelmed and have a defeatist attitude).

- "Oh, come on, do not exaggerate. Nothing is really going to happen!" (They do not see the writing on the wall).

- "Stop being so apprehensive, it will all work out in the end." (They have a very unrealistic, conformist attitude and disposition).

- "Don't worry, everything will be fine. God is watching over us." (They leave it to celestial powers).

Throughout this book, I will try my best to express my own thoughts honestly and directly. I do not want to go through this life without raising serious issues that affect our society and influence our future. Not to do so, to my mind, would simply be utterly wrong.

I will need to quote and refer to other sources of information from the past to illustrate, from different angles, my own critical thinking and personal interpretations, concepts, definitions, and trains of thought. It is imperative to mention that my views will be expressed and written without prejudice and with the utmost respect and the best of intentions at heart.

The views expressed here only reflect how I perceive things and personally feel about them. I am very lucky to live in a country in which we have a good degree of liberty, rights, privileges, freedom of expression, and, most importantly, freedom of choice.

Now, before we get into the essence of this book, let us start by listing the main positive human traits that, to my mind, have to be acknowledged as some of the most powerful and positive:

| | |
|---|---|
| Honesty | Patience |
| Responsibility | Honor |
| Humor | Decency |
| Reason | Self-esteem |
| Courage | Self-respect |
| Respect | Loyalty |
| Understanding | Hard Work |
| Perseverance | Trustworthiness |
| Self-respect | Compassion |
| Optimism | Wisdom |
| Sympathy | Self-discipline/control |
| Good judgment | Altruism |

Contrary to these, we also have some important negative characteristics, which we can refer to as "negative human virtues":

| | |
|---|---|
| Apathy | Lack of self-esteem |
| Disrespect | Arrogance |
| Manipulation | Possessiveness |
| Unreasonableness | Vulgarity |
| Harshness | Dishonesty |

| | |
|---|---|
| Traitorousness | Vengefulness |
| Carelessness | Laziness |
| Fear | Unscrupulousness |
| Sadism | Hostility |
| Ignorance | Lack of self-discipline/control |
| Lack of self-respect | Obstinance |

The Greek philosopher Plato (born in 428 BC) who founded in Athens the first real institution of advanced learning, "The Academy," once said that the key human virtues were four: wisdom, courage, self-control and justice. Plato considered them to be, virtues at the time, what we nowadays consider as "universal categorical imperatives," that are a must for every human worldwide to have and apply. Without crossing over into science and textbook discourse, this book will simply open a down-to-earth perspective that anyone can understand and capitalize on, using an analysis of five specific categories amalgamated from the traits just listed. These contradictory traits are what make us such a fascinating species compared to those of the regular animal kingdom that roams planet Earth.

As previously mentioned, this book is the first of a series of three, all with the same self-improvement goals that every human being can strive towards for a positive impact on their lives and on this world of ours. We are born, live, and die within the confines of an established society based on rules, regulations, and civic norms and behaviors to which we need to adhere to the best of our abilities. Otherwise chaos is inevitable.

We all have a responsibility to promote awareness of the issues of concern in our modern society, so that, as a team and with an enriched perspective, we can try to build a better world together. It is vital to begin this process as quickly as possible for the safeguarding of current and future generations. We need to keep in mind that, in 2015, we were approximately 7.2 billion people on this planet and, by 2050, the forecast is to reach the 9 billion mark. Can you fathom the demands on our planet to feed and provide goods and services to this constantly increasing population? Can you even imagine the amount of garbage we will be producing by that time worldwide?

If you cannot fathom or imagine the answers to the two questions mentioned above, then stop for a few minutes, and really think hard about it. It is our responsibility as part of the human race to do so. I truly and humbly hope that my series of books will assist average people to get motivated and start working together in a cohesive and coordinated manner to give humanity a chance for a better future.

A famous Hollywood actor called Al Pacino once said: "Never let the influences of the modern world affect your morals and who you are." Unfortunately, the majority of the population is falling victim to our various modern societies' marketing and trends, regardless of whether these trends are good or bad.

Regrettably, people succumb to peer pressure easily. This is mainly due to lack of proper education, strong will, or to the absence of clearly defined goals and convictions. This is pushing all of us deeper and deeper into becoming a runaway society, like a brakeless locomotive that needs to substantially slow down immediately and (I hope) eventually stop. The same thing needs to happen to the various societies we now live in. I reiterate; I do not expect all to agree. That is impossible. I cannot write everything I want in this runaway trilogy either. As mentioned previously, it is only part of the foundation of what I want to express and share with every reader.

## CHAPTER ONE:  A SECOND CHANCE IN LIFE

How many times have you asked yourself the following?

What would I do differently if I had a second chance to be a kid again?

Well, you are not alone! This thought has crossed the minds of literally every human being, especially of those who have left the teenage years behind. We all regret what we did not dare do, and we all know that there was always room for improvement in what we did at a certain time in life and, above all, in the choices we made.

There is a famous South American writer named Jorge Luis Borges who wrote about this subject and came up with many thoughts that touched people's hearts and, above all, people's memories. Here is one memorable quote:

> If I could live again my life, I would try to make more errors, I would not try to be perfect and I would try to relax. I would try not to take things so seriously. I would risk more, travel more, observe and enjoy the sunset and sunrise more often. I would climb more mountains, swim more rivers, and go to new places I had not been before. I would focus more on the real obstacles and problems rather than those imaginary ones that never came through in life.

Mr. Borges said he was a very sensible and prolific person throughout all his life. Yes, he did have fun, relaxed, and had amusing moments, but if he had the chance to do it all over again, he would try to have nicer and more affable moments than before.

According to Mr. Borges, life is made out of what he called "moments in life." Those moments will never come back, so his message was to always live the moment. To live and enjoy the present. Mr. Borges once wrote that, when younger, he used to bring along a thermometer, a hot water bag, his umbrella, and his parachute wherever he went (metaphorically speaking of course), but that if he were to live again, he would travel light. That if he were granted the chance to go back in time, he would be barefoot from early spring all the way to late autumn—he would dance more and play more with his children. He was almost 85 years old when he wrote those sad and beautiful thoughts.

Personally speaking, I remember what my grandfather used to say: "I regret those things I did not dare to do, regardless of the circumstances at the time, and my own disposition for adventure, for daring, and for experiencing new things." He used to tell me that, when we die, we will not leave behind all that we have danced, eaten, and enjoyed. That nobody will ever take that away from us. We will take our life experiences to our tomb. We all know that we leave behind belongings, but our personal experiences do not stay behind. They tag along with us when the time to depart this world knocks at our door. And unless we write a book of our life, our personal experiences will forever disappear and be completely forgotten.

My grandfather insisted in living life in an orderly manner, daringly, with lots of enthusiasm, and, above all, with dignity and respect. He used to say, "Respect for others starts first with respect for oneself." He insisted that "if you learn to respect yourself, respect for others comes easily, comes naturally." People will pay attention and follow your lead if you respect yourself first. They will respect you if you set a good example initially, which shows others that you are coherent and loyal to your values, your discipline, and your goals, and that you have a high sense of dignity and honor for your own self. Even the Dalai Lama has always maintained the importance of following the three Rs: "Respect for self – Respect for others – and Responsibility for all your actions."

Since some people have not had the chance to read the kind of philosophy expressed by Jorge Luis Borges, the Dalai Lama, and other esteemed thinkers, I would like to bring to the attention of some readers another example I feel confident many will relate to. This is the well-known UFC fighter, George St. Pierre, who, in a Bacardi Canada advertisement, used as a slogan something he believes in and that his followers should too. It goes like this: "Respect Yourself, Be Yourself, Know Your Limits."

To my understanding and interpretation, this means that self-esteem, self-respect, and self-control for Mr. St. Pierre are attitudes that are very valuable for him and for everybody to strive for. He is a respectful example in sports philosophy for all generations, not just the young.

## Life Quality vs. Materialistic Lifestyle

Based on the previous statements and ideas, I cannot help but bring to the table what the fortieth Uruguayan president, José Mujica (2010-2015), once said: "No material belongings are worth as much as life, and this is fundamental." To respect life is to respect yourself and others. Mr. Mujica has always stayed true to who he is, to his thoughts, and to his convictions. He still teaches and preaches using himself as an example. He has always lived humbly, covering all his needs without ostentation.

Mr. Mujica gave a fabulous speech, very different from those of the rest of the dignitaries who attended Rio de Janeiro during the G20 Summit on June 20, 2012.   While the dignitaries of other countries were talking about sustainable development and rescuing the masses from the claws of poverty, Mr. Mujica adhered to his agenda by saying that the world is being ruled by globalization and ruthless competition. He stated very clearly and accurately that our societies are being ruled by hyper-consumerism and that this is ultimately affecting our already ill planet. He has always been concerned that other countries seem to believe that, if consumption is tackled, this will slow down the economies of scale and call forth the ghost of stagnation.

According to Mr. Mujica, this is not the problem, because we do not need to grow to sustain a proper and well-functioning economy. The problem is that other countries seem to absolutely believe that, if you do not grow, you stagnate and your economy stops.

While this is far from the truth, we have to acknowledge the fact that, as our population grows around the world, we need to feed more and more people, dress them, and provide housing and all sorts of other necessary goods and services. This alone will expand or accelerate the growth of any country, but at the expense of our planet's health and well-being through irreparable damage to our soil, water reservoirs, and overall environment. That is what Mr. Mujica was concerned about. Personally, I believe he is 100 per cent correct and also that the real problem stems from the population explosion on this world. We are not respecting the limitations or the balance of things that the environment has to offer.

Our planet does not and will not negotiate with us and with our unrealistic demands on Mother Earth. Everything will sooner or later give in, if we keep putting too much pressure on our globe. One of these days, the planet will react violently to the punishment and damage we are inflicting on it due to human overpopulation and our relentless over-consumption syndrome. In fact, it has already started. The amount of natural disasters such as fires, mudslides, and flooding during 2016, 2017 and the beginning of 2018 have been off the records and some, have never been seen before. Just because we have the right and the ability to have nine or ten children does not mean we should. The same philosophy applies to material things. We need to be responsible for our own behaviors for the benefit of our planet.

Our natural resources are being depleted due to unethical, indiscriminate, selfish, and unstoppable exploitation to cover not only human needs but human greed as well. This will be dealt with in more detail in my second book, "Our Runaway Globe." Overpopulation and hyper-consumption, along with the relentless desire of humans to have more and more and be richer and richer, are destroying the planet. Mr. Mujica gave an excellent example of a regular light bulb that you buy in any store or market, which provides 1,000 hours of use. But the technology has existed for decades to make a light bulb that can provide over 100,000 hours of use. In fact, with current LED technology, we really have no excuses, especially if LED technology comes down in price (which it is). LED means light-emitting diode, which is more efficient than compact fluorescent lighting (CFL), which we all know is even more efficient than old regular light technology. LED consumes less energy than any other regular low-energy lights. Mr. Mujica then went to make the point that things are made purposely to have a short useful life. That is the perfect example of the United States' marketing focus, now copied and being applied all over the world in many industries.

Mr. Mujica said that societies and their economies are focused on sustaining civilization under the concept of "use and discard." Therefore, the 100,000-hour light bulb cannot be manufactured. It would represent an obstacle to a "sustainable economy." This is wrong, but, as he said, we are trapped in a vicious cycle with strong political and economic ties. He stated that it is time to start fighting for a different culture, one that cares for our planet. He insisted that he was not promoting backwardness, simply trying to explain that, if we do not change, we will continue to be in worse and worse trouble, because we are not controlling the market; the market is controlling us. This is dangerous. He brought to our attention that, since ancient times, thinkers such as Epicurus (Greek philosopher), Seneca (Roman philosopher), and even the Aymara people (indigenous people of the Andes) have said: "A poor man is not one who has little, but rather one who needs more and more and more." It is a cultural issue and part of human nature, but it is ultimately not good and beneficial for future generations and, above all, for the well-being of Mother Earth, the only planet we currently have to live on!

This hyper-consumerism is promoted and encouraged by

modern marketing of course. Companies sell their products directly, but also through TV, pop music, and movies. The entertainment industry is not only selling its products, but the unfulfillable dream that everyone can be a star, can be rich and famous with houses in a very big city, with many sporty and luxurious cars, private jets, and have fun all the time with no hard-productive work.

This creates a high level of dissatisfaction with ordinary life. In the past, no one could aspire to be a star, because one usually had to be born into the "right" family, although that is not the correct way either. We need to get satisfaction from average situations that positively affect our society, not just as stars, but also as average citizens. We all need to be honest and realistic about our surroundings and ourselves. The main objective of Mr. Mujica was to show that we can achieve happiness if we change our attitude towards our "need" for excessive and indiscriminate consumption. He said:

> I salute the efforts and agreements made in the G20 Summit here in Rio, and I will adhere to them, as a ruler.
> I know some things I am saying are not easy to digest. But we realize that the water crisis and the aggression to the environment is not the cause. The cause is the model of civilization that we have created. And the thing we have to re-examine is our way of life. We need to start working in favor of human happiness, of love on earth, human relationships, caring for children, having friends, having our basic needs covered, precisely because this is the most precious treasure we have—happiness. When we fight for the environment, we must remember that the essential element of the environment is called human happiness.

Ken Hagan, in the Canadian magazine Zoomer (July-August, 2012), interviewed Sir Richard Branson about his efforts in trying to convince companies to make a serious effort to do business with the well-being of the environment in mind. Branson is a self-made billionaire entrepreneur who among many other things, wrote a book called "Screw Business as Usual."

Hagan quotes Branson as follows: "Business as usual isn't working, resources are being used up; the air, the sea, the land are all heavily polluted." Branson wants companies "to turn capitalism upside down – to shift our values from an exclusive focus on profit, to also caring for people, communities, and the planet." Hagan also cites Branson's challenging but true and interesting statement that "every single business person has the responsibility for taking care of the people and planet that make up our global village. I have been convinced that this is the way forward, if the planet as we know it, and life as we know it, is to survive."

Yes, I agree fully with him, but I will add that every human (not just at company levels) should make their own personal efforts to evaluate their own actions. These actions need to be aligned with the best interests of the societies they live in and, at the same time, should hold hands with the best interests of the environment and ecosystem (all flora and fauna and its interaction with humans).

Yes, I totally agree with Sir Richard Branson that we need to re-examine our way of life and that we really need to make an effort to change. But this has to be done on an individual and daily basis, so that the societies in which we live can stop the relentless degradation of our quality of life. Examining and changing your way of life sets you apart from the average passive person. It means you have grown and achieved maturity and are guiding your daily living more intelligently and efficiently. It means you are happy in your own skin and comfortable with your surroundings. Unfortunately, we tend to live in very selfish societies basically driven by competition and avarice.

## Greed vs. Moderation

In a very interesting article called "The Psychology and Philosophy of Greed" (Hide and Seek, October 8, 2014), Neil Burton, M.D. wrote:

> Greed often arises from negative experiences such as parental inconsistency, neglect, or abuse. In later life, feelings of anxiety and vulnerability, often combined with low self-esteem, lead that person to fixate on a particular substitute for what he or she once needed but could not find. Greed is the only consistent human motivation, and produces preferable economic and social outcomes most of the time and under most conditions. Whereas altruism is a mature and refined capability, greed is a visceral and democratic impulse, and ideally suited to our dumbed down consumer culture.

There is no doubt that greed also tends to isolate people, and that isolation itself brings a high degree of selfishness and unhappiness. Altruism, on the other hand, opens new doors in society. It is the antithesis of selfishness and therefore tends to provide strong feelings of satisfaction and happiness. It provides a deep sense of self-esteem. Therefore, we should all start by doing small, simple altruistic activities to try to get away from greed. But we need awareness so we can then apply a strategy for altruistic action.

This reminds me of what actor and producer Clint Eastwood once said: "Respect your efforts, respect yourself. Self-respect leads to self-discipline. When you have both firmly under your belt, that is real power." This helps me confirm that self-respect and self-discipline (self-control), though not always easy, help in pushing away greed and are the key elements to improve our standards of life individually and in our society.

We should learn from other societies, such as some tribes in southern Africa that emphasize people's allegiances and relationships with each other. They focus on altruistic activities, while setting greed aside. Some believe that "Ubuntu" is a very good example of an African philosophy in that corner of the world. The Ubuntu idea is based on trying to answer the following question: How can one of us be happy when others are sad? The philosophy of Ubuntu is "I am who I am because of who we all are."

"How can I fill up my stomach when others are starving?" they ask themselves. Archbishop Desmond Tutu in his 1999 book "No Future Without Forgiveness" offered a definition of Ubuntu as follows:

> A person with Ubuntu is open and available to others. Affirming others, does not feel as a threat that others are able and good. This based on a proper self-assurance that comes from knowing that he or she belongs in a greater whole and is diminished when others are humiliated or diminished, when others are tortured,

oppressed and continuously suffering.

Nelson Mandela gave this example to illustrate Ubuntu:

> A traveler through a country would stop at a village and he didn't have to ask for food or for water. Once he stops, the people give him food and entertain him. That is just one aspect of the Ubuntu philosophy. Ubuntu does not mean that people should not enrich themselves.

The question therefore is: What are you going to do to enable the community around you to improve and better themselves, so you can also improve in parallel with them?

The Franciscan preacher Jorge Bender, from Argentina wrote a book titled "Africa no me necesita: yo necesito de Africa" (Africa does not need me: I need Africa). He explains that Ubuntu means: "I am because you are; a person turns human through other people surrounding him." He says that, in those African tribes, if somebody is smarter or better, they feel more secure and at ease because they grow up and protect each other as a group. If somebody is humiliated and treated badly, everyone feels oppressed, frustrated and hurt.

Well, that is certainly not echoed in the America. It does not happen in the rest of the world either, for that matter. For the purpose of this book, America means the American continent, which goes from Tierra del Fuego in Argentina, through Central America and all the way to Northern Alaska.

Our society is definitely not based on Ubuntu principles. Ours seems to be based on competition, greed, survival of the fittest, accumulation, selfishness, bullying, lack of respect for others, and to some, lack of consideration for the communities in which we live. Guess what? Hypocrisy seems to always prevail. All this is not bringing long-lasting happiness to our societies. It is only temporary. Just take a minute and evaluate the world we are living in. Are we surrounded by peace, by harmony, by a crystal-clean environment, by stress-free days, by full happiness, and by real, true friendship?

If your answer is "Yes," you belong to one per cent (or less) of the world's population.

## Identity Issues in People

It is well known that the youth in general are having a hard time trying to find their identity. Most people do not know where they stand in society or where they are heading. In fact, the majority live with the wrong attitude towards their peers, while living in a society in which they are either bullies or bullied (victims). Few remain neutral, but if they do, it is due to strong convictions and values. This is one of various reasons that, in many schools in North America, we have problems such as unhappiness, assaults, murders, student complaints, instability, and even suicide. That does not mean all youth are in need of help, but a high percentage of students have serious issues of belonging, fitting in, and, above all, being happy.

This reminds me of an article, "Words for Teenagers," that, according to the Pierce County Tribune, dates back to 1959, although some critics say that it was Doris S. Burville who originally authored it as "Letter to a Teenager" in 1955. Based on these sources, The New Zealand Herald published not too long ago (Aug 8, 2014) an article written by Amelia Wade entitled "Kiwi principal sends teen message viral... 53 years on," which tells how the principal of Northland College, John Tapene, decided to share Doris Burville's words of wisdom for all teenagers. Allow me to quote this important and 100 per cent accurate message for teens to re-read and adults to fully understand.

John Tapene started by quoting the main complaints that usually get teenagers into trouble. These are:

"What can I do?"  ….  "Where can we go?"

Tapene then adds:

"Always we hear the cry of teenagers, 'what can I do, where can we go?' My answer is this:

> Go home, mow the lawn, wash the windows, learn to cook, build a raft, get a job, visit the sick, study your lessons, and, after you have finished, read a book. Your town does not owe you recreational facilities, and your parents do not owe you fun. The world does not owe you a living, you owe the world something. You owe it your time, energy, and talent so that no one will be at war, in sickness, and lonely again. In other words, grow up, stop being a crybaby, get out of your dream world, and develop a backbone, not a wishbone. Start behaving like a responsible person. You are important, and you are needed. It is too late to sit around and wait for somebody to do something someday. Someday is now, and that somebody is you.

New generations tend to have some identity issues (e.g. gender, ethnicity, race, religion, intelligence, popularity, and others) and seem to be driven always by immediate gratification. Luckily, we still have down-to-earth, progressive, hard-working, and responsible young people, though unfortunately these numbers are dwindling with time and are starting to be the minority. They will have to strive and work harder than we did to overcome their peers' bad example and lack of cooperation, which nowadays is very influential and a real burden on progressive students.

We have to remember that, in the 60s, 70s, and 80s, the children everyone wanted to emulate in class were well behaved, had all the answers, and were known to be disciplined, organized, smart, studious, dedicated, and intelligent. They were examples for the rest of the class to follow and the pride of the teachers and the school system itself, which used to push hard so that students could improve themselves and be better citizens in the future.

It now seems that the student who gets into trouble, who is loud and lazy or sometimes comical or a bully, is usually the "cool" one. Other students want to emulate and be like the cool person, whom they might actually dislike or even be afraid of. They need to pretend as part of their survival strategy, that is their desire to belong and not be picked on. In reality, they themselves become what they fear or dislike.

Nowadays, the kid in class who is well behaved, organized, studious, respectful of others, and has almost all the answers to the teacher's questions is considered to be a "nerd" and often bullied. Go figure, but it is the crude and cruel reality. In today's society, that nerdy kid is not cool. This is the reason such kids are usually picked on, become very lonely and sometimes can even be pushed to commit suicide.

Even though today's youth "seems" to be smarter and to possess faster thinking processes than previous generations, in my eyes, they are not necessarily smarter and definitely not more intelligent or logical than previous generations. Children are growing too fast nowadays and do not have the time to develop better values in life. They are bombarded by technology, sex, aggression, war, advertising, and many other negatives through their cell phones, TV, film, video, and other electronic means. They do not seem to live reality to the full. They have no time to enjoy and appreciate nature, real friendship, or love for themselves. Do you know how many millions of youth worldwide would not be able to differentiate, recognize, or simply enjoy the smell and aroma of pine cones, flowers, rivers, moss, oceans, certain vegetables and fruit, herbs, cattle, farming fields, early mornings, lakes, and so on?

## The Misconception of the Younger Generation

I insist that the young people of today are taking almost everything for granted without looking at other realities beyond their borders. Many tend to live in a world of dreams based on immediate desires and gratifications. More youngsters lack common sense, discipline, and patience. They seem to want things now, before they have earned the right to have them. Many parents even promote that. They also believe their children deserve everything and that everything will last forever and that everybody around their children are wrong and their child is the only one who is right.

One of the main reasons for this is that, in North America and in other lucky places around the world, the young generations have never seen or been in any war within their own territory. They only hear about war through the media, through TV, newspapers, computers, and magazines. Their society has been stable and protective towards their communities and their own citizens. They (me included) have definitely been extremely fortunate in this respect.

In such a peaceful environment, parents have managed to provide everything to their children in excess and have overprotected them. In doing so, they have betrayed the essence of parenthood by bringing up many kids who do not have any sense of obligation and responsibility and who appear to lack understanding of the real world, of justice, of respect for others, and overall appreciation of their belongings, their surroundings, and their own personal future. Many of these children, luckily the minority but steadily increasing, tend to be capricious, selfish, and self-centered. Again, not all are like that, but the numbers are growing steadiy.

They literally do not care a rat's butt for others they do not know. *Absolutamente nada!* That, is sad and worrisome.

They bite the hands that feed them (Mom and Dad, who many times live in fear of their own kids), and their social behaviors seems to lack a single shred of respect for themselves, for others, and much less for their environment. But you know what is the worst part of all? They do not even seem to realize this or be aware of it. They seem to wear horse blinkers and are only focused on fun things to do and their own personal rights. Immediate indulgence and fun are their burning and twisted desires, and obviously, their ultimate, consistent, and long-lasting goals. I truly hope I am wrong, but these entitled young people are due for a rude awakening from the financial, environmental, and world peace points of view. Regardless, it has turned out to be so bad that many parents are changing their feelings towards having children. In fact, MacLean's Magazine (February 2018) published an article entitled "I wish I never had kids. There. I said it." According to the author (Anne Kingston) women in Canada feel "Trapped, suffocated and fed up. Why more and more women are no longer afraid to admit they hate being a mom."

In my personal opinion, an interesting example of the above overall picture is the case of Ethan Couch, the so called "affluenza teen." In New York, Jana Kasperkevic reported in an article in the US News (December 30, 2015):

> In 2013, Couch, from Keller, near Fort Worth, admitted killing four people in a drunk-driving accident. At the time, his lawyers argued that he suffered from "affluenza," and, because of his privileged upbringing, he was not able to fully understand the consequences of his actions. Affluenza is not an officially recognized condition, but instead of being sentenced 20 years in prison the then 16-year-old was sentenced to rehab and 10 years' probation.

Apparently, these types of kids, brought up without proper manners, education, or sense of responsibility, do not know right from wrong (as even psychologists say). It is painful to admit, but some children nowadays can literally get away with murder, though it is arguably not their fault as much that of their irresponsible parents who, in many cases, bring up monsters instead of children.

I know that some of you are saying or thinking "Come on, they are just kids and they will grow out of it." Unfortunately, I feel that only a few will eventually grow out of it. The rest will not change and will be so behind and frustrated in life (by, for example, the high levels of unemployment of recent graduates, many of whom are still living at Mom's and Dad's) that they will not be able to snap out of it in time. They will most likely fail profoundly to catch up with the so-called nerds, who work harder and smarter and will probably be their bosses in the future.

The same denialism happened when people like Albert Arnold Gore Jr., known to the world as Al Gore (ex-vice-president of the US), was trying to convince the world about the "warming of the planet." A majority of his audience did not want to accept this and questioned his scientific research and unfortunately, some still do. At the time, the great majority said the alarming facts he highlighted were simply part of the normal cycle of our planet; others said he was exaggerating. To the world's surprise, he had been accurate all the time, and now many cities around the world are building dykes eight to 12 feet high, or even higher, to protect themselves from rising sea levels at a cost of billions of dollars in taxpayers' money.

If we do not make an effort to accept reality, we will continue killing our planet. This is definitely not a matter of higher powers or of another natural climate cycle alone.

We need our younger generation and current leaders to believe, and believe profoundly, with open hearts and minds, and begin to take some serious action. Otherwise, just a few selected humanoids, if we are lucky, will end up escaping our own destruction and colonizing another planer to save the human race from itself. But for that to happen, we need to speed up our work geared towards technology advancement. This is the main reason space exploration is such an urgent issue nowadays. In saying this, I am not being negative but only realistic. In fact, a good example is what Elon Musk, the founder and or co-founder of Tesla Inc., SpaceX, Solar City, and Neuralink among others, is trying to achieve. His main goal is to change the way humans think and see progress. He has been trying to teach people around the world that our species needs to change towards the use of renewable energy, making production and consumption sustainable on planet Earth. He believes, like thousands of other scientists, in the possibility of human extinction and the reason he has been pushing hard on outer space exploration and colonization. His dream is to colonize another planet such as Mars and further in the future, the closest exoplanet if technology allows. As the CEO and CTO of Space Exploration Technologies, he has been working hard in the improvement of rocket technology to make space exploration more viable. According to various sources, SpaceX has the leading technology for rocket engines, which provide the best thrust-to-waist ratio. Science Vibe News of October 28, 2016, published the following in an article in reference to Elon Musk:

> "The future of humanity is going to bifurcate in two directions: Either it's going to become multiplanetary, or it's going to remain confined to one planet and eventually there's going to be an extinction event." Influenced by Isaac Asimov's Foundation series and views space exploration as an important step in expanding—if not preserving—the consciousness of human life, Musk said that multiplanetary life may serve as a hedge against threats to the survival of the human species. An asteroid or a super volcano could destroy us, and we face risks the dinosaurs never saw: an engineered virus, inadvertent creation of a micro black hole, catastrophic global warming or some as-yet-unknown technology could spell the end of us. Humankind evolved over

millions of years. In the last sixty years, atomic weaponry created the potential to extinguish ourselves. Sooner or later, we must expand life beyond this green and blue ball—or go extinct.

Of course, Musk is an exception and an extraordinary person, business man and human being. But what about the average individual? Personally, I strongly believe in the abilities of the young to learn and adapt quickly to new circumstances, but I have my doubts about whether they are building strong enough characters to confront the mighty damage our parent's generation and our own are leaving behind.

## Awareness Required in Parents

To achieve success in coming generations, the parents of today need to be aware of the strengths and weaknesses of how kids have been brought up for at least the past 25 years. Some of the important problems that require immediate attention in my view are:

### Speed of growth

Children are now growing up very quickly, many with only a single parent. In the past, children used to *be* children; they had the time to enjoy a healthy upbringing at a slower pace, away from violence, sex, and drugs. Today's kids experience these problems through TV, movies, the internet, cell phones, and tablets. Peer pressure at a young age is much stronger than before. Many children, with only one parent at home, are barely receiving all the essentials. The great majority do not have enough quality time with the parent, who cannot inspire, explain, and guide the children as he or she would like. This is to the detriment of the children's life experience. Single parents are already making an amazing effort to provide the bare minimum for their families with today's high cost of living and, at the end of the day, are simply exhausted. I truly feel for single parents, their children, and the challenges they daily confront. It is a complicated situation. We need to remember that the quality time the single parent provides to their child is worth a lot more than another new pair of sneakers.

Children are always pushing to know "everything." I did too! But I was told that certain things were for children and others for adults. The problem is no longer one of keeping them innocent a little longer and protecting them from learning too quickly about the truth of Santa Claus, the Tooth Fairy, and Peter Pan. By age ten, they already know about STIs, drugs, sex, murder, rape, abuse, aggressive bullying, vengeance, sadism, etc. From my personal point of view, it is too early for children to learn things like that; in North America, they do not all live in areas where they need to wake up so early to the crude realities of life around them in order to survive.

## Violence and narcotics at all levels in the school system

Teenagers are attracted more to sex and alcohol than to books, sports, and an orderly life. This is just human nature, unless they are taught differently. Unfortunately, they are now bombarded by movies and advertising that promote sex, drugs, and violence, and they feel cool if they give in. This affects them negatively through poor grades, poor school attendance, and overall poor performance.

Stabbings, shootings, and other aggressive behaviors are seen more frequently everywhere and seem to happen more often in families with lower levels of education or in low-income urban settings where parents are trying very hard just to make a living. Yes, it also happens in wealthier families, but at a lesser rate. During 2017 and the start of 2018, the youth and opioids problems in North America has escalated, reason why many young people are dying every week.

## Lower educational standards in our school system

There are many schools throughout North America where the policy is to pass every student regardless of academic knowledge and abilities. The education system at elementary and high school levels, especially in Canada and the United States, is very lax and forgiving, and dangerously less competitive than other countries. Schools are bringing up weak-spirited children with unrealistic expectations. Not quite what the world needs to save itself from self-harm or self-destruction. That is one of many reasons that the children of new immigrants in Canada and the United States often excel above and beyond their counterparts despite the handicap of having to learn a new language. The discipline enforced by their parents outweighs their initial lack of language, social know-how and integration.

## Weakening of ethical and moral values

Children are growing up with a false sense of security that overshadows their ability to be aware of their future reality. They live with constant peer pressure and a strong desire to attain more stuff (goods and services) regardless of the economic or environmental impact.

Sound values, good ethics, and moral sense have not been imprinted in them adequately, pushing them to potential future derailments in their professional careers. For example, instead of promoting the concept of savings, we are pushing our children to be mundane and object-oriented (banal, utilitarian, and materialistic) by providing them with everything they want.

It is a noble idea to try to provide everything, but, in the end, parents spoil their kids, who lose a sense of reality and grow up thinking they deserve and have the right to anything. If their friends have something new, they need to have it too or the peer pressure would be "unbearable." Often, this is why many parents live in debt and never seem to catch up. If this is the example we provide to our children, then that is what they are learning and, in turn, will teach their children, creating an even bigger problem in society. It's a metaphorical black hole that can end up destroying itself without being able to escape from its own negative and destructive gravitational forces.

The things we really need to provide our children during the early stages of their lives (besides the basics of food, clothes, and shelter) are love, attention, and interactive quality time together. Parents should spend time with them in activities such as conversing, cooking, reading, playing, gardening, planning, dreaming, laughing, etc. among many others.

The young do not understand or accept this problem. They believe that, just because they want something right now, it has to happen immediately. They need to learn that if something does not happen immediately, this does not mean it will never happen. Patience needs to grow within the spirit of younger people. They need guidance, teaching, and supervision. They need to try harder, consistently, and with full focus and devotion. If they work for it, rewards will come. Guaranteed! This is taught at home first through the use of a powerful and sometimes painful word, "No." I believe it is imperative for parents to learn when to say "No" and for children to learn that both parents mean it and adapt to it.

Unfortunately, the opposite attitude is reinforced in the school system. Kids are allowed a very loose rein without being required to learn the value of discipline, effort, and dedication. Contrary to "No," the word "Yes" comes more easily to most parents, who are too afraid, lazy or ignorant to be consistent, determined, and tireless in the proper educational upbringing of their children, which is for their own good.

## Reading vs. fun time

The young generation is not focusing enough on books and lectures and, therefore, not putting enough time and devotion into studying and developing better working habits. Instead, they always seem to have fun first and then cram in a few hours of studying, only to forget what they learned a few days later. There is a strong need to guide them in expanding and reinforcing effective strategies to make their days more productive, with schedules involving less amusement and unproductive time, while placing more attention on activities that will have a positive impact on their future productive lives. Competition is fierce out there. The better prepared they are, the greater the opportunities ahead of them. For example, although some countries like Finland only demand an average of three hours of homework per week, in many other country, students have a heavier load of homework. Aside from their daily assignments, they are also involved in other productive educational activities such as languages, music, high-tech hobbies, sports and outdoor activities.

This is the reason why the average North American student

scores much more poorly in international competitions than their foreign counterparts. Of course, we excel in certain tests every now and then, but foreigners generally have a notorious lead. The truth is that, in most international tests, students from Asian and European countries come in ahead of our students, and the gap has just been getting wider in the past two to three decades.

One of the businesses I once had was a school for English as a second language (ESL), which I ended up selling. We also used to offer afternoon classes related to languages, music, chess, painting, etc. I will never forget the answer of a local mom when we offered our afternoon services for her two children (eight and nine years old). She said: "My kids do not need more learning. At school, they make enough effort, and I do not think they can take it. They also need to rest, relax, and have fun." Those kids only knew English, and they were back home by 2:30 pm. Imagine the waste of talent of those two little kids who, at that age, were eager to learn and could absorb new skills and knowledge like sponges! As a parent, you need to be on top of your children like a hawk. Remember, you are a parent and a tutor first. As the years go by, you can then be their friend after they are mature enough to understand and appreciate the difference.

I once read the thoughts of a smart and down-to-earth lady called Jennifer McGrail. A married woman and mother of four children who loves writing and home schools her children. She excels in writing articles, anecdotes, thoughts, and sayings, and shared with the world an idea about "the path less taken" that I really need to quote:

My promise to my children: I am not your friend. I am

your mom. I will stalk you, flip out on you, lecture you, drive you insane, be your worst nightmare, and hunt you down like a bloodhound when needed because I LOVE YOU! When you understand that, I will know you are a responsible adult. You will NEVER find someone who loves, prays, cares, and worries about you more than I do!

She also made an observation that I totally agree with: "Never spank when you're angry. Give yourself time to cool down, so that you can then spank calmly and without emotion." This was written by Ms. McGrail as a way of expressing her care for her children. In my eyes, she does not mean it literally or aggressively, but with sincere care and deep love. As parents, we need to be determined but loving at the same time. If we only keep helping, overprotecting, and stretching our hand out to our children, some will end up ripping off our arms. Just take a look at how many kids control their parents with tantrums and bad behaviors. They do it publicly, and it is uncomfortable and annoying for the parents themselves and the people around them. But the kids have been allowed to get away with murder. Everybody else is afraid of saying anything, because the kids' parents will jump down their throats like wildcats, though on many occasions the parents themselves are afraid of their children's reaction in public, even if they will not admit this.

## Active vs. passive life

Children and teenagers are meant to be active, not sedentary. But the use of more and more technology is making the new generations physically lazy, which is ultimately affecting their health and brain. Being physically inactive promotes obesity. Children who are overweight and obese also tend to have less self-confidence and lower self-esteem, which will have a negative impact on their social behaviors and achievements. Their inactivity will have a serious impact not just on their own physical and mental health but will increase the overall cost of medical services for the society overall. If they do not change, such children will have fewer opportunities later in life. It induces them to be more reclusive and less outgoing. These children need our help to make them aware of the dangers of their situation, the alternatives on hand, and the specific and tailored solutions available, because not everybody suffers the same issues. Custom-made solutions are very important in almost every case.

## Students and stress levels

Nowadays, more students are complaining about stress. Many want to harm themselves, and some even think about suicide. That is nothing new, but the percentages now are definitely much higher than in previous generations. In my view, parents and some schools are to blame for the sudden increase in the levels of stress and in the higher percentage of students harming themselves.

Why? The over-protecting of children before and even during high school does not train and prepare them to deal with tougher situations or with future obstacles and stressful realities. Mom, Dad, and their school cannot solve all their problems, so when they are forced to solve them themselves, a great number of students do not know how to do to it. Their levels of stress then grow to intensities and proportions we have never seen before.

In addition, many schools pass every student regardless of performance. Some schools do not even provide grades for fear of "damaging the psyche of the student" and, soon thereafter, having to confront an angry and aggressive parent. When I grew up, schools always gave grades, and if you did not study and know your subjects, the teacher would fail you. You would have to repeat the year, period. And guess what? Nobody grew up traumatized for the rest of their lives because of repeating a year, but I guarantee you they learned their lesson, which was beneficial for their future development.

Nowadays, the philosophy in many schools is not to "traumatize" students, so they are passed regardless of whether they learned the material or passed the final exam. Sure enough, further on in life, a moment comes when only the good students succeed in university and get the real opportunities. The bad and weak students are weeded out. That is when reality kicks in, and Mom and Dad cannot do anything about it at that point. It is usually too late. That is when a student's stress goes through the roof, and they start either hurting themselves or even going to the extent of committing suicide.

Recently, there have been various studies done on students and stress. A good study was reported in the Globe and Mail (April 25, 2015). This was a research done by the University of British Columbia in the spring of 2014 at Vancouver Technical Secondary School. The four main conclusions of this study that I want to bring to the reader's attention are the following:

1. 79 per cent of the students confirmed hearing another student calling somebody anti-transgender or anti-gay words.

2. 33 per cent of students intentionally hurt themselves.

3. 69.2 per cent of the students complained of waking up feeling tired and unrested.

4. 35.4 per cent of students said they did not have enough time to do their homework.

Point 1 shows how more and more students lack a basic sense of education and respect for each other. In my time, we had bullies calling other students names like this too, but they were only two or three in a class of 30 students. It was the minority, but nowadays the percentage of bullies seems to have increased, especially behind the screen of their computers where they feel safe and brave. They are just cowards, but life will catch up to them; it always does. Facebook and Twitter are perfect means to perform negative social acts like cowardly bullying.

But through these and other types of social media, you can also find the most motivating, caring, and positive comments and ideas. No doubt it depends on the education, ethics, and integrity a teenager has been taught and trained throughout his or her upbringing within their families. They say that "the apple does not fall far from the tree."

Point 2 proves how today's students cannot handle stress like previous generations did, and it is getting worse. I personally do not remember a single student harming him or herself as a result of not being able to deal with school stress. We did not have special psychologists to deal with student matters. Even with full or part-time psychologists in schools, the problem keeps escalating, so what is really wrong in our society?

Point 3 shows how students are running free, doing whatever

they want, going late to bed, and not sleeping enough. Any human being knows that we need our sleep to feel good and rested next day (eight, nine, or ten hours depending on the individual). If we do not sleep enough, our stamina and mental sharpness are not the same next day. In fact, it is as simple as knowing that to quench our thirst we need to drink water. Lack of discipline inside a youngster's home promotes unhealthy habits like not sleeping enough, which they ultimately end up paying dearly for in the future.

Point 4 shows that at least a third of students lack the skills to be efficient with their own time or to know or care to prioritize their activities, instead of doing their homework first and then whatever they fancy afterwards. For example, they always seem to want to be connected with their friends through their iPhones or computers before and during their homework, the reason that, on many occasions, they run out of time to do the work properly. Homework helps build some discipline in life.

## Stress, suicide, and prevention

When children are brought up overprotected and with free rein, without knowing deeply the boundaries of do's and don'ts, they get confused and out of synch with reality. A great majority grow up to be frustrated and incapable of solving their own problems effectively and efficiently when they encounter real-life problems. If we add the fact that our school system is so easygoing and lenient in dealing with bullies (a social cancer in North America), failing to impose serious consequences, then we can understand why many students are making more and more suicide attempts.

Due to general bullying, along with higher academic tension

and difficulty, a growing majority of students simply cannot take the pressure. They are not well-prepared or trained to deal with bullying. Again, the rate of dropouts and suicides is increasing. Fortunately, at some high schools and in almost all universities, students are finally starting to confront bullies openly and in an organized manner. Some schools are providing more demanding levels of control. Students seem to be responding positively to these efforts.

Schools are constantly being offered a so-called "suicide prevention package," which does not necessarily stop the attempts. To some critics, it is just a moneymaker and a misuse of public funds. There is an interesting article by Tom Blackwell in the March 19, 2015 issue of the Calgary Herald entitled "Suicide Prevention Measures Criticized." This article talks about mental health issues in schools and about how Stan Kutcher (psychiatry professor and Sun Life Chair in Adolescent Mental Health) and his colleagues from Dalhousie University confirm that there is no evidence that expensive suicide prevention packages work.

On March 9, 2015, Dialynn Dwyer from Boston.com (staff member) wrote: "Suicide is the third leading cause of death for adolescents aged 10 to 24 and results in approximately 4,600 lives lost every year in Canada, according to the Centers for Disease Control and Prevention." After considerable research, it all seems to indicate that suicidal incidents have increased so much in the United States alone (followed closely by Canada and other countries) that they have developed various suicide prevention systems or programs that cater to this alarming and growing national problem.

The article in the Calgary Herald cites two very well-known

educational programs called Yellow Ribbon and Sign Of Suicide (SOS). These programs offer to raise awareness about suicide and related subjects among students and staff while screening students for various risk factors such as depression. But these programs do not stop there; they also assist in creating community awareness. They offer sessions inside and outside the schools while trying to get parents involved as well.

Stan Kutcher and his colleagues proved that there was no successful correlation between universities using suicide-prevention programs and a decrease in suicide attempts compared to universities not using these programs. Kutcher's study carefully followed and analyzed various Yellow Ribbon and SOS programs over ten years to evaluate their efficiency. The results showed that students were seeking less help in universities offering those programs compared to other universities that have never used similar programs at all.

Whether these suicide prevention programs work or not is irrelevant for our analysis however. What is relevant is the fact that there are more students seeking help to avoid thinking about suicide than in previous generations. Some critics say that this is due to the way many parents and schools overprotect their children. It appears they lack good and efficient teaching techniques to promote independent thinking and strong self-development. Harsh punishments for perpetrators are lacking in our society as well.

In my view, we now bring children up to be weak or even worse, making them believe they are the best and the smartest when they are far from it. We are bringing up children who live in their own world, and when the gift-wrap tears and their protective bubble pops, they are then forced to jump into the real world, where they are stunned by the harsh realities of life. They simply cannot take it, and, added to the bullying syndrome out there, they end up attempting or committing suicide. Why is it that, in previous generations, this topic was almost unknown and scarcely talked about but nowadays is all over the schools and the national news? This is definitely something we should all seriously think about, isn't it? Well, this brings to memory the following:

- Against bullies and cowards ... "Don't let someone else's opinion of you become your reality" — Les Brown, businessman.

- Against lack of character and strength ... "If opportunity does not knock, build a door" — Milton Berle, comedian.

I remember my father always used to tell me: "a bully will always be a bully until the victim gets dressed with courage, decides it is enough, and draws the line."

## Mysterious and Forgotten Games and Activities

It is important to instill in the younger generations an interest and love for outdoor activities and sports. Not everybody is sports-oriented, but there are many activities in the outdoors not related to sports that promote a dynamic and healthy approach to life. Even when children are not interested in sports, they can play with friends outside, enjoy their back yards and their local parks, go hiking in the mountains, stroll along rivers, go bird watching, or simply go for a walk.

As wild or strange as it might sound to some readers, and acknowledging that times have drastically changed, we could also try bringing back just for fun and socialization "some" interesting healthy games and activities such as:

Yo-yo, Cowboys and Indians, bicycle races, tops, wall tennis, hide and seek, water games, any sport game (e.g. soccer, volleyball, baseball, basketball, etc.), water balloon fights, archery, catch, collecting bugs and leaves, sidewalk chalk games (e.g. hopscotch), jacks, barrel of monkeys, pickup sticks, camping out in your friend's back yard, playing Frisbee with a friend or your dog, building your own race car with wood and ball bearings, making your own bow and arrows, building a tree house, playing paddle board, baking cakes or cookies, making sugar popcorn and selling it in your neighborhood, skipping rope, playing marbles, visiting friends and going to a museum, local fair or any social event with them, reading a favourite book on the branch of a favourite tree, swimming at a pool or lake, playing water polo, playing board games (e.g. checkers, Monopoly, backgammon, chess, Snakes and Ladders, etc.), card games, playing with your dog or cat and teaching them new tricks, feeding the squirrels and the birds, playing with a top, creating your own music band with friends, learning poetry and reciting it to friends, playing treasure and scavenger hunts, cops and robbers, hula-hoop, playing Robin Hood or The Vikings or the Three Musketeers, creating your own home theatre, playing tag or dodge ball, designing and building your own kite and letting it reach the skies, putting on a play and inventing your own dance routines, target shooting, asking Grandma to teach you how to cook, knit, or sew, asking your grandfather to teach you carpentry, gardening, iron work, etc.

The range of activities is limited only by what parents and other family members can teach or by children's own imaginations. Unfortunately, a great number of kids and teenagers are bored to their skulls or glued to their TVs, computers, or cell phones and, when challenged to do something else, in an already defeated attitude they complain: "but what can I do?" Go figure!

## Younger Generations vs. Older Generations

Some people believe that the new generation is better prepared than the generations before them to handle change and even perhaps the stress that comes along with change. This might be partly true, but we also need to keep in mind that the new generation is out of touch with reality in many instances, which makes it less able to handle stressful changes. However, it certainly adapts more easily and quickly to technological changes, at least in the electronic and computer world.

For the younger generation, the understanding of computer hardware and software comes more naturally and therefore a lot easier than for previous generations. In fact, although most of us use desktops, laptops, or tablets, the younger generations and professionals have started already to rely on super computers and quantum computers, which can be 500,000 times faster than their predecessors. They are currently "playing" with them in private and government projects, applying special algorithms to evaluate the exact probability of events such as terrorist attacks to try and stop them. This is just one example among other endless uses for these progressive computers. Regarding general life experience, previous generations were kept naive longer by their parents but given stronger values and principles, making sudden life changes less stressful for them. Nowadays, children in elementary school are being taught early in life about sex and drugs. This is too early for my taste, but then these things are experienced a lot earlier in life today. Also, many agree that, regrettably, the new generation has serious problems with history, geography, politics, socializing, communicating, establishing intelligent dialogues about what is happening around the world, integrating, and cooperating in the civic development of their community. They tend to live in their own technological world, which makes them less efficient in their overall social skills, as well as more selfish and less prone to teamwork.

Some people believe that the new generation is smarter than previous generations. This is definitely not accurate. It only seems that way because younger people have been exposed earlier than their predecessors to adult subjects and to very fast technological changes. Their naiveté and innocent imaginations have been stolen earlier in their life by our modern society. They do have better skills to deal with information technology and are fortunate to be able to access new information and knowledge at the click of their keyboards.

However, this does not mean they are necessarily more intelligent or better equipped for life. In fact, they are more ignorant in world matters and in social skills than previous generations by far. They do not read as much as previous generations, so their verbal and written skills are limited in comparison. They have a harder time expressing their thoughts clearly and professionally. Even worse, they believe they know more than they actually do.

## IQ Test by Generations

Please refer to Dr. James Flynn of TED Talks – ted.com — where he explains the "Flynn Effect" and how the older generation scored an average of 70 points in IQ tests and nowadays the average is 130 points on the same tests. Why? Because, according to Dr. Flynn, the current generation deals better with abstractions and with a wider range of issues. They are better able to multitask than older generations. Lateral thinking has developed more strongly throughout history, giving modern generations an edge over earlier ones. However, this does not mean that this generation is smarter. IQ tests are not necessarily good measures of intelligence, as Dr. Flynn admits. In fact, he has uncovered through his research that the younger generation is weaker than older generations in their overall vocabulary and are actually suffering a mental decline. There are fewer bright people on average today than in earlier times.

This is a big concern. The average attitude of today's youth is to have a fun before hard work. They want their prize before earning the right to it. One of Dr. Flynn's most important conclusions is that human beings of today keep more up to date than their predecessors, because information travels faster, but they are definitely not smarter or more intelligent.

They tend to be more current in state-of-the-art matters, more adaptable and resourceful, but they are not necessarily more astute, bright, wise, brilliant, shrewd or bold. In fact, they have started to fall behind in these matters. In general, they lack the positive attributes of being dedicated, organized, disciplined, and respectful. They are less willing to follow procedures, and sacrifice focus, discipline, and work for quick personal enjoyment and fulfillment.

## New workforce is ill-prepared for today's marketplace

In the United States, a joint press release was published in May of 2016 by the Conference Board, the Partnership for 21st Century Skills, Corporate Voices for Working Families, and the Society for Human Resource Management. Their report is entitled "Most Young People Entering the U.S. Workforce Lack Critical Skills Essential for Success."

According to this report, the economy of the United States is vulnerable because today's younger generation is ill-prepared. They lack important traits such as: critical thinking, teamwork, communication skills and common sense. They score low in reading abilities, comprehension, retention, mathematics, and lowest of all, in writing.

As per Ken Kay, President of Partnership for 21st Century Skills, the younger workforce "lacks the basics plus an array of applied and social skills, from critical thinking to collaboration to communications." According to the report, they have a hard time putting together well-written memos, letters and technical reports. Employers complain that they are deficient in critical thinking, proper communication, and problem-solving skills and have to be retrained to cope with the demands of the working world. This represents a big challenge and a high cost for any company, reason why many small companies do not risk hiring them.

Yes, recent graduates have a big disadvantage when compared to previous generations in terms of overall communication, teamwork, and writing skills. Unfortunately, they do not realize this, or if they do, they do not want to accept it. They need to be taught how to follow instructions, methods, and procedures, and to be creative at the same time. They also seem to be deficient in logical reasoning, common sense, and analytical ability. Previous generations were better prepared to perform their jobs without the need of being retrained in matters that sometimes go back deep into their upbringing during the early stages in life, both at home and in school (from elementary all the way through high school and undergraduate studies).

The same situation is being experienced in the Canadian work place due to our lax education system over the past 20 years or more. Unfortunately, it is not getting better. In fact, there are discussions about not having to teach the younger generations calligraphy, because computers seem to be replacing that need. Although alarming, it is also my opinion that some people with obtuse minds and weak logical thinking believe this is the way of the future. But what happens when there is a power outage and their batteries run out?

## Speed of Change and Parental Influence

We live in a world of astonishingly rapid change, and it is not slowing down. On the contrary, it is speeding up. Technology is advancing by the minute. So, you better learn the ropes and go with the learning flow, or you will remain behind and turn into a slow-moving mastodon, both mentally and physically.

Regarding the speed of technological advancement, the newer generations have the ability to adapt faster and thus enjoy an edge over older generations. They are mentally stronger as well as faster in their overall ability to handle the technological changes of the present and those of the future. However, knowing the problems of the younger generations, a question arises in my mind. How many will actually develop the right attitudes, dispositions, and overall strength of character to take advantage of those improved skills, and how many will succumb to their insecurities or to their false sense of superiority?

Fortunately, or unfortunately, parents along with the schooling system are the sculptors of their own children. Now, allow me to insist on a fundamental upbringing problem that needs to be crystal clear. I am not trying to sound preachy with what I am about to reiterate, but I want to make a strong point about something that can be very difficult for some individuals to accept. Parents are often mistaken because they lack clarity to see or even accept the truth.

They think they have done everything right during the upbringing of their children, and they have real problems dealing with their mistakes, regardless of whether there is an obvious detriment to their children's current and future behaviors. Why? The reason is simple. We are humans, and we dislike accepting our errors openly. Who does? Unfortunately, only a few have the courage to take their blinkers off and accept their shortcomings. Therefore, I need to stand firm on the following nine thoughts and realities that our society is having trouble admitting:

1. Mistakenly, parents want to be their children's best friends instead of being just their parents and mentors first. In the future, they can choose and try to be their friends if the opportunity presents itself.

2. Parents in general lack the character and determination to deny capricious requests and say "No" to their children. But even more difficult is to stand firm in their position individually and as a couple. Parents' weakness of character or indecision is ultimately reflected in the children's misbehavior. Children know very well how to capitalize on the weakest link, that is, the softest parent. Teachers are also sceptical and uncertain in denying certain things to their students, because they are afraid of losing their jobs due to the overreaction of some parents who have a sick, over-protectionist syndrome. Nowadays the school system and many parents are apprehensive of "psychologically affecting" their poor little children if they say "No" and stand firm behind their decision. In my view, they should demand the proper attitude from the young and help them develop a stronger character to improve their future chances in life.

3. Providing children with everything whenever they want it is simply irresponsible and even unethical in many circumstances. In fact, it is seen by many as abusive. For example, allowing a child to have unhealthy fast food and sodas for dinner is undoubtedly going to damage the child's overall health and promote obesity. This should be considered abusive towards the child, who in many cases does not know better. Those parents either do not see this, or they simply do not care, and therefore deny their weakness every time they are confronted about it. These parents usually lack character, strength, and energy to firmly disallow their child something he

or she wants, and maintaining their position in a firm and decisive manner. This has a serious detrimental impact in the children's future.

A good example is when the children want to do several activities during the day, and Mom or Dad drives them around town for hours catering to their every single and last desire instead of saying "No, that's enough; we are not doing so many things, so just choose one activity and let's stick to it." Another example is when children want to watch another program or want to go to bed an hour later and parents succumb to their persistent attitude instead of saying, "No."

Why? Because parents should know that a regular routine is the best for their children. Children need adequate sleep. Saying "No" is not being abusive; it is simply being a good and responsible parent. It is hard and sometimes even painful to be strong and stand your position, but for the child's sake, it needs to be done. We have the responsibility to teach them the proper boundaries, along with respect for their parents.

4. Parents who yield to the capricious demands of their children are literally robbing them of something useful and beautiful. Yes, those parents are taking something of critical importance away from their own children by giving them everything. It sounds strange, but they are taking away their children's sense of pride, appreciation, and accomplishment in getting things done on their own through their own energy, work, commitment, and sacrifice.

Many parents seem to need to listen, learn, and have the courage to implement, in coordination with the other parents in many instances, proper in-house rules for the benefit of their children and themselves. All of this has been thoroughly researched and explained in many different books by various authors, including the popular Dr. Phil McGraw (Dr. Phil).

A well-known TV program called Nanny 911 has dealt with these subjects. At different times, all the nannies (Lilian Sperling, Deborah Carol, Yvonne Shove, Stella Reid, and Yvonne Finnerty) tackle the children's and parent's issues head on. Just Google either of the above two sources for a plethora of information, which however requires reading with an open mind and understanding. We all need to learn how to say "No" to our children, if we truly care about them and want the best for their future. This is unmistakable and undeniable!

5. If children want something, they are relentless, but Mom and Dad need to be firm and united. Otherwise it is natural for children to put pressure on the weaker parent, who ends up always giving in and making a fool of the other parent in the children's eyes. This causes stress and miscommunication among family members and, if it continues, can even develop into separation or divorce, which has been on the rise on the American continent (and specifically in North America—Canada, the US and Mexico). As per divorcewealth.com, about 38 per cent of marriages in Canada end up in divorce before their thirtieth anniversary (although other sources say it is closer to 45 per cent).

As reported by the Daily Infographic, the rate of divorce in the United States is 50 per cent (although other sources place it between 51 and 53 per cent). Mexico's divorce rate is said to be 15 per cent. Mexico tends to have stronger family and religious values, and it is a fact that stronger family values assist in bringing down the divorce rate. A worldwide table of the divorce-marriage ratio put together by Wikipedia using very reliable sources confirms the above statistics.

6. In general, history has proven that those children with responsible parents who "sacrifice" their time, energy, and efforts to guide, teach and educate them until they have the skills and maturity to apply what they have been taught are those who will be more successful and the true leaders of our future societies.

7. Good, responsible parents protect and teach their children to grow physically and mentally healthy, and to be strong, knowledgeable, and skillful, with as many competitive assets as possible (e.g. languages, musical skills, sports, reading inclination, hobbies, volunteer work in their communities, etc.). Parents do not necessarily need to have money to provide extracurricular activities to their children. There are government programs, libraries, community sports facilities, public parks, church programs, and many other extracurricular school activities. With a strong will and desire, parents will always find the way to do it.

8. To provide children with the basics in education, parents need to provide their children with competitive skills above and beyond the basics. To accomplish this, both parents need to work in cohesion, harmony, and with absolute dedication, along with making extra efforts and sacrifices. Some children need more attention than others to learn the ropes of life, but ultimately all will learn if taught properly by their parents. All of this starts at home. You cannot wait for children to learn these things at school; it will simply not happen. They will grow up lacking a competitive edge over their peers, which will certainly make the difference between failure or success and

between frustration or happiness. All of the above can be achieved more easily if parents are not divorced.

9. If you want to nurture a tough but a reasonable and understanding child, then as a parent you need to lead by example, while being tough and a teacher first. If you want to raise a weak and a disadvantaged individual, you just need to be a weak and "friendly" parent and give in to your child's every whim. Parents must train their children to obey if they want them to succeed. That is a challenge already suited for even the best parents.

## Dr. Benjamin Spock's "Damaging" Legacy

On July 14, 1946, Dr. Spock published a book that revolutionized how mothers brought up their children in the United States and in other parts of the world. This book was called The Common-Sense Book of Baby and Child Care. It has been widely analyzed, criticized, damned, and praised. Whatever the case may be, after families in the United States and Canada started following his recommendations, Spock became a household name during the 1950s, and many children of that time were known as Spock children or Spock babies. His influence on the upbringing of babies during the 50s and 60s was dramatic. His philosophy was to treat each child as an individual but to raise them with "natural loving care," avoiding being harsh and strict like previous generations. Spock indirectly discouraged respect for authority and openly discouraged what many called direct training and obedience.

As expected, it is human nature to take things to extremes and not always be rational and balanced about matters such as bringing up your own child. You cannot dump previous theories and adopt new ones just because the new ones sound good and are in fashion. But many people did. Few balanced both theories wisely. People in the US and Canada went too far and left important discipline aspects behind, which got lost in the "natural loving care style."

Unfortunately, as the generations go by, the overprotection, pampering, no-boundaries concept, and reinforcement of the idea that each child is the best child has exploded in our face and come back to haunt us.

An article worth citing at length, "How Dr. Spock Destroyed America; Exclusive" (January 27, 2009 in WND Commentary—News Alerts, also published by Imaginative Worlds) by Reb Bradley asserts that Spock's childcare book cultivated narcissism in millions. He says:

Parents began to feed self-indulgence instead of instilling self-control – homes were becoming child-centered. As parents elevated children's "freedom of expression" and natural cravings, children became more outspoken, defiant, and demanding of gratification. In fact, they came to view gratification as a right.

Spock wrote his book in response to a cold, authoritarian philosophy of parenting that had been dominant in America. For years, parents had been told to withhold affection from their children, not to touch them too often and not to respond to their tears. Understanding of children had not been encouraged, and fathers had played a minor role in their nurture and care. These things distressed Spock, and they would have upset me had I been born back then. Children need our tender affection, understanding, and respect.

However, Spock's solutions reflected total ignorance of the hedonistic bent of human nature and fostered an over-exalted sense of self-importance in children. Homes became hotbeds for narcissism, entitlement, and victim-thinking. I wanted to quote the above excerpt, because it is very well written, and I could not agree more. In fact, how weird and difficult to understand is the fact that the grandson of Dr. Spock committed suicide. His name was Peter, and he was the son of one of Dr. Spock's sons, Michael, who worked as the director of the Boston Children's Museum. Peter himself was working part-time while studying at the University of Massachusetts in Boston. Then he simply jumped from the roof of the museum to his death. Nobody knows why he did it, but some critics wonder if going too far to the opposite in educating children (without proper boundaries) can cause problems of a different style, even to the extent of leading to suicide. I guess we will never know, and I personally believe it was not the case, but you always wonder. Why are the suicide rates in students going up every year? Could it have to do with the way families are bringing up their children with too many liberties and no boundaries in sight?

To read more points of view as to how Spock "destroyed America," please refer to the following site:

wnd.com/2009/01/87179/#Mq2lkLE7t6DxE0My.99

## A True Story

The following is a true story that happened to a dear friend of mine who also left Mexico for better opportunities. Even though he gave me permission to go ahead and write his story, I cannot mention names due to our confidentiality and privacy understanding.

My friend was married and had two children. A girl and a boy. The daughter was a beautiful, smart girl and the boy very amicable, handsome, and intelligent. The father, who we will call Juan from here on, came from a middle-class family and grew up knowing the values of hard work, savings, honesty, integrity, self-esteem, and true love. For Juan, his children always came first and then himself. Juan was always willing to sacrifice his own comfort and needs for those of his children.

Juan went to private schools assisted by scholarships, loans, and his parent's savings. Juan's mom and dad taught him by their own example through dedication, sacrifice, and hard work.

Juan had two brothers. The three boys studied for their master's degrees abroad through a combination of government loans and scholarships. One of the brothers got his doctoral degree as well. Mom and Dad taught the three boys, in perfect synchronization, matters of ethics and values based on study first and then having fun. They were very strict with them but very loving at the same time. If any of the brothers did not perform in school, they were punished until improvement was apparent. It was the time in which a good spanking or even perhaps the use of a belt was still acceptable. The three boys got a good spanking or a good belting every now and then. But they grew up to be productive men in society, with good professional achievements and zero traumas or frustrations. According to each brother, those spankings, beltings, and punishments only made them stronger. Again, none of them was traumatized, like today's society wants to believe. In fact, the three turned out to be quite successful in their own country and in the international arena as well. They owed their success and strong characters to the rigorous, relentless, and strict education imposed by their parents, combined with understanding and unconditional love. Both Mom and Dad were always in the same frame of mind and used the exact same strategy with their three boys in order to be consistent, equal, fair, and progressive. Juan's parents always told the three boys that honesty, morality, and truthfulness would set them apart. They needed to be true to themselves and always follow the law of self-respect and respect for others. They emphasized that, in life, you need to develop a high sense of integrity and honor and that these are fundamental for healthy growth, stability, and maturity.

Now, my friend's wife, who we will call Consuelo, came from a very rich family. Her mom and dad gave her everything she wanted in life except true and unconditional love. They pampered her to the extent of affecting and distorting her inner values. At home, she had servants of all types, gardener, pool man, kitchen maid, chambermaid, and a police guard for the street paid by them and their neighbors, for security purposes. Consuelo went to the best private schools and university. She grew up with two sisters and one brother. All spoke fluent German and English besides their native Spanish. None of Consuelo's siblings studied for master's degrees or PhDs abroad. They immediately started working in some of their dad's companies. They belonged to a very privileged financial and economic group in Mexico. They enjoyed various vacation houses in their country of origin and abroad.

Consuelo's two sisters and brother seem to be average professionals who appear to be doing just fine regardless of always having the table set for them. None ever started from scratch or succeeded through their own personal efforts and sacrifice. It was all handed to them on a silver platter. Fortunately, they seem to have responded to the required family level needs and turned out to be good and productive professionals. At least, that is the last I heard a few years ago.

Consuelo's mom and dad offered their four children expensive vacations locally and in foreign countries. They used to go to ski resorts in Colorado, beautiful beaches in San Diego, expensive golf courses, on cruise ship vacations, African photographic safaris, and many others. They were even sent to Europe for private lessons and courses of different types— from language, to cooking and baking courses, to technical courses related to their business and industry in order to improve their company's success in the future. All this is very good if you have the money and the work ethic, which, at the time, seemed to be the case. However, they failed to provide Consuelo with a true understanding of the work ethic or with an overall appreciation and value for things. It is said that there is always a black sheep in the family, and in this case Consuelo turned out to be the "chosen one." Unfortunately, she never cared, because she has always been "fresh like a lettuce."

Consuelo never knew the value of a hard-earned dollar or the requirements of being a good, responsible mother and wife. She always thought that being her two children's friend was more important than being a parent. Therefore, she always acted accordingly. She never really mentored the children as a responsible parent would. Good times and fun were her understanding of being a good mother, because she was also brought up like that, having been the first child in her family. She was spoiled rotten compared to her two sisters and her brother.

Consuelo's dad was a very successful, self-made man. But he was very possessive and wanted all his sons-in-law and daughter-in-law to be very close and work for him. In fact, they all did end up working for him. He controlled them completely. He bought a big property, which had a house for each of their children and their new sons-in-law and daughter-in-law. He wanted to have everybody under his umbrella and absolutely under his influence. This was one of many reasons why Juan suggested that he and Consuelo go to another country and start a new life instead of being pressured and controlled by her family, which Consuelo constantly allowed. The family always flashed their money and social position in Juan's face and everybody else's. They were very insecure socially, so they needed to show they had money.

Juan thought that, with distance, the influence and pressure on Consuelo from her parents would diminish. Unfortunately, Juan was mistaken. He was too young to know better and too naive to understand the strong bond and umbilical cord between Consuelo and her mom and dad, especially from the cultural background in which she had been brought up. Consuelo's dad was of German descent and her mother was a real Mexican native.

Finally, Juan and Consuelo decided that they wanted to make

their future abroad, so they emigrated to an English-speaking country. Three years went by in the blink of an eye, while Juan worked very hard in their new, but still semi-foreign, country. Consuelo did not work. She was a stay-at-home mom and used to travel very often to meet her parents at any of the vacation houses they owned. Juan and Consuelo had their first daughter in their new country three years after their marriage. Juan mistakenly thought Consuelo would then settle down and finally grow roots in their new country without having to travel so much abroad to see her parents.

But Consuelo's behaviors and overall way of being started changing after the birth of their daughter, and even more after the birth of their second child, a baby boy. Everything circled around her children and herself. Nothing else was important, and unfortunately, she took extreme positions and attitudes on her daily behaviors, which portrayed her as an absolutely and totally different person than she was before. This was very damaging for the family. As many women like her do, she always used her children as the reason or excuse for whatever she wanted to do herself, regardless of whether it was bad for the children. Unfortunately, Consuelo's values and priorities were clearly different from those of Juan. For Consuelo, traveling an average of six months a year and taking the children with her, who meanwhile were also missing school, was normal and justified. Consuelo's mom and dad wanted to see their grandchildren constantly, and Consuelo just wanted to be traveling. Money was not a problem. They had plenty. Nothing could stop them from doing what they wanted, even if it was the wrong thing to do.

This situation brought many other inconveniences and hardships into Juan's and Consuelo's relationship. Juan was doing very well financially, but never well enough to compete with Consuelo's family. The most important differences between Juan and Consuelo were their values and their priorities. This was due to the obvious differences in their upbringing, and it was tearing their marriage apart.

Consuelo was never taught to grow and mature with time, to really appreciate what she had. She was a child in a woman's body. She wanted everything immediately and did not appreciate the sacrifices that Juan made for her and their children. Juan bought them a brand-new house in a very nice neighborhood. Six months later, the house was not only very messy and dirty, but also mistreated, with toys everywhere, dishes and food all over the counters, clothes unwashed, kids up late at night and very hyper, being fed fast foods. And the list could go on and on. The worst was that the values and morality that Juan held dearly to succeed in life were totally different and never acknowledged by Consuelo. While Juan made an effort to pay for extracurricular activities for their children (such as piano lessons, German lessons, and soccer), Consuelo did not consider that important. She only wanted to cater for and play with her children.

The piano teacher told Consuelo and Juan that their daughter was gifted. At age four, she played over 30 melodies with an amazing accuracy and ability. She knew how to read the musical notes and make beautiful music on the piano keys. The daughter also had amazing and definitely above-average physical abilities for sports, while the son was more oriented to intellectual matters and possessed amazing and contagious charisma.

Consuelo lost her way (or never really had it). Her true self was steadily emerging. She did not have any self-esteem, self-respect, or self-control. She gained a lot of weight through eating disorders, lack of exercise, constant traveling, and by being very inactive in her daily life. Her real dark self was pouring from her pours from within. She lost her modesty, her lady-like attitude, and her integrity, but she continued using the children as shields and as an excuse and justification for everything. Consuelo always insisted that she did everything for the benefit of the children, who were always playing, eating outside, going to parties, sleeping late, and traveling endlessly. Due to this, they were constantly falling behind at school.

Today, neither of my friend's children speak German. At first, this language was spoken at Consuelo's house very fluently due to their German background. But Consuelo thought English and Spanish were enough, and that the German language would only mix them up. German was soon forgotten. She never talked to them in German again.

To date, the daughter does not play any piano because Consuelo got tired of taking her to piano lessons and refused to do it anymore. Consuelo was a stay-at-home mom, so she did not work or have any other serious responsibilities, and it was simply not a priority on Consuelo's list to take the children to piano lessons or any other type of lesson. She instead continued her habits of bad parenting until Juan and Consuelo ended up divorcing.

Money is good to have, but it can affect your focus, your reality and your real targets in life, while slowly destroying your soul—especially if, in a couple, values and interpretations are abysmally different. Yes, opposite poles attract at the beginning, but not for long. They are opposite and different for a reason. Couples need to be similar to each other and possess the same values and morality. They require holding hands happily in a family environment with common goals, or things will eventually crumble and collapse.

Note:

Once again, it is important to mention that this is just one example of a couple that happened to be my close friends. I could bring to the table many other examples in which the ugly character was the man and the woman was the victim. Especially in the area of marital loyalty, men seem to fail more often by fooling around with another woman, while making a regrettable mistake, thinking they will never be caught.

Unfortunately, the ones most affected are children who, in many cases, grow up not knowing the truth of what happened, with insecurities and frustrations that most likely will affect their future performance as human beings in their own marriage.

## The King and the Falcons

All these comments and stories bring to memory a legend about the King and the Falcons. There was once a king with two falcons. One flew beautifully all day long, but the other did not how to fly and was always perched still on a branch of a tree. The king asked everybody what to do to make the other falcon fly. Nobody came up with an answer, so he decided to offer money to whoever could provide a solution.

Next day, when the king woke up and approached his window, he saw both falcons flying. He asked his servants to bring him the person who had made the other falcon fly. When they brought him to the king's balcony, he was asked what he had done. The farmer said, "I just cut off the branch where he used to sit all day long, and he immediately started flying. The falcon realized he had wings and had no choice but to use them."

Sometimes children (like the falcon) do not know what they are capable of doing, so parents have to teach them self-confidence and trust in themselves. Not to the extent of encouraging them to grow up conceited, vain, and arrogant, but just to believe in themselves and dare to try things with confidence and perseverance. They need to know that everything is possible, if they try hard and persist with a positive and happy attitude. They also need to be conscious and realistic, to know when to stop and let go! Some children live within their own fear, insecurity, lack of confidence, and diminished values. Others are totally the opposite, that is, they live without fear, thinking the world circles around them. They live with a cocky attitude, conceited, bold, and impudent.

Every extreme is bad, and that is why parents should get involved and guide their children to a medium range of normal self-esteem in which they should be realistic and confident about themselves, down to earth, progressive, respectful of themselves and others, and always with a positive attitude. It is not easy, but it is not as difficult as it might seem. A high percentage of parents simply lack the discipline, stamina, or vision to guide and educate their children properly.

Unfortunately, at school (including university), I never saw courses about:

• Being a better parent.

- Loving and respecting your partner (wife or husband).
- Keeping romance alive at home.
- Loving and respecting your children.
- Taking care of a marriage.
- Practicing loyalty and honesty during marriage.
- Educating your children.
- Bringing up a happy and unified family.
- Respecting the elderly.

I truly believe some of these courses should be mandatory and part of the curriculum in high school or even university. Humans in general, especially at the childhood stage in most of North America, tend to live in a comfort zone. Take them out of their comfort zone, and they get nervous and stressed out. But life is about constantly pushing the boundaries of our comfort zone. Sometimes this happens consciously, and sometimes it happens accidentally. We need to strive to find our comfort zone but also be ready for a change, if need be. It is imperative to train our children from an early stage in life. This is what the Arab legend of the king's falcon is about. The falcon did not know it could fly until somebody cut off the branch where it was peacefully perched, forcing it out of its comfort zone. From that moment on, the falcon never stopped flying, because that is what it was born to do, though it had not known this. The sky was its new and better comfort zone and, above all, its natural environment.

You will be surprised to know that many people do not even realize that there are many different comfort zones out there. Many people live with their original values, fears, limitations, or selfishness. In those zones, what seems to prevail is the past, and the past denotes stagnation in a different time zone. It is not positive or progressive to remain there. But everybody has dreams — they want results and new opportunities; unfortunately, not everybody is willing or eager to take risks and work hard to try to achieve those opportunities. Not everybody is willing or even capable of walking and venturing in new trails with new challenges.

When I was younger, I was taught to respect and improve myself, and so I used to think that everybody would strive for new and higher plateaus. For me, the mere fact of trying something new came relatively easily, with little or no stress, because that was the way I was brought up, the way I was trained by my parents and my school system at the time. But as I have grown older, I have come to realize that not everybody wants to risk and dare for better comfort zones or higher plateaus. But that is all okay. That is the beauty of being different. Also, as you grow older, your attitude towards new risks and challenges changes, sometimes drastically, to the extent that, at certain ages, "people do not want more cheese, they just want to get out of the mouse trap" (old Mexican saying). By this, I mean that some people are cozy and happy in their own little world and do not want new challenges. They are happy in their safe world, which they know well. "Why fix it if it is not broken?" they say. Why take new chances and face new challenges? If you have found a nice comfort zone, it is okay not to search for new opportunities or new risks, that is, for more "cheese."

Nowadays, my goal is not to take big risks anymore. At least, not like I used to do before and as younger people than me ought to be doing now. At over 50 years old, I need to be cautious and measured. I might not have the time to recover if things do not work as I planned. If I were 10 years younger, I would definitely risk more in search of a better return in life.

If everything works out fine, and I keep enjoying good health, my goal is to be happier, not necessarily richer or powerful. When the time comes and I leave this world never to return, my money, possessions, and power will be left behind for others to enjoy, but my happy experiences throughout my short existence on earth will leave this world along with my memories and my body. So, the question in life should really be: Whom do you really work for? For yourself or for others? You have to make a conscious decision. Choose wisely, because life is too short. I am sure that most people have heard the following question: Do you want to be happy, or do you want to be the richest person in the cemetery?

After a certain stage of one's existence, and after achieving a certain level or status in life, why work more or harder for others? The goal should be to reduce stress, prolong life, and enjoy whatever we do. I would rather enjoy life to its maximum, along with the people closest to me, whom I love and respect. But hey, you have to be happy with that decision, which means that you have put your time into being productive and hard working for many years prior. You have to be honest with yourself and make that balanced decision about when to slow down and switch from: "I need to do" to "I want to do."

## Appreciation of our Comfort Zone

We need to learn how to treasure our own comfort zone at any stage in life while always being open for improvement, even after retirement. I want to fly freely like the king's falcon for the rest of my days, and fly freely in search of health, relaxation, happiness, and a productive life. I want to fly consciously, knowing how fast time goes by, knowing where I am and where I am heading. I want to learn how to really appreciate life on a daily basis and be happy during my daily activities.

I also want to learn how to do it as soon as possible. I am tired of being in sixth gear all the time and at full speed; I am tired of being at a continuous level of stress that blocks my ability to enjoy my ride through life. I need to be conscious of time. I have failed myself there often. Time is slipping away through my fingers at a scary warp speed. Life is passing by in the blink of an eye, yet it is amazing how vividly I can remember when I was 10 years old. It is like it was yesterday! What happened? How did time go by so fast? I remember blinking and, guess what, I had suddenly finished high school, and I was already 18 years old, then I blinked again and I was 22 and had just finished university, then I blinked again and at 24 had finished my master's, then I blinked again and voila, 10 years went by, then 20, then 30 years. I am afraid of blinking now. I will be 60 years old next year, but mentally I still only feel about 20. Definitely not 60, though I have to acknowledge and accept I am getting older.

Luckily, I have the right frame of mind. I am positive and conscious that "youth is wasted on the young," who do not seem to appreciate or realize what they have when they have it. They believe they do, but they really do not. In general, almost everybody appears to take their youth for granted and feel it will last forever. I made that same mistake myself when I was younger, at least for a while. I know better now. I have not been taking anything for granted for the past ten years. I have finally learned (unfortunately only recently) to enjoy life, enjoy the moment, and try to be happy on a daily basis, conscious of what I have and what surrounds me. Not thinking of what I do not have or that I wish I had or could have had. Let's face it, the list would be endless, regardless of how much power, money, and possessions I may have acquired. So we need to learn to draw the line and put a stop to our desire of wanting to do and have so much more. When young, you definitely need achievements and material things, but this "need to be" or "need to have" tapers off with time.

I have liberated myself from many memories, many things that weighed me down. I should have learned how to do this at an earlier stage in life. I failed there, but heck, life is not easy, and I am very far from perfect. It takes a lot of work and sacrifice if you want to succeed and have a stable and healthy family and retirement. Pay attention—don't have a lazy retirement but one that is productive, healthy, proud, and full of activities that you choose to do for yourself, your family, community, friends, and country. Yes, it is never too late to change and improve yourself. Never too late!

Everybody should stop living in the past. That (and excuse my French) is an asinine way to live your life. Once again, I have to admit that for many years I only had in mind my own goals, my desires for a better future, my sacrifices for that more stable future. I forgot to live in the present. That present now is a thing of the past; it is gone and never will return. I should have learned to live in harmony and in a more balanced way by appreciating the course of time...at the time. Now I take advantage of my past experience to try to mold a better future without letting go of the present. The present needs to be cherished at every second. If we see a long winding road ahead of us, it is because we are looking at the future without living the present. That should be stopped as well. We should pull our head out of the mud, wipe our eyes, and enjoy the present. There is not a more important moment than the present. The past is dealt with. The future is yet to come. That is undeniable; the past is gone, and we have no idea what the future will bring. Every step of the day has to be achieved with consciousness, love, and happiness.

Regardless of your present situation and condition, remember: immediate gratification does not last long. We require working for it and, when achieved, cherish it with devotion, truth, and passion. We can sculpt our life the way we want it to be, so it is imperative to start shaping it now, but we have to choose the proper hammer and chisel to do so. It is important to select the right tools, so we can achieve the most beautiful sculpture we can imagine.

Making an effort to appreciate, honor, and respect oneself is crucial. I truly believe that the above requires to be done soon if people want to better themselves. You can start right now. Any minute of the day, any day of the week, is a good minute or day to start. Self-esteem, self-control, and self-respect are the sparks that start the engine in the right direction in search of a better life, with less stress, more quality, and overall personal satisfaction. Isn't that what we are all trying to achieve? Life is not a result of pure destiny; it is a result of your own choices, decisions, actions, and your will to exercise them properly.

## In Search of Balance and Harmony

Brihadaranyaka Upanishad is a collection of Indian scripts. Its roots come from a combination of Hinduism, Jainism, and Buddhism. These scripts and their overall philosophy include many beautiful sayings and thoughts that can be applied intelligently to everybody's daily life, without falling or getting into any specific religious thoughts. A few that I really like and agree 100 percent with are the following:

- "Life is the way you want it to be."
- "You are the result of the deep desires that motivate you."
- "Your will is a reflection of your desires."
- "Your acts are a reflection of your will."
- "Your destiny is a reflection of your acts."

Swami Krishnananda has written a lot about the Brihadaranyaka Upanishad and how to lead a more productive life in The Divine Life Society, which in my opinion, is interesting and worth reading with an open mind and a neutral perspective. Alex Krawciw Levin wrote Lotus of the Heart, a summary of the Upanishads and a perfect guide to the philosophy, which can be briefly explained as follows:

> The Prashna Upanishad (The Breath of Life) explains the specific manifestation of this energy in the story of six seekers of self-realization. The sage Pippala answers their questions probing the forces at work in the universe and our world.

> Among the questions is "What powers support the body… and which is the greatest?" Pippala answers: "The powers are space, air, fire, water, earth, speech, mind, vision, and hearing. All these boasted 'We support this body'. But prana, vital energy, supreme over them all, said: 'Don't deceive yourselves. It is I … who holds this body together." Naturally, that question is followed-up with "Master, from what source does this prana come?" And answered: "Prana is born of the Self. As a

man casts a shadow, the Self casts prana into the body at the time of birth so that the mind's desires may be fulfilled."

Part of his message is that we need to see the full and complete reality in front of us. We will then have a chance to find or discover perfect harmony, because everything must be in harmony. Everything must be balanced, but it needs to come from our true desires and from within. We just need to find it and accept it as such. We must open our eyes and our heart. This will bring us peace and happiness. Once again, it seems easy, but it is difficult to achieve. We have to be aware of this and try passionately and vehemently on a daily basis.

This brings me to something I read many years ago. At the time, I loved it, but I did not do much about it nor did much to keep it in mind on a daily basis. I let my instinct kick in instead and reacted spontaneously, without thinking about what an old Cherokee man told his grandson about the battle that happens in the inside of every person when he stated:

Every person has two wolves inside battling each other constantly. One wolf is evil. He is the personification of envy, hate, sadness, arrogance, selfishness, guilt, resentment, inferiority, lies, false pride, superiority, jealousy, and ego. The other wolf is good. He is the personification of harmony, peace, serenity, humility, nobility, benevolence, trustworthiness, empathy, generosity, compassion, faithfulness, and happiness.

Then, the grandson thought hard and long and, after meditating for quite a while, he asked his grandfather, "Which wolf will win the battle, Grandfather?"

The old Cherokee answered: "The one you decide to feed!"

Well, was the old man right or what? We have the option to feed the evil side of us or the good side of us. Every human being has both sides. Of course, there are various degrees of evil and goodness, but every person on planet Earth has both. It is a matter of choosing which to respond to. Which wolf will guide your specific actions or reactions in a specific moment and throughout your whole life? Will we be a good person or an evil person? Everybody has the power to decide.

Everybody is independent in thoughts, decisions, and actions. Of course, we are influenced by our surroundings, but in the medium and long term, we have the power of being who we want ourselves to be. Nobody else but us has that powerful decision! Good decisions in life build up our self-esteem and our confidence, leading us to happier paths in this world. The future is definitely in our own hands.

## Reacting Positively to Events in Our Daily Lives

An author called Stephen Covey wrote a book entitled "The 90/10 Principle" that has changed the lives of thousands of people. The principle is accurate and fascinating. He says that only ten per cent of your life is related to what happens to you. The other 90 per cent depends on how you react to what happens to you.

What does he mean by this? Well, that we really do not have any control of 10 per cent of the things that happen to us. If our bicycle or car breaks down, there is nothing we can do about it. It simply broke down for some reason usually out of our immediate control. What is important is how we react.

You cannot control the weather, but you can control how are you going to respond to it. The same applies to human relationships. If somebody does something to us and says something to us, there is nothing we can actually do about it, but we can control how we are going to react to it. We should not let others control our reaction or response. You can make a conscious decision how to react and respond. Is it the evil side of you reacting and responding, or the good side? However, your response will bring consequences, good or bad. But they are based on your own reaction.

Here is a down-to-earth and mundane example. Your son or daughter knocks over a glass of milk during breakfast, spills it all over the table, and even splashes you all over. How do you react? In that moment, you have the choice of letting the accident ruin your day as well as that of your son or daughter. If you get mad, that's it. You have then decided to change that day for the worse, but if you react in a controlled way, then you can even capitalize on what happened and make a better day out of that incident. You can let your child know that he or she lacked attention and that everything has repercussions, but approach it with love, as a concerned parent and mentor should do. Smile, then go and change. The child will learn a lesson without you ruining the day for everybody.

Again, it is difficult to do, but if you do not even try to make an effort to keep the 90/10 principle in mind on a daily basis, then you do not have a chance to control who you are and the direction your day will take you, that is, the other 90 per cent of what is going to happen. Your reaction will cause an automatic chain reaction of events (good or bad) thereafter. Now, it is extremely difficult (though if there is a will there is a way) to stay centered and educate your child not to spill the milk again, being firm in your guidance but kind in your manner. That child will understand the message and try hard not to do it again. You need to be firm and make them understand that there will be consequences. You will also need to fulfill that promise, if it happens again! Then both of you will go on with your daily activities without a bitter taste and without having to deal with an event like that again.

Another example. You are at the airport, and your flight gets delayed several hours. There is nothing you can do to avoid that delay, but there is everything you can do to control your reaction after the delay is announced. You can choose to get angry, shout at the flight attendants, raise your blood pressure, increase your stress level, feel frustrated, and complain to others about your problem. But what if you decide to tell yourself: "Take it easy, there is nothing I can do." It is out of your control, so if you cannot enjoy the new and sudden course of your ride that day, then at least be civilized and peaceful with the new set of circumstances. Try always to keep your cool and your class.

We need to make the best of our efforts to relax, smile at adversity, rearrange our schedule, let others know about our delay, and keep our cool and our poise. Avoid getting stressed out and try to be pleasant with others and portray a positive, easy-going attitude. Remember, what goes around comes around. Our vibes tell a lot about ourselves and can assist us to encounter and accept a new set of circumstances. We might meet somebody we would not have met if that flight were not delayed. This is not destiny; it is just a fact.

This reminds me of a saying that goes like this: "Things happen for a reason that sometimes reason itself does not understand"—but accept the new things with a smiling face. Personally, I do not fully believe that everything "happens for a reason." This is like giving up and leaving the future to celestial forces. But many people do. If they are happy with that and achieve peace, well, that is great. Good for them, and just let it be. Science, intellect, and our own actions and reactions are what I believe in. Our will and conscious actions determine what happens later. But if something out of our control develops, we need to make an effort to understand it, adapt to it, and accept it wisely. You and the people that surround you will definitely be happier as a result. This might sound, to some, a bit like being in denial. It is normal to feel anger and frustration, but it is how we vent or react that can be even more explosive. For example, it is healthy to come home after a hard day of work and talk about the day's challenges, but if this goes on forever or builds up the stress even more, it is time to stop and change the conversation. Bringing positive vibes and thoughts home, is the way to go.

## CHAPTER TWO: RESPECT FOR ONESELF AND OTHERS
(Self-Esteem, Self-Respect and Self-Control)

### Self-Esteem

Self-esteem is the ability to evaluate yourself in a positive manner and to hold yourself in high regard. From a psychological point of view, self-esteem is the overall emotional evaluation people have of themselves, that is, the interpretation or perception that people have of their own self. Everybody has a specific attitude or disposition, which is often the "pillar" for the judgment of their own value, worth, and position in society.

One of the best definitions I researched is that of Nathaniel Branden (Canadian-American psychotherapist and writer), who defined the concept of self-esteem as "the experience of being competent to cope with the basic challenges of life and being worthy of happiness." Branden goes further and explains that self-esteem is a feeling of personal confidence and security to face life's challenges, daily duties and responsibilities, and overall actions in society.

If we possess a positive and altruistic attitude, our self-esteem grows higher and stronger, but if we are selfish and negative, then our self-esteem will sink to levels from which we may not be able to recover. There is not necessarily always a direct correlation between monetary compensation and self-esteem. If we act in a selfish and negative manner, regardless of how much more money we are making, our self-esteem goes down. Therefore, we need to work two or three times harder and smarter to rationalize and accept a higher opinion of ourselves, which would bring a higher self-esteem. We cannot have self-esteem with a self-destructive attitude. This is simply impossible! Some people can never get enough money. Others keep building assets but never self-esteem.

## Self-Respect

Now, let us also evaluate what self-respect is. There is definitely a big difference between self-respect and self-esteem. According to Nathaniel Branden, self-esteem is just a general feeling of personal worth and personal intrinsic value. But to respect something or somebody means to accept them as is. Our societies depend on the idea of self-respect.

We need to accept our limitations to be at ease and at peace with ourselves. If you do not accept yourself, you risk not ever being happy. That, to my mind, is a no-no!

My grandfather once told me: "If you can change it and it has a solution...why worry? But if you cannot change it and it does not have a solution...why worry?" Since I was a kid, my parents told us to change those things that are dynamic and able to be changed but not waste our time with things that are beyond our control or influence.

Ellen J. Langer, psychology professor at Harvard says:

> A person with self-respect simply likes her– or himself. This self-respect is not contingent on success, because there are always failures to contend with. Neither is it a result of comparing ourselves with others, because there is always someone better. These are tactics usually

employed to increase self-esteem. Self-respect, however, is a given. We simply like ourselves or we don't. With self-respect, we like ourselves because of who we are, contrary to what we can or cannot do.

I agree with this statement, but I feel there is more to self-respect than just accepting myself the way I am. To my understanding, this does not indicate that I necessarily respect myself fully. I believe respect starts from accepting yourself but does not end there. I do respect and like myself, but I know there is much room for improvement. I like myself because I know I am also capable of improving every day. It is important to state the difference between accepting yourself, liking yourself, and ignoring or not caring about your potential and how you really fit in your community and overall society. In my view, liking yourself does not mean you completely respect yourself.

Let me explain a bit further with a brief example. For a minute, just imagine you are in an average fast-food restaurant or coffee shop, and you see a couple eating on the table beside you, making lots of noise, talking with their mouths full, spraying food particles while they eat, dressed very sloppily or dirtily, dropping food on the table and on the floor, and when they are done eating, getting up and leaving a real mess behind them. From my personal point of view, these are uneducated low class people, self-centered, messy, disrespectful, and rude. It is obvious they do not respect themselves, much less others.

Now, allow me the benefit of the doubt. To my mind, these types of people lack any kind of manners and are extremely selfish. But they are smart enough to know that they are misbehaving. Even when others glare at them, they do not care. Such people live in an oblivious, insensitive, and unconcerned state of mind with absolute disregard of how they portray themselves in society. They have lost interest in how others perceive them and whether they are ridiculing themselves or not through their Neanderthal-style behaviors. They totally lack self-esteem, but they have also lost respect for themselves. But guess what? These types of individuals are everywhere and they are procreating. I am not a psychologist nor a psychiatrist, but as a businessman with education, experience, and good behavior throughout my life, I can certainly distinguish if a person has self-respect or not.

I refuse to believe that people like these, with all the negative attributes described above, respect and like themselves. I object to believing they sincerely and deeply like and accept themselves the way they are. They are either too lazy or ignorant or do not care to make the slightest change to better themselves. In my own perception, these types of people do not even feel ashamed of their primitive behaviors anymore. They have lost respect for their own persona and, obviously, for others. Again, these kinds of people are defined in my dictionary (and of all those people I researched) as people who have very low or no self-esteem at all and suffer an uncivilized and impolite way of living their daily lives.

Another short example: just for a moment, assume you are in a public place, and the fellow beside you is on the phone almost yelling about subjects and matters that are clearly (or should be) personal. I find that very rude, and it definitely invades other people's personal space. Now, what if I get my own phone and pretend I am also talking to somebody loudly and non-stop? I am sure that even that person will find this uncomfortable, confusing, and irritating. So why does he or she do it? Could it be because of ignorance, stupidity, rudeness, total lack of education, absence of class, or simply absolute lack of self-esteem and dearth of self-respect? Or is it just that they do not care? A person with self-respect acts with pride and confidence, not with absolute disregard. A person with self-esteem, self-respect, and self-control always acts with a strong feeling of behaving with dignity and honor, contrary to the two examples above.

People with a lack of self-esteem, self-respect, and self-control are less prone to guilt or to accepting blame, less likely to avoid uttering lies or to feel either regret or discomfort. They simply tend to have an attitude of "I do not care" or "whatever" and have no remorse for wrongdoing. They are comfortable in their Medieval-style world and behaviors. As my grandfather used to say, "they are fresh like a lettuce within their own skin", that is, with no guilt or remorse whatsoever.

Amazing! The worst is that there is nothing anybody can do or say. We need to turn a blind eye. What real choice do we have? Some are worse than animals, and, trust me, I am not about to start domesticating them.

Although self-esteem is based on how you evaluate yourself, mood plays an important role in this. People's moods or states of being change more often than we think. So many different matters affect people's moods—the weather, the music they are listening to, the amount of sleep they got the night before, what they ate that day, what they drank, their bosses or peers' influence, their levels of stress, etc. If these factors change the following day, people's moods also change.

There are no fixed rules or permanent points of comparison to evaluate self-esteem; therefore, there is no specific accepted foundation. However, there is a direct correlation between mood and the evaluation of your own persona. If people are affected by their environment, they can adopt a negative state of being, a negative mood, and create a low self-evaluation. This is contrary to when they are happy, because they will then evaluate themselves more highly. People in distress tend to be in a negative mood and therefore have a low self-evaluation.

On the other hand, self-respect is based on how you act and what you do and is directly related to your behaviors. Here we do have specific previous foundations regarding the moral and ethical things to do. Yes, to the surprise of many, there are moral and ethical ways of behaving in every specific situation within our society, which helps to govern the boundaries of evaluating self-respect in people. A friend sent me the following quote from nononsenseselfdefense.com:

> Self-respect is based on demonstrable facts. Facts that, although they are created and influenced by you, exist independent of you. Facts that are not subject to change unless you actively enact that change by your actions.

Therefore, it is a fact that certain behaviors by people in society are considered wrong and may even be penalized by law, but people keep on doing them (e.g. spitting in the street or parking a car using two or more parking spots). Why? Because either they do not care, or there are no immediate penalties, or they lack respect for themselves and for others in their community.

They do not feel guilt, nor do they feel ashamed of their actions. They coexist among us with a primitive-style attitude, until they are caught and sanctioned. Initially, their self-esteem is irrelevant or might even be high, but after being caught, it might collapse.

The problem with self-esteem is that it is in people's own perception, but self-respect and respect for others is measured by society in various ways. There are behavioral standards that we need to abide by. But many people tend to be lazy and do not care, so they go beyond the boundaries of self-respect, thinking they have the right to do and act as they please. This is simply wrong. It denotes total lack of respect for themselves and for others.

If you spit in the streets of Singapore, you are breaking the law and can be seriously punished. But if you spit in any North American city, nobody really tells you a thing. People are afraid of a disrespectful and challenging reaction by the perpetrator either verbally or physically, if they tell the person spitting that he or she should not do this. But when a person spits, he or she is certainly behaving without pride and dignity. By definition, it is a disrespectful action towards others and themselves. In other countries, it is rightly penalized by law. Why should we endure the spray of spit in the middle of downtown and keep on walking without even knowing if our friendly spitter is sick and spreading some kind of illness?

As bad as it might sound, the average spit is a combination of somebody else's saliva and mucous, sometimes even with a secret potent combination of germs, blood, tobacco residue, and their own DNA package. Yikes, is that disgusting or what? It is disrespectful, vulgar, and aggressive, and make no mistake, it is also truly heinous and repugnant to many people.

But hey, that is only me and my own upbringing and standards. Tell that to the average teenager or to any baseball player, and they will certainly have a different opinion. Some have developed and perfected such a good technique that they will hit their target with the accuracy of a llama or a cobra, and I am not kidding. They even have spitting competitions. That must be very "entertaining". Go figure!

This reminds me of what a very well-known nineteenth-century writer called John Stuart Mill, who was one of the most influential philosophers in the area of social and political theories, once wrote: "It is better to be a human being dissatisfied, than a pig satisfied." Unfortunately, there is an expanding minority, now reaching alarming levels in North America, that does not understand the depth of what J S Mill meant by this quote, or simply does not care. They would rather live in their own piggish style life, distancing themselves from the dignified concept of a human being.

## Self-control

Self-control is the most powerful tool human beings have to achieve progress, to master themselves, and to have a stronger chance to succeed. It is a very powerful psychological, self-regulated trait that empowers people in their quest to triumph in sports, business, politics, or hobbies.

Self-control is the golden key and the most essential tool to achieve goals more efficiently while avoiding emotions or impulses we might regret in the future and that could derail us from our goals and from achieving success. Self-control allows us to control our desires, behaviors, thoughts, and emotions. Those who have self-control have the most powerful weapon against those who lack this magnificent trait.

We all need to regulate and master our desires, reactions, and impulses to avoid making mistakes and to promote accuracy, determination, and a faster and more efficient method of accomplishing our goals. There is a very good article in Scientific American magazine entitled "Conquer Yourself, Conquer the World" by Roy F. Baumeister, which was published in April, 2015. Dr. Baumeister is a social psychologist and professor in the Department of Psychology at Florida State University. In his article, he writes something worth quoting at length:

> The ability to regulate our impulses and desires is indispensable to success in living and working with others. People with good control over their thought processes, emotions, and behaviors not only flourish in schools and in their jobs but are also healthier, wealthier, and more popular. They have better intimate relationships (as their partners confirm) and are more trusted by others. What is more, they are less likely to go astray by getting arrested, becoming addicted to drugs, or experiencing unplanned pregnancies. They even live longer. Brazilian writer Paulo Coelho summed up these benefits in one of his novels: "If you conquer yourself, then you will conquer the world."

Experts in psychology now concur that even self-esteem, though very important, is secondary to self-control, which is the key to harmoniously living, working, and succeeding with others. But self-discipline is a difficult virtue to master, unless it is taught from a very early stage in life. It is a challenge to have the willpower to control our emotions and actions, but if we train our thoughts and desires, we can achieve higher degrees of self-control.

Self-control should and can be taught to children. If a dog can learn not to eat a fresh steak placed in front of his snout, a child should be able to master self-control. Police and military dogs require a high degree of self-control to work with the police and military forces. The same thing applies to rescue dogs and dogs used for handicapped people. Their owners and whoever gets to know them revere these dogs, if the dogs are trained properly.

Unfortunately, children do not get taught self-control to the degree they should at the early stages of life. Tantrums and capricious acts follow when they are told something different from what they want. Parents give in, and that is when the possibilities of a more successful life start declining, compared to the children of parents who, in coordination, stand strong in their principles, while providing the same degree of love and attention at the same time.

Moderation in life is the key to progress and success. As Roy F Baumeister, explains in his article entitled "Mental Muscle Building," willpower is a mental muscle that can be trained:

> I have come to the conclusion that self-control, which might also be referred to as self-regulation or willpower, works something like a muscle does. In particular, it seems to "tire" after a workout. Several hundred studies in many labs have now replicated the basic finding that, after exerting willpower, people have less left over to complete a second choice.

To me, this implies that working hard to build self-control requires training and getting to know oneself in order to succeed in the medium-term and long-term in matters that are important to us. These matters are crucial to achieve our goals and to open the possibilities to succeed above and beyond others. This is done through moderation and self-monitoring.

According to Baumeister, "new findings suggest that any brain changes occurring in addicts do not lead to a loss of self-control. People can often choose whether to give in to a craving or resist." But, he adds, willpower and strength of character disappear once addiction takes over.

On April 22, 2017, there was an article published by TMZ (thirty-mile zone) entitled: "American Airlines mother allegedly struck by stroller, tried fitting large buggy on plane." The employee was immediately suspended pending further investigation. I truly feel for the employee because passengers in general either bluntly abuse or disrespect the policies of the airlines in relation to what they can or cannot bring on board. Nobody really seems to care whose luggage space is above people's seats anymore. First come, first served. If it is empty, they tend to shove their suitcase in while disrespecting and challenging others. Sadly, the employee's frustration pushed him to act in an unjustifiable manner, though I feel confident he tried to do his job the best possible, like they always tend to do. Unfortunately, he lost perspective and control of the situation. But in an effort to be fair with the employee, let us evaluate the other side of the coin and the reason of what triggered the situation and caused all this to happen.

A woman with twins and a double stroller challenged the rights and the security of other passengers while ignoring the policies of the airline. In my opinion, her lack of sensibility and respect for others might cost an employee his job who was pushed to act inappropriately by an intransigent and selfish mother of two. She was specifically told that her stroller was over 20 lbs. and too large to go in the plane with her. That she should check it and leave it at the gate. The message was crystal clear. But she refused and insisted on taking it with her, causing a big scandal. If one exception is ever made, the airlines would need to allow everybody to do the same. They cannot discriminate, so just imagine the chaos if they were to allow exceptions.

Now, the really unfortunate social problem is that the average person fails to see that the mother of the twins wanted to bully and push her way in, disrespecting company policies and threatening the safety and comfort of all other passengers. It appears she only wanted to impose her "rights" selfishly, with total disregard to the system and security of other passengers. To other people, the woman seemed to have used her children as a shield (or as a weapon) and started sobbing out loud in an exaggerated, pretentious manner, and completely out of control. She alienated others to the extent that an orangutan-minded individual sprung up his seat and wanted to punch the airline employee.

We live in a world that if you expose yourself as the victim (right or wrong), you have a lot more to win. You can step on others' rights with total disregard and nobody has the courage to say anything because they are afraid of being accused of being intolerant, racist and cowardly. In reality, it is the person's rights that are being violated by another disrespectful individual, who tends to be the real coward. In this specific case, it was the mother of two playing the victim of a situation she herself instigated. Again, I agree that the attendant reacted incorrectly and should have controlled himself and expose her for what that woman really is, a troublemaker and to some, an exaggerator, abusive and a hypocrite. Unfortunately, only the end of the situation was caught on video, which is exactly what went viral and American Airlines, afraid of being sued perhaps, decided to publicly state: "We are deeply sorry for the pain we have caused this passenger and her family and to any other customers affected by the incident. The actions of our team member captured here do not appear to reflect patience or empathy, two values necessary for customer care. In short, we are disappointed by these actions."

Next day, an article by TMZ confirmed that the mother and her children were upgraded to first class on a later flight home to Argentina. My background is Latino, and I know very well that in the Latino culture people tend to be more "expressive" or "exaggerated." That is what they tend to do. In fact, there is a saying that goes: "*Niño que no llora, no mama*", which literally means, "A kid that does not cry, does not suck". In English, it is usually translated as "If you do not ask, you do not get" or "the squeaky wheel gets the oil." The mother of two was "crying" (no teardrops but sobbing out loud) totally out of control for something that apparently was not justified.

Are the "rights" of one person more important than the rights and safety of other passengers, along with the internal policies of companies representing us all and providing us with a professional service? Is this a paradox perhaps? In my mind, no matter our gender, no matter our job, no matter our position, we all require to treat others with respect, comply with the system, and acknowledge the trust laid upon us by others without abusing it, or allowing it to be abused by others.

Do you think that nowadays everything should be accepted and that everybody should mind their own business, except those who lack respect for others and interfere in somebody else's private space, but if stopped, they cry abuse, racism or whatever? Don't we need to re-connect with our principles, basic ethics and traditional morals to avoid a society out of control and gear it back on track? In today's runaway society anything goes, nothing is wrong, things will be fine, tolerance is a virtue, total acceptance is a must and blind faith should prevail, but many believe that this will continue until one imminent and irrefutable day our society will abruptly fall on its knees and bust its teeth, changing its optimistic smile forever. The best way to stop a runaway society is to jump into the driver's seat and intentionally slam on the hydraulic brakes and bring it to a total halt. Acting in a politically correct or incorrect fashion, is sometimes irrelevant. It is important to regain control of the future of for our community and us. Responsibility and integrity should be our motivational factors to stop the declining moral and ethical standards in hopes of rescuing our society. To illustrate this better, I want to quote the following:

- One way to stop a runaway horse is to bet on him – Jeffrey Bernard.
- Our runaway judiciary is badly in need of restraint by Congress – Phyllis Schafly.
- One way to stop a runaway society is to take responsibility – Rafael Carreras.
- Our runaway society is badly in need of self-esteem and self-control – Rafael Carreras.

## Self-control, narcissism and self-confidence

Self-esteem and self-respect are very important, but they cannot be achieved if we have no self-control. We live in the most narcissistic epidemic of times. Backward people are confusing narcissism with self-esteem and confidence. Many seem not to know the difference. We should not brag about ourselves or have excessive self-admiration or self-love, because we might fall into the abyss of self-centeredness, believing that everything revolves around us, which is a shallow and dumb mistake, but many do not see this clearly.

Narcissism, to me, consists of self-admiration and self-absorption. It is a disease that induces failure through not living in reality. It represents a high degree of egotism and egoism. Some go to the extent of being, without realizing it, egomaniacs. Some people consider narcissists to have too much self-confidence (and I agree). Narcissistic people do not care about other's needs and preferences. They have a continual attitude of believing that their needs are above and beyond those of others. Being narcissistic is a very sad way of living a life, and in the end, very unproductive.

We used to be taught humility, quietness, modesty, simplicity, and moderation. These traits seem not to exist anymore in the younger generation, who live surrounded by excessive social media, weak and dissimilar parenting styles, easy access to any service or product, and the crazy idea that you can be anybody and do anything. Real life and their personal human limitations will teach them that self-confidence and trust in themselves are the essential tools to succeed, along with self-control. If you have self-esteem, you can respect, love, and believe in yourself. These are crucial elements for developing a strong degree of self-confidence without venturing into the darkness of narcissism, which only leads to frustration in life.

In an article, "Kiddo Knows Best" in the June 2015 issue of Scientific American, Andre Alfano writes that parenting styles can make the difference between bringing up a self-confident child or a "narcissistic nightmare." Alfano reports that the University of Amsterdam and Utrecht University in the Netherlands concluded that "children of excessively praising parents were more likely to score high on narcissistic qualities but not on self-esteem." She also mentions that they found that lack of parental warmth showed no link to narcissism.

## Millennials vs. Generation X and Baby Boomers

The most recent generation cycles, per Strauss and Howe, are commonly known as follows:

- G.I. Generation (b. 1901-1924) - Heroes - Early 1900s.

- Silent Generation (b. 1925–1942) - Artists - The 20s and 30s.

- Baby Boomers (b. 1943-1960) - Prophets - The 40s and 50s .

- Generation X (b. 1961-1981) - Nomads – The 60s and 70s.

- Millennials (b. 1982-2004) - Next Heroes - The 80s and 90s.

- Post-Millennials (b. 2005 and onward) - iGeneration or Founders.

There is no doubt in my mind that the Millennials (aka Generation Y) are the least well-behaved and the least adapted to their communities. They have serious social issues and behavioral inconsistencies. Obviously, we cannot generalize, but I am referring to the great majority. Having said that, the older generation (Baby Boomers) is catching up with similar issues and inconsistencies in many areas, especially related to the use of cell phones and social media. They are also showing symptoms of cell phone and social media addiction, instead of setting a better example for Millennials. Let me explain by using a well-known 15-minute speech about

Millennials made by Simon Sinek, an author, motivational speaker, and marketing consultant in the United States.

According to Sinek the Millennials are narcissistic, selfish, unfocused, self-absorbed, emotionally unstable, arrogant, pompous, with low self-esteem and, therefore, high insecurity. But Sinek says that their worst characteristic is their high degree of entitlement, that is, Millennials believe they deserve special treatment in everything, along with the best of opportunities for quick development and guaranteed achievement, such as faster promotions, better salaries, extra benefits, etc.

To my mind, Sinek's video is excellent in about 95 per cent of what he brings to the table, but I believe he makes one serious and alarming omission or mistake when he claims that all the Millennia's social deficiencies and behavioral inconsistencies "are not a fault of their own." Sinek insists several times that it is not the Millennials' fault at all but that of their parents and teachers only. But let's face it, even a three-month-old puppy knows the difference between right and wrong in peeing inside or outside of their den. Metaphorically speaking, Millennials also know very well if they are "peeing" on their own future or not, but their self-righteous attitudes is stronger than their will to accept responsibility and make an effort to positively change that negative attitude. Millennials definitely know better, because from a very early stage in life, they could differentiate between good and bad, right and wrong. Most importantly, they are experts in taking advantage of their parents' and teachers' weaknesses by pretending not to see and understand the right thing to do. The reason why I was surprised by Sinek's comment of taking away their share of responsibility, like parents and teachers have done throughout the life of the Millennials.

Many parents praise their children in everything they do regardless of how well or badly they do it. Many teachers also praise all their students for fear of "traumatizing" some or in fear of parental retaliation. When Millennials are launched into the real world, therefore, their self-esteem comes crashing down, because they realize their substandard background and capabilities and that all they have been told has been exaggerated. They stop being proud of who they are, and the blame game starts. They are in for a cold shower and immediately realize they are not as special as they were told they were, thus sending their self-respect to a dark and lonely abyss.

Millennials also tend not to have true and sincere friends that understand them and are willing to support them in the middle of the storm, no matter what. Almost all their friends are simply 'digital friends." Most do not develop deep relationships. They simply do not know how to do this. In their social media "relationships," they are strong and secure at first, but at the click of a button, they are dropped by others and devastated if they are not followed or texted back.

Sinek notes that constant social media interaction produces high levels of dopamine in users' systems. This is very addictive, but when these superficial digital friendships are gone, the dopamine-highs become dopamine-lows, causing so much pain that many react with depression, drinking or drug addiction to ease their pain. Some even become suicidal.

According to Sinek, the Millennials' sense of patience is nonexistent, with which I totally agree. They all want immediate results and gratification without putting the time into things. They do not know nor want to sacrifice time and effort to achieve something. They do not realize that "easy comes, easy goes." To get to the top in any professional activity, they need to put in the required energy, time, and good disposition. Above all, they need to develop patience.

Without this capacity for patience, all of their talent, intelligence and creativity is futile, because they cannot focus on long-term goals. When they are told to follow procedures or to do this or that, many do not have the knowledge or maturity to realize that they do not know everything. They can be hypocritical and lie to themselves while camouflaging this with expressions such as: I did not know, I am sorry, I did not mean it, I will make it up to you, I felt depressed, I had no choice, etc. And then there is the worst expression of them all … "whatever." But guess what, they are mainly affecting their own personal lives in the medium-term and long-term.

Of course, we have to keep in mind that we also have brilliant young people among them, and we have to help them succeed and shine. They truly need our help, and we should all make a collective effort to assist them in some form or shape. Hopefully, we can also show them how to be grateful and appreciative, while helping them to erase their mistaken feelings of entitlement.

To make matters worse, generation Z, all those born in the early 2000s and onwards, have serious problems of their own. A good example can be found in the Feb 2017 issue of Maclean's magazine in an article by Aaron Hutchins entitled "Baby want a kale salad?" that satirizes "bringing up gluten-free, holistic, vegan, self-righteous baby; From chiropractic treatments for newborns to extreme diets for infants, inside the increasing and delusional new parenting craze." The article comes at a perfect time to back up a great deal of what I have written in this book. But still, so many parents do not understand (or want to understand), though I hope they start changing for the sake of their children, if they really love them. In this article, Hutchins observes:

- Parents can go astray despite best intentions. It is not something you want to play around with. It is your child's life.

- One child on a diet came with vitamin D deficiency, B12 deficiency, and the list was endless.

- We do not have alternative physics. But in health, we have this huge tolerance for non-scientific perspectives.

I encourage every parent to read this article. It will help them to see things differently, I hope.

## Changing your Conditions of Existence (Self-discipline)

There is no doubt we need to make a daily effort to control and guide ourselves to a better path. I recently read a book called Another Way To Live Your Life by Ernie Tadla. In Chapter 6, he writes about how thoughts can become things. I absolutely agree with him and want to quote some of his truisms:

1. "If you do not like your world, you have it within your power to change your 'conditions of existence' right

where you are, if you have the faith and consistent will to do so."

2. "If you continue in your present level of human functioning and thought, you will only experience your present level of human existence."

3. "This is your golden opportunity to take control of your life as never before, by getting control of your thoughts and emotions—your electrical and magnetic impulses—the blueprints of your future experiences."

4. "By your thoughts, you can change your personal future, if you will but heed my words, understand your true origins, believe in them, and use this knowledge in your daily routine."

5. "Whatever you hold steadfastly in mind externalizes."

Powerful true words. Tadla's key point, that thoughts become things, is something many other authors have also expressed in the past, but Tadla writes in a very refined and clear manner. So, if you really want to change the image of yourself (physically and mentally) and achieve higher self-confidence, self-esteem, and self-respect, then you need to focus on changing what Tadla calls your conditions of existence.

We need strong will and self-control to change those present conditions of our existence, but Tadla emphasizes that we have the power to create our own reality. Life is full of choices, and we have the power to make the best choices in the circumstances that surround us. If we think positively and make the right choices, our self-confidence, along with our self-esteem, rise to higher levels. It gets stronger. This does not necessarily come easily, but one can try to achieve it. Anybody can and should try. Remember, everybody has a choice. If there is a will, there's definitely a way.

## Tattooing and Piercing vs. Self-control and Self-esteem

We all know that tattooing and piercing have gone rampant in North America. This is neither good nor bad. To each their own, but the reality is that, as soon as we brand ourselves with a tattoo or pierce our body or face, we belong to a group which sends mixed messages to the rest of society. Those messages are not always for the best, whether we like it or not. But before we start talking about the correlation between low self-control and self-esteem and tattooing and piercing our own body or face, I would like to bring to the reader's attention a little bit of history about tattooing and piercing, so we can try to understand (if possible) why piercing and tattooing have gone rampant in our modern North American society, specifically in Canada and the United States, though not as much in Mexico.

Apparently, the English word tattoo comes from the Poylnesian word "Tatau" from Tahiti, which means to mark something. The word and the tradition of tattooing were introduced to Europe mainly by English sailors. Initially, tattooing was practiced largely by lower-class people. But as the years went by, some high-class people had small tattoos designed on their bodies, though usually hidden by clothing so as not to affect their status in society.

The purpose of tattooing and piercing is different among different cultures. Throughout history, they have been a crucial part of the tradition and ritual habits of many cultures. For example, in Japan, history indicates that the first tattoos were used to mark criminals. The criminal's first offence was marked with a line across the forehead, the second with another line, and the third by yet another line. These three lines formed the Japanese character for the word "dog" and meant that, after three strikes, you were an outlaw under Japanese law. These tattoos were done to mark prisoners as well, so that, if they escaped, they could easily be identified. Some soldiers in Japan also tattooed themselves for military purposes as well.

Some authors claim that tattooing has existed since between 12,000 and 10,000 BC. Tattooing and piercing have taken place throughout history on all inhabited continents during different eras and cultures, and have had a great deal of influence on various countries and their specific civilizations. Tattooing and piercing have expanded without barriers or borders through Europe, Asia, Africa, Australia, and America with the passing of time.

For a very long time in human history, tattooing and piercing were common only amongst sailors and criminals. Later in some cultures, it was practiced by a different group of people than that of the average citizen. In other cultures, it simply used to denote a lower class or an unwanted group of people. But times have changed drastically, and now it seems to be a common practice among many people in our North American society. Initially, tattooing was also common in circuses all around the world, which used to have, and still do, extravagant and exotic people.

These types of people and their circus environment have

always attracted the average citizen to a world totally different from a normal and accepted traditional society.

Polynesia has had some of the most artistic and intrinsic tattooing of all time. Polynesians believe that the power in the spirit of an individual is represented by specific, characteristic, and distinctive tattoos on the body or face. According to tradition, these tattoos also protected people against bad spirits throughout their lives. This form of expression has always represented a very strong cultural heritage in the country of origin and a big influence on other cultures, such as when British sailors first landed in the Polynesian islands.

In New Zealand, tattooing was a reflection of very refined artistry. In fact, it was more than just imprinting a design on the body; it was carving a design or specific lines and marks on people's bodies and faces. In the Maori culture, the marks on their faces denoted different statuses within their society.

In Peru, tattooed mummies have been unearthed dating from the 11th century AD. Women apparently practiced tattooing by applying a skin-stitching technique. Among some Peruvian tribes, some tattooed lines on the upper lip emulated mustaches and had specific meanings among their people.

In the early Greek and Roman empires, men and women used to tattoo themselves. Women thought about tattoos as exotic beauty marks, but Greek and Roman authorities used to tattoo slaves, criminals, and gladiators for recognition purposes. At one time, there were more tribes tattooed in the jungles of South America than anywhere else in the world. It was most noticeable in the Brazilian rainforest. Even the Vikings used to tattoo themselves. This was reported by other cultures that encountered the Vikings, which described them as pictures or art on the Viking's bodies and faces. The tattoos denoted power, strength, and stamina, and also indicated one's origins.

The Mayans in Mexico and Guatemala used to tattoo themselves as a sign of determination, courage, and status. They worshipped different gods, and their tattoos depicted those they worshipped the most. In other parts of North America, and specifically in the United States and Canada, different Native Americans tattooed themselves to reflect a specific position or status within their tribe. This was the case among the Chickasaw and Iroquois people, for example. In 1891, Samuel O'Reilly invented the electric tattooing machine, which helped popularize the tattooing tradition as an expanded and deeper artistic expression.

From Egypt to France, Peru to England, Japan to China, Australia to Thailand to the United States, all over the world at different moments in time and history, humans have practiced tattooing and piercing all over their bodies. Nevertheless, through many centuries, tattoos were mostly limited and related to five main categories: ancient tribes, prisoners and criminals, sailors, circus people, and those with psychological and mental problems.

According to Reef Karim, founder and director of the Control Center in Beverly Hills, UCLA, a centre that provides help for mental problems and addiction, tattooing is a modern form of social branding. In his article "Art or Self Destruction? Modern-day Social Branding" in Huffington Post Healthy Living (Nov 9, 2012), he asks: "Is tattooing art or self-destruction?" He then explains, from his experience and point of view, why people tattoo themselves:

People get tattoos for many reasons: for attention, self-expression, artistic freedom, rebellion, a visual display of a personal narrative, reminders of spiritual/cultural traditions, sexual motivation, addiction, identification with a group, or even drunken impulsiveness (which is why many tattoo parlors are open late).

And now about 35% of Americans have some type of long-term body art. What was once considered self-mutilating behaviors and a psychiatric problem has now become an "artistic expression" and a quasi-normative behavior.

## Are tattoos related to low self-control or self-esteem, or is it just an artistic expression?

This is a very difficult modern subject, extremely polemic and highly controversial for many. Some people still consider tattooing the social branding of a lower class, but others insist it is just an artistic expression of modern society. To each their own, and we need to learn and respect that. I personally believe that tattooing and body piercing are meant to express people's personalities, ways of thinking, and personal preferences at a specific time. For many, it is just to make a personal point. Unfortunately for some, today's trend could easily turn into tomorrow's regret. Therefore, many of yesterday's big-time trendsetters choose later on in life to remove those tattoos they once held very dear and displayed with pride.

Among the most important self-help subjects, we find the concept and practice of self-respect holding hands very closely with self-love. Unfortunately, many people lack confidence, faith, and conviction in themselves, bringing their self-esteem to very low levels. Due to that situation, some people end up disrespecting themselves, and this can be extremely harmful and dangerous.

These types of people usually need motivation from a well-trained third party or from loving family members. They need help to learn how to appreciate and respect their own persona. We are all unique individuals, and we all deserve fair and respectful treatment. We need to realize that we are all distinctive, special, independent people with unique strengths and weaknesses that need to be understood and accepted within the normal civic boundaries of the society in which we live. We all have the ability, and a fair possibility, to thrive, succeed, and achieve happiness. To my mind, self-respect seems to be the antidote to save and promote self-esteem; that is, with self-respect there is hope for self-esteem. A person with low self-esteem is a person with a broken spirit, which many people take advantage of.

People with low self-esteem need help and understanding. So how is self-esteem related to tattooing? In research by Marie Randle and Sue Aitken from Liverpool Hope University, reported at the annual conference of the British Psychological Society in Brighton, England, in April, 2009, participants from the North of England were questioned about their reasons for tattooing and where they tattooed themselves, while also answering a self-esteem questionnaire. The results were as follows:

> Findings highlighted the four main motivators for getting a tattoo: rebellion, aesthetic appearance, personal or emotional significance, and group affiliation. Men were

more likely to have tattoos related to their group membership (such as football teams or army regiment). However, women tended to have tattoos for rebellious or aesthetic reasons.

These motivational factors are directly related to self-esteem, according to Randle and Aitken. Therefore, they strongly encourage people to give serious thought and meticulous evaluation to their motivation for getting tattooed before they mark their body forever with a permanent design or symbol.

A good example of the need for caution is an advertisement released in March 2013 by Mars Incorporated for their snack called Combos. The advertisement used an image of good Combos and one of bad Combos. The good Combos image shows their edible snack, and the bad Combos image is of a wrinkled old woman in a bikini with an insane message tattooed on her back that reads "Forever 18," with something looking roughly like a butterfly design. For many people, she simply looks ridiculous, disgusting, and even aggressive. But hey, it is her right to do what she wants, regardless (to some) of her lack of logic, self-respect, common sense, and care for other's rights of privacy while invading their visual space with a totally provocative and defiant "artistic work" or attitude. For many, there are some rights that should simply not exist, because they infringe others' rights.

A neutral position is the best to keep peace around us, but we certainly need to build tolerance to higher levels. It is easy to misbehave and act and look vulgar, but not as easy to behave properly and act and look decent. It takes care, effort, and dedication. It takes self-control and discipline.

What does the average person say when asked why they tattoo their body or face? In general, they respond: "It is my body, it is my desire, it is my way to express myself, it is my life, and it is my decision. Period!"

Not happy or satisfied with this average answer, I performed a random and lengthy research and asked a wide variety of individuals about their tattoos. My last research was at the 3rd Annual Okanagan Tattooing Show, which took place on July 17-19, 2015, in Kelowna, BC. The respondents all had a few different reasons for why they tattoo themselves. They were all fascinating to talk to and listen to about their specific personal motivation for either piercing or tattooing themselves. The following were among the most common reasons:

- It is an artistic expression, and art is beautiful.
- It is a feeling of belonging or love.
- To tell their own story.
- Just because they want to.
- It represents a unique place and time in their lives.
- To look better by covering their body with beautiful art and memories.
- To start a healing process.
- To create a new personality and be somebody different.
- Because they succumbed to peer pressure but later acknowledged they made a mistake.
- To provoke a reaction and make a point.
- To attract others and experience a new approach in life.
- Because they made a mistake and did not fully realize what they were in for at first.
- To look feminine or sexy.
- To cover an old scar.
- To feel and look masculine and/or imposing.

- Wanting a tougher look for specific reasons and needs.
- To comply with a group or clan.
- Because …why not? Everybody else their age is doing it.
- To give them a sense of belonging and security.
- To position themselves among their own cohorts.
- It is the fashion and some people's overall artistic approach.
- It is a requirement and condition for belonging to a gang.
- It has a sentimental value for them.
- They do not want to forget something.
- They were feeling low and depressed then and needed a change.
- It is part of their religion, tradition, or beliefs.
- It shows their real values, where they come from, and who they are.
- It is a family thing and part of their ancestors and history.

Many psychologists conclude that tattooing is mainly done for one or more of the following reasons:

- Not liking their body and wanting to hide it.
- Old Tradition.
- An uncontrollable desire to make a point.
- Negative emotion and personality.
- Feelings of anger and frustration.
- Pleasing and satisfying others.
- Weakness and lack of self-control.
- Standing out to show one's distinctiveness in society.
- Impulsive character.
- Insecure personality.
- Artistic expression of modern times.
- Defiant and rebellious attitude possibly engaging in

dangerous behaviors.
- Borderline personality disorder.


## Main negative impacts of tattoos and piercing

Most people practicing or inflicting these tattoos and piercing techniques on their bodies, faces, and heads are not necessarily aware of all the dangers. Among the most important and common are the following:

- The risk of serious and detrimental psychological addiction.
- During the application and while healing, some of these markings can go beyond the threshold of pain that some people can endure.
- Subjects are prone to abscesses and skin rashes.
- Subjects are open to all sorts of infections such as Hepatitis B or C, HIV, tetanus, etc. Some infections can lead to death.
- Bleeding for long periods and scarring.
- Pierced objects interfere with scanners at airports and with medical equipment, putting subjects' security and lives at risk. They also risk having new skin grow over the jewelry.
- Risk of immediate or future severe allergic reactions.
- Subjects are prone to lose good job opportunities in industries in which tattoos are simply not accepted by many employers.
- Nerve damage and unhealthy subcutaneous growths that need removing.

Four Important Notes:

1. The Canadian Blood Services considers ineligible the donation of blood from all people with tattoos and piercings within the first six months after having the tattoos or piercings done. They represent a high risk for hepatitis C and other infections.

2. Tattooing and piercing seem to be a trend and a fashion. But we all know that trends and fashions tend to reduce and lessen with time. Is it wise to practice this trend then?

3. A friend of mine who is against tattoos once told me that he did not encourage his children to have them done. Why I asked? He said: "In an old wrinkled skin, today's beautiful tattoo of a dolphin will be tomorrow's orca; today's hummingbird tomorrow's vulture; today's skull tomorrow's waxy-droopy skull; today's seal tomorrow's walrus. And if that is not enough, some seem to want to accelerate the process by going to the beach and tanning themselves silly."

4. There is scientific proof that tattooing affect in some people the lymphatic system.

At the end (my friend said) "I give their average tattoo less than 15 years to look good. Let us wait and see how much they will enjoy them later in life."

**Tattoo healing**

Some people have serious and deep traumas in their life that are very difficult to surmount and leave behind. Many men and women with scars on their bodies due to physical abuse are doing their best to turn those scars and traumas into an artistic expression. Some say that an artistic tattoo will forever cover that physical scar and help hide their trauma. With the aid of tattoos, they leave behind their frustrations while achieving peace and harmony for their future.

They cover their corporal mark with a beautiful array of colors and an intriguing and unique artistic outline and drawing that will bring them satisfaction and a sense of well-being. It helps them to let go of a damaging and stressful memory, which will contribute to heal their pain, grief, and suffering. This brings a better standard of life both for themselves and the people around them.

## Tattoos in the workplace

This has been a serious subject for debate in many arenas. Many employers cannot ask people to cover their tattoos in their working environment, and this is causing problems at work.

According to Ms. Nicola Middlemiss in an article in HRM Canada (April 07, 2016) entitled "B.C. hospital backs tattoo employee," there was a lady named Ms. Marie Molloy in the city of Lake Country, BC, who found a tattoo in the shape of a skull damaging, terrifying, and extremely offensive. A nurse "shoved it in her face," infringing her right to peace, calm, and a safe recovery. According to the article:

> Molloy's effects of a previous operation were exacerbated by the rheumatoid arthritis in her larynx and

her abnormal small airway. Struggling to breath, Molloy was fitted with a full-face, by-level positive airway pressure mask and given the sedative Ketamine. When she finally came around several hours later, Molloy says the only thing she could remember was her nurse's skull tattoo.

Complaints were made by Molloy's family members, but the hospital insisted that they do not, and will not, discriminate against staff with tattoos.

It is interesting where we are heading nowadays. People with aggressive tattoos, noisy, disrespectful and vulgar individuals, loud cellular conversations, and revealingly-dressed obese people have more rights and privileges than normal citizens whose personal space, visual space, and right to enjoy quiet and peaceful surroundings are being infringed, violated, overwhelmed, and stepped upon by perpetrators with their own "human rights" claims.

From my perspective, the ducks are shooting the hunters instead of the other way around. It seems this new breed of people has no deference or regard for others but only for themselves; their rights are above and beyond those of their cohorts, and they absolutely disregard the rights of others. But I guarantee things are going to change. Why? Because all human rights go both ways, not just one way. People whose rights are being violated can only take it for so long. It is human nature, and it is just a matter of time.

Canadians in general tend not to say a thing, because they do not want to offend or hurt the feelings of the perpetrator, but what about the person whose rights are being affected? I truly hope more and more people stand their ground for their rights when others are forcing themselves in, regardless of whether these others feel offended, hurt, or whatever the case may be. We need to draw the line. Again, respect goes both ways.

There was an article written by Stephanie Ip in The Province, published on April 22, 2016, entitled "Tattoos no longer issue for employers." Throughout her article, she wrote some personal thoughts and also referred to statements from other people in the human resources industry. Everybody knows that piercing and tattooing can be quite controversial, but the statements that caught my attention were those where Ms Ip, to my understanding, tries to justify them as accepted cultural norms, for example:

- Once a red flag in interviews, body art and piercing are becoming mainstream.
- Even Prime Minister Justin Trudeau has a tattoo of a Haida raven on his left shoulder.
- Some have done interviews with candidates who have visible piercings and body art, and sometimes it raises an eyebrow, but it is not something that they are concerned about.
- Does it impact their ability to do their job? I do not think so. That is not a reason to make or break a hiring decision.
- Ms Ip's personal view is that a lot of society needs to harden up just a tad.
- Trade industries don't care as long as you know how to use the tools.
- 72 per cent of all adults with tattoos said their ink isn't usually visible.

All of the above sounds nice in the world of tattoos. Outside that world, it is seen quite differently. It is an imposition to some sectors that are not willing to accept it openly. They silently and carefully discriminate against them. Right or wrong, it is not important, but it is a fact of life. Even the police and firefighters across North America get leery about tattoos and go the extra mile to see if any of those tattoos have any sort of affiliation with gangs, terrorists, or any other unlawful group. If in doubt, they will most likely not hire a candidate when they have others without tattoos but with the same skills.

This situation happens in any professional environment, although it is not openly accepted for fear of repercussions. Like racism, it is part of human nature for some people. Again, not openly accepted, but their silent actions and reactions prove differently, whether we agree or not.

Regarding Prime Minister Trudeau's tattoo, I wonder if that just adds to the reason why he is seen by some with doubt and mistrust, while others might identify with him and even see him as a worldwide celebrity? The real challenge is whether he is seen by his counterparts worldwide as an example to follow in the arena of politics, knowledge, experience, character to govern a country, delivering on what he promised, the protection of our environment and ecosystem, achieving multicultural integration, promoting the diversification of new industries, the creation of more jobs, control of inflation, protection against the devaluation of our Canadian dollar, etc. I sincerely want to trust that he will, but only time will tell.

I wonder why 72 per cent of adults with tattoos have them done on a part of their body that is not usually visible. Is it for fear of potential repercussions in the future? Aren't they proud of their artistic work? Are they insecure about what they are doing, but the peer pressure is stronger? Is it because they know that not everybody out there needs, wants, or has the ability to "harden up a tad" (as Ms Ip says)? With so many mixed messages out there, and whatever the reason any person might have, I still do not fully understand why so many people are branding their bodies forever. But guess what? That is the beauty of this world. We are all different, and we need to learn to live with each other in harmony and peace, doing our best to accept each other "as is." I am personally okay with that. To each its own.

## Artistic expression vs. symbol of rebellion

A writer for USA Today named Kim Painter published an article on May 15, 2016, entitled "Tattoos have gone mainstream, but they still carry risks." She starts by noting that, "if getting a tattoo is still a sign of rebellion, then a lot of Americans are rebels: 29 per cent of adults now have at least one tattoo, up from 21 per cent in 2012 and 16 per cent in 2003, a recent Harris Poll found." Painter adds that, according to the US Food and Drug Administration (FDA), as reported on its website, infections, allergic reactions, and various other negative reactions have been linked to tattoos.

The FDA is also apparently worried about the long-term effects on the body of the various types of inks and other chemicals used. Painter found that, according to the medical journal The Lancet, an average of 2.5 per cent of people tattooed or pierced get a serious bacterial, viral, or fungal infection. Some people suffer considerable health issues such as immune reactions and psoriasis flares, among many others. The Lancet review said that, even when tattoos are removed totally or partially through laser treatments, they can still have a long-lasting impact on an individual due to the ink breakdown in the body. Is this an overblown statement?

Perhaps, but the risks are there, though the immediate satisfaction of having a tattoo outweighs the negative impact 30 or 40 years down the road. By then, we will be old and wrinkled, so who really cares, right?

Some say that tattooing is just a way of rebelling against parents or social traditions. Once related only to low-class people, tattooing has now reached the level of the middle class and even some "high-class" people, if they still fit the category. It seems everybody nowadays is searching for their individuality, and that this is the reason some decide to tattoo or pierce themselves, regardless of what others might think about them. They just want to be different, make a statement, or show they are "artistically inclined." If tattoos strike some as kitsch, then they do not need to embrace them, though they need to learn to accept them, because it is now a normal thing that surrounds our daily lives. I just hope those who tattoo or pierce themselves do not live to regret it, as so many nowadays already do.

## Tattoo removal

Some tattoo removals can be painful and might not totally get rid of the tattoo. It depends a lot on the type of ink, how deep the ink is, how much ink concentrates under the skin, the types of colors used, the condition of the skin, and the tattooing method used.

The tattoo removal procedure through the laser method can be painful, very expensive, and time-consuming. Some surgical removal methods can bring serious complications. There are various products on the market that claim to remove tattoos safely and completely. These topical products have different specialties: erasing black ink only; erasing black and colored ink; for people with very sensitive skin; for various levels of effectiveness combined with laser methods, etc.

Any person wanting to remove their tattoo(s) needs to do proper research and talk to professionals about their own specific situation. Tattoo removals are not limited to laser methods and do-it-yourself removal creams. There are also intense pulsed-light therapy methods (very expensive) and other medical methods such as dermabrasion, but they tend to be very painful and leave some sort of scar.

Removal of tattoos is currently still very expensive. If you had a tattoo done for $250, the removal of that tattoo (everything else being normal) will cost an average of $2,500. However, nobody I talked to guarantees that the tattoo will completely disappear or that the cost will not go higher, if more treatments are required. Some people just go for the cover-up method. A new tattoo is designed to cover the previous bad tattoo or camouflage an unwanted one.

## Negative Actions Crush Self-respect

Many people nowadays believe that anything goes, and so they go through life with the attitude of "who cares!" These types of people do not really care about the consequences of their actions. They have the wrong attitude and only convey the wrong message and tend to create real conflict and, in many cases, self-inflicted pain and frustration.

To the dismay of a few, a good example of this was a political figure in Canada named Robert Ford (known as Rob Ford) who was the mayor of Toronto for some time and, later on, elected to city council.

<u>Seven Important Notes</u>:

1.  The following example is without prejudice and is only my personal opinion. I will use Rob Ford as an example to illustrate the antithesis of some human traits from the educational point of view. Why Rob Ford? Because, aside from being based on facts available in various public domain sources, Mr. Rob Ford was an example that transcended our borders, and also because most people have heard of him all across North America and beyond. This is also a free country with freedom of speech, as long as it is done with respect and based on true events. Last but not least, it is important for our younger generation to fully understand what is right and what is wrong.

2.  I personally would like to start by emphasizing my sincere and deep condolences to all the family members of Rob Ford, who passed away March 22, 2016. I also want to send my sincere condolences to all his followers and fans.

3.  Mr. Rob Ford passed away at a very early age, only 46 years old. He was a good family man, a successful businessman, and a devoted public servant. He is remembered as well for being totally committed to his constituents and totally devoted to serve the City of Toronto. He was passionate about being a public figure and showed this on a daily basis. He was also known to have been the

most easily accessible politician that Toronto has ever had.

4.   There is no doubt Rob Ford was ambitious, bold, and audacious. These are important traits to succeed as a politician and to achieve many great things, as he did for the City of Toronto and its people. Among his main achievements as a politician, he:

- Made strong improvements to the Toronto Transit Commission (TTC) and made it an essential service to all in Toronto.
- Succeeded in reaching a new collective agreement for full-time and part-time city workers.
- Improved Toronto's emergency medical services (EMS) and Toronto's fire services.
- Rebuilt public trust in the Toronto Community Housing Corporation (TCHC).
- Made Council more accountable and transparent in what they did.
- Reduced the excessive numbers of city staff.
- Helped balance the operating budget of the city of Toronto, while saving several millions of dollars.
- Contracted garbage collection to third parties.

5.   Unfortunately, if we were to portray his life as a silver coin, we can all attest to the fact that one side of the coin was always buffed and shiny, while the other side was dull and dark.

6.   In today's age, people sue anybody for the slightest reason and with the minimal excuse on hand. They either just want to retaliate and harm the other party, regardless of whether they are right or wrong, or they are simply looking for money.

Therefore, people are afraid of expressing their personal thoughts freely and accidentally rubbing, without malicious intention, other individuals the wrong way. But let's face it, when people read the truth about themselves or their loved ones, only a few "can handle the truth," so they lash out by suing immediately, regardless of the consequences and whether they are, or are not, utterly wrong.

Unfortunately, when the plaintiff (an individual bringing a case against another in a court of law) fails to succeed due to lack of facts, they often only get a slap on the wrist instead of a big hefty fine or even jail time.

7.   When the tragedy of Charlie Hebdo happened in Paris, many people lost their lives due to the deadly terrorist attack. The next morning, almost all Parisians were on the streets protesting against the attack and in favour of protecting their freedom of speech. This was echoed all around the world. Unfortunately, Charlie Hebdo ridiculed and made fun, with apparent disrespect, of others' faith. We are supposed not to discriminate against any other belief, worship or creed, so many people wondered why did Hebdo do it?

The bottom line is that, to many Muslims, Hebdo's mockery was simply unacceptable, and this is why unfortunately a few extremists reacted violently the way they did. Regrettably, their reaction was even worse and, in the eyes of the rest of the world, absolutely unacceptable. But nobody should be afraid of writing the truth if it is expressed based on facts, with respect and courtesy, which I always try to do myself in anything I write the best I can.

While Charlie Hebdo has been construed by many as

inappropriate, rude, and insulting, I certainly do not want my readers to misunderstand my intentions when referring to Rob Ford's case as an example, and this is the reason I went the extra mile and got legal advice.

The truth always ends up floating to the surface. It needs to be said, and nobody should feel threatened, hesitant, or afraid of exposing "nothing but the truth," as long as what they say or write is based on facts and written decently, without ridiculing, offending, or insulting anybody. Everyone is entitled to his or her personal opinion, as long as it is based on and expressed through the above-mentioned premises. In my efforts to practice due diligence, the reader can refer to **Appendix 1** to read the letter I received from a law firm with their legal advice related to what I am about to write regarding Rob Ford.

## The dark side of the coin

Sadly, on many occasions throughout his political career, it appears to me that Rob Ford portrayed himself as acting with lack of self-esteem, self-control, and self-respect. As the mayor of the City of Toronto, it seems that he often behaved in a way that disregarded proper values and with a seriously unprofessional demeanor that neither the city of Toronto nor Canada as a country deserved. In my personal opinion, and regardless of his achievements as a mayor, he failed his city and his country by not portraying a professional and decent image as a politician, by not acting like a gentleman, by allegedly not behaving within Canadian laws (drinking and driving, and the possession and use of drugs). It appears he also publicly lied about this, and only when caught on video did he accept guilt. Apparently, he had no choice but to confront his previous lies. There were apparently no serious repercussions to match the level and degree of his actions. Any other average citizen would have painfully confronted some serious consequences.

To my way of thinking and that of many Canadians, his biggest mistake was to lie and provide the wrong example to the younger generations, who are Canada's future. Simple as that! Especially in his professional position as a mayor, his antics and rude behaviors placed him in the news around the world and embarrassed him and almost all Canadians. In my view, he did love his country and the city of Toronto. But it seemed he loved attention more, though it also appeared he did not care at what cost he got it. According to some critics, he might have taken advantage of an omission in the law to not get fired due to his actions. But to my eyes, he seemingly failed to have the dignity to resign from his public duties. All across the country, there were feelings of embarrassment, humiliation, and concern about why he was elected to such a reputable and honorable position.

The reader can easily Google the name of Rob Ford and confirm that the media said several times that his addiction to crack cocaine and alcohol impaired his performance and caused him to perform poorly in his daily duties as a public servant. To many, it appeared that he portrayed himself as a victim in a relentless campaign of public deception. He literally disrespected his position as a mayor and, in my own personal view, he let down the majority of the people who actually voted for him and trusted him to represent them. Sure, there are always exceptions, but they are the minority.

I am legitimately concerned that history will make a hero out of him after his death, while sending the wrong message to emerging and future generations. In the eyes of the world, our famous Canadian "tolerance" is now in question, is misinterpreted and, in some scenarios, is creating a damaging international reputation. As Canadians, we need to refocus, stop misunderstanding the meaning of tolerance, and get a grip on reality to be once again well respected in the various international arenas.

Ford developed a reputation for being abusive, using harsh language, and allegedly being physically aggressive while at work. Is this the way even an average person should behave? Is this a way a politician that represents the city of Toronto and ultimately, the Canadian flag, should behave? Is this the example that we all want for our children, our school system, overall citizens, and other politicians? The consensus is **NO**— capital, bold, and underlined!

Unfortunately, it appears to me that Ford literally humiliated himself; he mocked his own actions, and he acted without self-control, while portraying himself on the bad side. He provided a really bad example to younger people, many of whom, in their naivety and youthfulness, ended up being amused by him, with some even thinking of him as "cool." But does the young generation really feel proud of his actions? Hard to provide a definite answer, but I sincerely doubt it.

It was so, so bad, that even the media abroad talked about him in a negative light. The majority of Canadians were embarrassed when he showed up on Jimmy Kimmel's late night show for an interview. In fact, Jimmy Kimmel said things such as the following: "I see you are dressed like a magician." (Rob Ford had a bright red tie and a bright red pocket-handkerchief.) Later in the show, Kimmel even offered to send some proper ties for him to wear. Jimmy Kimmel, in good spirits, even made fun of Ford's weight, asking him, "Realistically, how high can you jump?" Ford just laughed and said, "You will be surprised how fast I can move."

Then Mr. Kimmel asked, "Why are you here? What good can come from this? Have you ever seen the show? Imagine my shock when you actually answered your phone?" In the meantime, Rob Ford was laughing nervously, but regardless, he went ahead and responded that he was there only for the "customer service" he likes to provide. Kimmel, surprised, said, "But I am not even your customer."

According to Mr. Kimmel, people in Toronto were very angry that he had Rob Ford on the show. It was a slap to all Torontonians and to Canadians overall. To many Canadians, and to people in the United States, it seems that Rob Ford portrayed himself as a clown with problems such as drunk driving, domestic abuse, homophobia, and an inability to tell the truth. Mr. Kimmel even showed him some taped videos in which Ford made himself look so unbelievably bad that almost all Torontonians were very uncomfortable and offended that Rob Ford had been interviewed by him in a sarcastic way and outwitted.

Somewhere during the interview, Rob Ford was so uncomfortable that he started sweating like a fountain. Mr. Kimmel got up and started patting Ford's forehead with what seemed to be a handkerchief. People who liked Ford shunned the show because they were angry at how Mr. Kimmel made fun of the Toronto mayor and apparently humiliated him. Luckily, they were the minority.

## Actions Speak Louder than Words

To my understanding, and according to my upbringing, if the example of Rob Ford does not illustrate a person with lack of self-esteem, self-control, and self-respect, what does?

David Shum wrote an article that appeared in Web Producer Global News on August 28, 2014, called "Rob Ford's behaviors as football coach revealed in school documents," where he revealed, using school documents, that:

> Mayor Rob Ford's behaviors is yet again under the microscope following the release of documents revealing disturbing details of when he was a head coach of a Toronto high school football team. The Globe and Mail and Toronto Star are both reporting Thursday that Ford allegedly threatened teachers [and] appeared drunk at a practice for students. It all occurred in the months leading up to his dismissal as a football coach at Don Bosco Catholic Secondary School.

In "News Toronto and Greater Toronto Area" (Toronto Sun, March 24, 2014) there is an article by Don Peat, city hall bureau chief, entitled: "Rob Ford 'bad behaviors' on work, personal time." Peat writes:

> Newly released Project Brazen 2 documents confirm police investigators have interviewed eight former Mayor's office staffers and those interviews do not paint a pretty picture of their former boss, including substance abuse, drinking and driving, and physical altercations with staff.

In an article, "Rob Ford 'disruptive' in rehab" by Jennifer

Pagliaro, city hall reporter, and Kevin Donovan, investigations, published on Tuesday July 8, 2014, at thestar.com, the reporters stated:

> Mayor Rob Ford pushed and scuffled with fellow rehab residents and was so verbally abusive that he was kicked out of his group therapy program, according to people who have knowledge of his two month stay at Greenstone rehab clinic. These accounts of what one person referred to as "destructive behaviors" stand in stark contrast to Ford's recent public statements that he had a healthy experience in rehab and took his recovery seriously. Ford broke things, got into fights with other residents, said one source. Other residents felt intimidated. They felt he was a bully.

In Canada, various laws prohibit the use of illegal drugs. If you are caught using either cocaine or marijuana, or driving under the influence, an average citizen would end up behind bars and with a criminal record. Well, our ex-mayor Rob Ford was caught in videos smoking crack and driving under the influence, and I still wonder if he was dealt with properly, that is, with the proper rigour of the law upon his shoulders, like any average citizen would have endured. In my view, nothing negative really happened to him. Without being literal, it is rather like the expression: "he got away with murder." That is an insult and a slap on the face to all Canadians and a horrible example to the younger generation, our children, and their future. To make matters worse, Ford even wanted to run again for Mayor. Go figure!

Again, the younger generation, in many cases, is inexperienced and naive, so they find all this funny; yes, tragically funny, the reason why, in my personal opinion, so many ignorant and shallow people wanted to vote for him once more.

Again, in my personal view, the above shows a total lack of self-esteem, self-control, and self-respect. It is also contrary to very important and crucial values such as honesty, integrity, dignity, and loyalty.

Both Rob Ford and his brother Doug have been audacious. Rob tried to stay in office and run again for mayor until he unfortunately met with his health issues. He was voted in as a counselor all the same. Doug ran for mayor but did not win. One aspect I have to admit is that their slogan "Ford More Years" was very good, though, luckily for many, it did not work in the end!

It is well known that people have the government they deserve. They elect people for office, undoubtedly without doing proper research. In today's day and age, it is very easy to research things on the Internet with a very confident and reliable depth of investigation. If a candidate is known to be very social and knocks on people's doors to meet them in person, this does not necessarily mean they are a good candidate to represent a city's interests.

Dismissing everything regarding Rob Ford for a moment, and completely independently of him, I suggest we all keep in mind that history shows that the worst swindlers and con artists are, and need to be, very personable, friendly, down to earth, smiling, concerned about your well-being, attentive, and helpful in order to gain your trust and then, after a while, they can easily (without remorse) cut your jugular. It is important to try and see behind their mask and behind the scenes, so proper research on their background is required. It is not easy, but the bottom line is that people put their future in the hands of elected politicians.

People should be encouraged to watch less TV and get informed by reading newspapers, magazines, books, and, above all, surfing the Internet and accessing reliable sources of information. The latter is not always the most dependable, but it opens perspectives and invites thinking and better reasoning. Research the background of that specific candidate and his or her family's background as well. As a good example, please just go ahead and click at "Rob Ford's family background," and you will find in less than 10 seconds many sites that cover this in good detail.

For example, an article in the Globe and Mail by Greg McArthur and Shannon Kari, published May 25, 2013 and entitled "Globe investigation: The Ford family's history with drug dealing," reveals that:

- "Doug Ford, Rob Ford's brother, sold hashish for several years in the 1980s."

- "Another brother, Randy, was also involved in the drug trade and was once charged in relation to a drug related kidnapping."

- "Their sister, Kathy, has been the victim of drug-related gun violence."

Now, not everything is bad news. Rob's family was poor, but apparently, they managed through hard work and good business instincts, to build up a strong financial position for themselves in an industry-leading company in their hometown. I do not know if they did this ethically or not, and it is not my business. I truly do not care. But what I do care is how they performed from there on in the public light, because this affects every Canadian. They seem to be a very tight family, as it should be. Blood is thicker than water, and I guess we all know and agree on that. But I always keep in mind the following Mexican sayings that have been around for hundreds of years for a very good reason:

- *El que con lobos anda, a aullar se enzeña.* "If you go with wolves, you learn to howl."

- *Dime con quien andas y te dire quien eres.* "Tell me who you are with and I will tell you who you are."

- *Genio y figura, hasta la sepultura.* "Genius and style, until you die."

In summary and in my own view, people do not change that easily, and they tend to join and get along with people similar to themselves, their own "clan." They position themselves in society according to who they are, what they are, their mutual interests, taste, preferences and overall style of living, along with similar ethics and moral values or lack thereof.

For more information about Rob Ford and his family, please refer to a book called Crazy Town by Robin Doolittle (Toronto Star reporter and author) about the Ford family. A very interesting book.

Not everybody falls for the bad news. Other parts of Canada

had strong reactions to the Ford story. A good example is an article published by the Kelowna Daily Courier (Section C, May 8, 2014), "Rob Ford's follies prompt Okanagan town to introduce code of ethics for councilors," which quotes Lake Country Mayor James Baker explaining: "We realize that if we had a Rob Ford-type of character on council doing stupid things, there really wasn't anything we could do about him or her." Therefore, they changed their code of ethics to avoid getting stuck with a counselor who did not comply with "all applicable federal, provincial and local laws in the performance of their public duties."

Respect for oneself and others is of crucial importance (at least it should be) in the public eye. The duties and responsibilities of a person in public office should be performed with honor, responsibility, dignity, respect, and admiration for that public position, for our Canadian values, and ultimately our flag, which is waved worldwide.

In Maclean's magazine of March 14, 2016 (page # 25), an article by Jason Markusoff entitled "Get Out Of Town: Across Alberta, frayed town councils are cracking down on cantankerous mayors" explains that in the city of Gibbons (Alberta), Mayor Doug Horner was stripped of his mayoral powers by council in a unanimous decision. Why? This was apparently due to past bad behaviors. Albertans are cracking down on cantankerous politicians. I believe every other province in Canada should act accordingly. Cantankerous bad-tempered, argumentative, and uncooperative politicians are now considered a chronic syndrome in Alberta and in many other provinces. Markusoff wrote: "Mayors have also been Rob-Forded in Fort Macleod, where the diminished chief magistrate sued the town and lost; and most recently in

Manning, where Mayor Sunni-Jeanne Walker's alleged transgressions were never made public." These cantankerous politicians need stopping, and laws need changing before that happens, so politicians like Rob Ford won't happen again.

Without proceeding further on this subject, I would like to raise a few questions and allow readers to answer them themselves in order to clarify their own judgments.

| QUESTIONS | YES | NO |
|---|---|---|
| 1. Was Rob Ford a good politician? | _____ | _____ |
| 2. Would I want Rob Ford as a mayor? | _____ | _____ |
| 3. Was he a good role model? | _____ | _____ |
| 4. Did he represent Canada properly? | _____ | _____ |
| 5. Was he well-respected worldwide? | _____ | _____ |
| 6. Was he an honest and humble man? | _____ | _____ |
| 7. Did he have high values/ principles? | _____ | _____ |
| 8. Should smoking crack be allowed? | _____ | _____ |
| 9. Did he show self-control and respect? | _____ | _____ |
| 10. Was he a potential Prime Minister? | _____ | _____ |
| 11. Was he fun to watch and follow? | _____ | _____ |
| 12. Should he be a Canadian hero? | _____ | _____ |
| 13. Did he work hard for the poor? | _____ | _____ |
| 14. Was he a man of high morals? | _____ | _____ |
| 15. Would I like him as a co-worker? | _____ | _____ |

If you gave four or more "yes" answers, you should have belonged to Rob Ford's team (or a real fan of his). I personally would not give more than one or two "yes" answers, and that is the beauty of this world; to each their own, as long as we know where we stand and do not pretend otherwise.

All the situation regarding Rob Ford is not very surprising to many Canadians, when you actually have the Prime Minister Justin Trudeau, who on Apr 24, 2017, publicly accepted that his father used his contacts and position in society to clear his brother's name (who died in an avalanche 20 years ago) to avoid a criminal record after Michael Trudeau was arrested for using pot, something that people with little means do not enjoy the luxury to clear their name. Trudeau publicly admitted his father contacted his friends in the legal world to clear Michael's name because "he was very confident that we were able to make those charges go away", Prime Minister Trudeau said. Why admit guilt publicly? For many reasons, being the most important his effort in introducing the government plan (his plan) to legalize marijuana. This has many Canadians worried about driving and killing under the influence of marijuana, and the ability to prove, without a shred of a doubt, that a criminal act has been committed. Tolerance and acceptance, to many Canadian, should not be applied in this category. It remains to be seen if his administration is doing the right thing for our society overall, because of course, people who like marijuana or need it for medical reasons, are all in favour. I would be too if I needed it for medical purposes, but I would not drive or operate heavy equipment under the influence. But, will everyone be disciplined as well?

## Strategies to Improve Self-esteem and Self-respect

There are various ways and methods to improve self-esteem and self-respect. In my view, the most important and efficient can be summarized in twenty-two specific actions:

1. First of all, we all have a duty to be kind and noble with ourselves. We have an obligation to cherish and take care of

our bodies and our minds. Therefore, learn how to respect and love yourself. The best ways of doing this are to sleep and rest enough for your needs, stay away from processed foods, eat as fresh as you can, read something every day, be responsible in school and at work, learn something new every day, do some exercise regularly, and follow a dress code that makes you feel better.

2. It is urgent and of utmost importance to stop disliking or hating ourselves, as many people do. We all have something in us that is very valuable to share with others, and that others will listen to with interest. We need to focus on our good sides, not our negative sides. We are also an important part of our dynamic society's fascinating puzzle. We should never abuse ourselves physically or mentally. We should absolutely avoid self-torture. Our daily duty should be focused on pampering ourselves (in a disciplined way).

3. Make an effort to go deep into your heart and soul and see who you really are. Rediscover your true self. We change with time, so we require self-evaluation often. What makes you happy, and what does not? Feed the first and starve the latter. Study your true-life force, your emotions, and your passions. Be aware and fully conscious of what makes you tick.

4. Stop comparing yourself with your neighbors, your peers, your friends, with better-off people or with people who are fitter than you or smarter or more intelligent. We are all given different physical and mental characteristics, features, and tools at birth. Yes, we are all different, but we are also capable of improving ourselves, if we really want to. We need to truly desire to change and better ourselves, but without comparing ourselves with the best. Comparisons do not make sense and

only chisel your true spirit away into the lonely and dark emptiness of space. However, there is still value to having a role model to use as inspiration. Yes, you can compare yourself and say, "I'd like to do and achieve what they have done" and try to improve an aspect of yourself, but not in a demoralizing or obsessive manner.

5. We need to take off the mask that protects our crystal-clear identity, and if we do not like what we see, make a conscious effort to change. What I mean by this is to consciously change the attitude of our own persona for a more positive attitude and a better portrayal of ourselves.

6. We need to reinforce our hope, trust, and faith in a better future. We have to help our own selves, before any external variable, force, or celestial power can assist us. It is in us to change; it is in us to improve. My grandfather used to say: "Help yourself first, then God will help you."

7. Take wise advantage of your power of choice. Every morning when you wake up, look at yourself in the mirror and decide how you want your day to be. Feel good about yourself, and do something good for yourself that day. Brush your teeth, wash your face, take a shower, comb your hair, put on some make-up, trim your beard, and apply some lotion or perfume if you wish, so you can feel better immediately. You will only attract positive vibes and results.

8. To boost your thoughts and feelings (your mental approach and attitude), take a few minutes every morning to meditate, to reason, and actually envision how your day is going to take place. Make it happen. We all can!

9. Be realistic about what you are changing in order to feel better every day. Go slowly, with easy attainable goals. If you want to change too much and too fast, the odds are you will only succeed for a very short time. What good is that? You need changes that last forever! You need realistic and achievable expectations: one step at a time.

10. Every day when you awaken, I strongly encourage you to open the blinds and let the light come in, then make your bed immediately. It will instantly assist you in your daily efforts to feel responsible, organized, and valuable, and to feel worthy of a good and successful day. Look around you, and you will undoubtedly find people who like you and need your company, thoughts, example, or support. Feel good about this. Strengthen your efforts to better yourself under the bright light.

11. I want to emphasize the fact that we need to dress in clothes in which we feel good about our persona, not necessarily just comfortable clothes. Many people use tights on bodies that should not wear them, because they are either extremely obese or very old. I honestly encourage these people to dress with a sense of decency, modesty, and discretion. Get rid of the attitude of "who cares." YOU should care for your own persona. You will be surprised at your immediate achievements.

12. Expand your friendship and networking and spend time with people as much as possible. Socialize. It enriches your soul and promotes vitality, enthusiasm, better spirits, and inspiration. All of these are very valuable for change.

13. We must work hard every day but also take time to enjoy something we like doing. Do your daily homework, and, at the

end of the day, do something relaxing just for yourself. We need to pamper ourselves wisely, rationally, and with common sense. Pat yourself on the back at the end of the day, but ask yourself if the pat on the back is proportionate to the effort you put in throughout the day. If the answer is yes, then pamper yourself, but if the answer is no, give yourself only a small pat on the back, but do it.

14. It should almost be an obligation to sit down with the family for dinner. Take advantage of this to discuss positive matters, and make it a pleasant supper. Turn off the TV and your cellular phones. Nothing bad is going to happen. Do not read anything while eating with others at the table. Reading at the table curtails your communication with others and is also considered bad manners. But if you live alone, at least try to make supper a very special moment. Play your favorite music. Listen to your favorite motivational tape or video or read something pleasant that fills you up with good thoughts and vibes.

15. We need to stop leaving things for later or another day. The moment is now. We live in the present, and we need to start doing things now instead of leaving them for "mañana." We also need to be very conscious of time. Do not leave for another day what can be tackled today.

16. We need to make a habit of saying positive things to others. Acknowledge others and do something good for them if possible. Put aside negativity and selfishness. That alone will improve our days and make us feel better.

17. It is imperative to improve our small, daily habits: organizing our closets, tidying our room, shining our shoes,

walking upright, looking others straight in the eyes, smiling more, shaking hands with vigor, saying "please," "thank you," "excuse me," etc.

Honor and dignify yourself on a daily basis through these minor things that ultimately have a powerful impact on others, on how you are perceived by them, and on how you feel about yourself. Remember, you are unique, you are a human being, and you are valuable. Treat yourself and others better, and feel pride in doing so.

18. According to an article published by the Mayo Clinic website ("Healthy Lifestyle – regarding self-esteem," mayoclinic.org), we need to challenge negative or inaccurate feelings and become more aware of our thoughts and beliefs. The article specifically mentions not mistaking feelings for facts, avoiding negative self-talk, not jumping to conclusions, forgiving yourself, encouraging yourself, using hopeful statements, and practicing daily mental filtering.

19. We have the liberty and freedom to change or expand our knowledge with activities such as reading, dancing, sports, different hobbies, poetry, painting, wood work, cooking lessons, music, gardening, volunteering, etc.

20. If we truly want to improve, we have an obligation to seek higher degrees of honesty, integrity, and truthfulness. This will certainly help us to reduce stress and conflict in the future.

21. We have to be more respectful of others, which will assist us in engaging in a more powerful relationship with them. This will strongly influence our ability to lead or follow. Respect and self-esteem are directly correlated and help others trust us.

22. Seek help or assistance in all the above, if you do not have what it takes to achieve true awareness of who you are and what to do to improve. There is nothing wrong in asking others for help.

More self-esteem = more self-respect = more respect for others = more trust from others = higher leading capacity.

As a leader, you improve your self-esteem and self-respect when echoed by others who have engaged their trust in you. With self-esteem and self-respect, people develop confidence, which is a crucial element for leadership. Then the following question arises.

## What Exactly is Leadership?

- Leadership is the power to influence others into following your direction and guidance with their own goodwill and full commitment.

- To lead is to have an impact, to affect, to command, and to have the proper influence and repercussions on other people, on your followers.

- Leadership is to inspire and persuade people to follow your vision and your goals.

For some people, a good leader is someone who guides and influences people without making it obvious, that is, when his followers are so devoted and convinced of the specific goals that they do not even realize they are being given or granted a specific course of action, a new mission with a better vision. A good leader can also make people sometimes believe it was their own idea. A true leader does not necessarily need to be acknowledged as such, but needs to complete and attain the end result of their vision while giving full credit to others, the actual doers. True leaders yield the overall idea and success to their team. They guide their team to reach the vision in their mind so that the team can "discover" it and feel ownership. It is only then that people are willing and eager enough to put their brains, knowledge, time, and their heart and soul, to work to achieve the vision and the ultimate goal. A leader is someone who provides confidence, trust, and a sense of protection while trying to accomplish growth and success.

Leaders, like other people, have either hard skills or soft skills. The hard skills are those learned throughout life. They are the knowledge and experience you need to perform a specific job. The hard skills of an astronaut are the knowledge of physics and mathematics, for example. But an astronaut could require other hard skills such as strong analysis and engagement in intelligent conversations to solve problems, be a driven person, and have the ability to solve problems head-on.

Contrary to hard skills, soft skills are based around your ability to communicate with other people. They are the interpersonal skills that the human resources industry calls "people skills." These represent the ability of leaders to interact with other human beings regardless of their backgrounds. Diplomacy, caring, understanding, patience, listening, flexibility, empathy, and constructive criticism are only a few examples of the skills that form the foundation of interpersonal communication.

According to the great German writer and statesman Johann Wolfgang von Goethe, a leader is "a great person who attracts great people and knows how to hold them together." It is a real challenge to choose the right people, but it is a bigger challenge to keep them working together in pursuit of common goals understood by everyone while trying to achieve these goals in harmony.

A true leader still stands out when the initial target is not necessarily accomplished, but keeps the group tightly together while regrouping ideas and strategies to try again with the full devotion and commitment of everybody involved. To achieve this, the true leader needs to maintain a cohesive group philosophy, true beliefs, and a very simple and focused goal.

Former US president Theodore Roosevelt once said: "The best executive is the one who has sense enough to pick good men to do what he wants done, and self-restraint enough to keep from meddling with them while they do it."

"A ruler should be slow to punish and swift to reward," said Publius Ovidius Naso, known as Ovid. He was a Roman poet who strongly influenced Milton, Dante, and Shakespeare.

According to Bill Gates, "as we look ahead to the next century, leaders are those who will empower others." These leaders will enable and permit others to enjoy authority and apply it to the right cause.

As previously mentioned, it is of utmost importance to reiterate that true leaders have a high sense of self-esteem, self-respect and self-control, which is immediately reflected in respect and esteem for and from others. True leaders always go the extra mile, using enthusiasm and innovative approaches. They have a strong sense of initiative and good communication and organizational skills, together with an excellent risk management approach. A true leader has the ability to set priorities and take responsibility for the outcome.

## True Leader vs. Pseudo-Leader

A true leader is different from leaders who just happen to be leaders due to circumstances and the roll of the dice. These people are what I call pseudo-leaders. Some examples of how pseudo-leaders achieve leadership are:

- As a result of a political party's strategy.
- By being mistakenly voted for due to either ignorance or because there was nobody better to vote for.
- By inheritance.
- By owed favours.
- By bribes and corruption.
- By coup d'état (e.g. revolution or internal uprising).
- By military invasion.
- By seniority.
- By mistake or pure luck.

These types of pseudo-leaders do not have what it takes to be true leaders. They lack souls of steel and integrity.

Above all, they lack "magic," which is shown in their lack of humility, nobility, and modesty, all parts of the natural self of a true leader. A friend of mine named Robert Tunstead (whom I call Don Roberto) once told me that a true leader needs "courage and guts of steel." This confirms a good quote about leadership from the Chinese philosopher Chan (Master) Fuchan Yuan who says, "there are three essentials to leadership: humility, clarity and courage."

One major problem in today's society is that the great majority of leaders fail to have the traits of a true leader. They lack humility, clarity, and, above all, courage and guts of steel. Unfortunately, these so-called leaders usually also possess great vanity and distorted egos; they are full of themselves, do not acknowledge mistakes, and love to blame everybody else for their own failures. What is worse, they do not even realize or acknowledge that they lack the attributes of true leaders. The main characteristics that make a pseudo-leader are all or some of the following:

- Lack of honesty and integrity.
- A "know-it-all" attitude.
- Limited vision and poor communication skills.
- Inability to read or feel the needs of other people.
- Lack of focus and understanding.
- Lack of innovation and guts to take calculated risks.
- A high degree of arrogance and a sense of invincibility.
- Lack of hard or soft skills (as defined previously).
- Selfishness and lack of coordination regarding the common goals of their society.

These pseudo-leaders go through life blinded by power, unless they surround themselves by a capable, prudent, and strong team with a vision and a mission. But for that to happen, they require a minimum level of honesty and integrity. Former US president Dwight Eisenhower once said, "The supreme quality of leadership is integrity."

## Achieving Integrity

The question then arises of how to achieve and maintain integrity. Human history has proven that you do not need to have integrity to be a leader, but you do require it if you want to be remembered as a good, positive, and true leader. To my mind, there are nine minimum requirements to achieve integrity as a leader:

- Acknowledging the work of others and respecting ownership and boundaries.
- Being truthful with themselves and others.
- Being responsible for their actions if they fail, but proud, humble, and courteous if they succeed.
- Being courteous, simple, respectful, and very clear in all their actions.
- Going the extra mile in providing help or guidance to others who need it.
- Tackling obstacles honestly.
- Listening carefully and interpreting things honestly and responsibly.
- Taking the bull by the horns to avoid mistakes and achieve positive change.
- Valuing their principles and, if they stumble or fail once, getting up trying again with head held high with strong and healthy pride.

Integrity is taught and learned from an early age and continues throughout a person's life. It has been said, and confirmed through centuries, that integrity allows a person to be humble and to put pride aside.

These are not just traits that a true leader should have, but also what any positive and constructive, mature man or woman should aim for and ultimately achieve. But we need stamina, persistence, strong will, and full commitment, which, unfortunately, only a few people have. It is easier to let go and give up. This is the reason why there are few true leaders in the world. Integrity, pride, and honesty should be taught early in life, first at home and then reinforced at school.

## Crucial Factors for Being a Successful Leader

Once somebody asked Mr. Jim Pattison (a very successful Canadian businessman from Vancouver, BC) what made a leader successful, and he answered that it was the result of three specific factors: "Focus, focus, and focus."

Successful leaders, need to satisfy and please as many people or followers as possible, but you cannot please them all. There is no one specific formula for success, but this brings to my mind a quote from editor and journalist Herbert Bayard, who said: "I cannot give you the formula of success, but I can give you the formula for failure – Try To Please Everybody." Indeed, if you try to please everybody, you are certain to fail. The key to success is to please yourself while trying to achieve your goals in unison with common objectives. That's when you will succeed.

You definitely need a vision and a mission, and then, with absolute determination, you need to try to achieve them, regardless of whether everyone will agree with you or not. This seems to be a bit of a selfish attitude in the eyes of many, but if successful leaders are true to their personal values, principles, and ethics, then their goals are matched and will run parallel to those of the great majority of the community or society being led. Therefore, leaders should be absolutely conscious that they cannot and will not satisfy everybody.

## Are Leaders Compromised during their Leadership?

Absolutely yes. Their own people, legal systems, and overall surroundings compromise every leader. They start by working within their own personal boundaries of self-esteem and self-respect but also make an effort to do so in tandem with those same goals of their community or society—under altruistic and specific promises, specific guidelines, unique laws, and definite and distinctive public and private goals.

Unless you are a ruthless conqueror like Genghis Khan or a mass murderer like Adolph Hitler, you will always be compromised as a leader by your overall surroundings. What makes a great true leader is when that person, given their specific limiting circumstances and conditions, balances and chooses the best course of action for the benefit of the great majority. A good example is the US president Barack Obama, who was elected by the people but also had the support of major companies and industries with special interests in mind.

In an effort to provide a well-researched, thoughtful, and carefully selected list of leaders throughout history, I began by first classifying the types of leaders into three essential categories:

1. Positive world leaders.
2. Famous and infamous military leaders.
3. Worst "leaders" (dictators and genocide perpetrators).

Please refer to **Appendix 2**, which contains an interesting and impartial list of leaders who, for better or worse, have been selected from various well-known sources. Among the most important sources we have are: thefamouspeople.com, biography.com, ranker.com, bio.com, businessinsider.com, time.com, biography and even Wikipedia.

Nobody can make a 100 per cent accurate list, because everybody knows it is impossible to fairly evaluate the different sources of information, points of view, and interpretations. Therefore, we limit ourselves to only a few examples per table under the categories previously mentioned in Appendix 2.

## CHAPTER THREE:  EDUCATION (Courtesy, Manners, And Ethics)

## Definition of Education

The concept of education has changed throughout human history. Currently, it has various connotations depending on where you are and who you are with. Education in general, and adequate access to it, has a magical and powerful impact on people who follow its path, in the form of unlimited opportunities that reshape their lives for the better. There are hundreds of definitions of education, along with many, many quotes. My personal favorites, and the most commonly accepted definitions of education, are summarized below:

- A poet from the United States, Robert Frost (1874-1963), defined education as "the ability to listen to almost anything without losing your temper or self-confidence."

- A philosopher from the United Sates, Allan Bloom (1930-1992), defined education as "the movement from darkness to light."

- Martin Luther King Jr. (1929-1968) defined education as "intelligence plus character." From his perspective, that was "the true goal of education."

- In "What Is Education?" (University of Chicago Press,2012), Philip W. Jackson describes education as "a profound philosophical exploration of how we transmit knowledge in human society and how we think about accomplishing that vital task."

To my mind, education is the product of learning, that is, the process of acquiring knowledge and turning it into positive habits, abilities, talents, and aptitudes that can be taught to the next generation in hopes of improving, with time, these skills and passing them on to the next generation.

However, in the context of this book, we are going to provide a slightly different angle or twist to the definition of education, one that society seems to have forgotten or left behind, either because it is not recognized anymore as important or is purposely ignored. Unfortunately, either cause is detrimental to our human behaviors, integrity, the care of our planet, and a proper and civilized development overall. Therefore, in the context of this book's objective, besides acknowledging education as the means for learning and transmitting knowledge, we will also define it as the level of courtesy, manners (including etiquette), and ethics that human beings are taught by their parents, teachers, or anybody else during their upbringing and then passed along to their own children.

The overall experience provided by higher education is consistently being expanded and is considered to be an infinite wealth of knowledge in its progression and accumulation. But what is happening to courtesy, manners, and ethical behaviors? They seem to be disappearing at an alarming rate and speed. Why?

The concepts of courtesy, manners, and ethics vary profoundly across cultures. Each culture has its own background and traditions and therefore follows its own ethical framework. Manners, and courtesies that are acceptable in one country may not be accepted in others.

Cultures are directly related to the moral behaviors, values, and principles that a society considers right or wrong. There are cultures in which discipline, respect, and good manners are considered very important for the development of each individual, but, in other cultures, these are of secondary importance or even unimportant.

What is "good manners" in one culture can be perceived as "bad manners" in another. For example, if, after an opulent dinner, you burp at the table, this can be perceived as rude and vulgar in North America, but in some Arab or Asian countries, it is an acceptable way of implying that the food was good and that you sincerely appreciate the meal.

Another example: While obesity is admired in South Africa, in North America and Europe it is not well regarded. In South Africa, obesity is seen as a sign of health and wealth; in North America, almost everybody relates it to bad habits, weak character, lack of self-esteem or self-respect, health issues, or a poor quality of life, but definitely not to health and wealth. Unfortunately, the average Mexican also sees a fat person as a happy and healthy individual.

## Intellectual or Cognitive Learning

Intellectual or cognitive learning concerns how information about new experiences is organized and learned. It is how individuals coordinate, process, and refine their ideas to help them make sense of the world. It helps people organize data and put it into practice.

In contrast, academic learning is generally related to the

knowledge acquired by people in school. Any kind of formal schooling and teaching is considered academic learning.

Everybody has an intellectual or cognitive education. This is based on specific emotional experiences, which strongly influence our learning and, therefore, our level of education (courtesy, manners, including etiquette, and ethics). Even environmental influences play an important role in acquiring knowledge through specific experiences, thoughts, and our senses. They all allow us to understand and view the world from different angles, while acquiring knowledge and developing the skills to retain this acquired knowledge. The real key is knowing how to apply the acquired knowledge to a positive and a productive action in our daily lives.

## Transformative or Life-Changing Learning

There is another form of education that focuses on the evolving changes required for the learner's evaluation and conception of the world they live in. This is known as transformative learning. In a January 2003 abstract, "Transformative Learning as Discourse" in the Teacher's College of British Columbia Journal of Transformative Education, author Jack Mezirow states:

> Transformative learning is understood as a uniquely adult form of metacognitive reasoning. Reasoning is the process of advancing and assessing reasons, especially those that provide arguments supporting beliefs resulting in decisions to act. Beliefs are justified when they are based on good reasons. The process of reasoning may involve such tacit knowledge as aptitudes, skills, and competencies.

Transformative education is based on two important dimensions, psychological and analytical (or methodical). These two dimensions profoundly influence our lives and lifestyles—our attitudes and behaviors toward others and even toward ourselves.

Transformative education displaces intellectual or cognitive education, and this is important as the years ago by. Transformative education is learned as you go along, with less effort than intellectual or cognitive education, where you need a higher degree of discipline and effort to achieve high levels of learning.

The concepts of cognitive and transformational education vary in every country and have deep repercussions on each country's economic development. Let me explain this better with a short but interesting story that I received through the beauty of the Internet in the form of an attachment from another friend of mine and that I managed to research and corroborate for accuracy.

## Short True Story About Yakult

This story is about the most important aspects of the entrepreneurial culture of Japan versus Mexico (or any other Latin American country). Mr. C.P. Carlos Kasuga Osaka (known as Mr. Kasuga), who has organized many successful conferences in the Republic of Mexico, wrote what I am about to relate. He is known as an exemplary Mexican entrepreneur who, as he says, "was born from Japanese immigrants but was properly assembled in the Republic of Mexico." For more specific references, you can find him on YouTube under his personal name.

Mr. Kasuga is the founder and general director of Yakult, S.A. de C. V., a successful and well-known company involved in the food industry. They currently sell over two million bottles of Yakult per day, which is a fermented mixture of skimmed milk with a specific bacterium to provide a probiotic dairy product.

One day, Mr. Kasuga was asked to talk about team work and about how he developed a very successful professional disposition in every worker employed either full-time or part-time by his company. They are all very good, efficient and loyal workers who form part of the Yakult corporate "family."

Among many things he talked about, what caught my attention the most were the following facts. Japan is a small country with slightly over 125 million people and with five of the 10 largest banks in the world. They have the highest longevity rate compared to all other countries, with the lowest criminal index worldwide and with a gross national product bigger than France, Great Britain, and Spain put together. Oh, by the way, Japan lost the Second World War and, in 1945, was pretty much in ruins, having suffered two atomic bombs (Hiroshima and Nagasaki). So, the question is: how did they come back so fast and so strong, and in less than 40 years? To what do they owe their high productivity? Mr. Kasuga says they owe it to three main reasons:

- Understanding of education.

- Attitude towards the environment and their surroundings.

- Attitude towards life and oneself.

## Japanese-Style Education

In Japan, education focuses very strongly on social and ethical aspects such as punctuality, honesty, respect, responsibility, cleanliness, and order. Their ethical values have always had very high standards. These aspects are very important throughout the everyday life of the Japanese, and they form an integral part of every employee in any company environment. According to Mr. Kasuga, there are a few important elements that are basic to succeed in life and in business:

- To be and feel good (happy with yourself).
- To do good (to be in good standing with others).
- To care what others think of you.
- To be happy with what you have and own (within the society you live in).

These elements make people positive, productive, confident, and successful, if they apply them properly. They increase the odds of being successful while focusing on being, feeling, and doing well.

Mr. Kasuga once cited the example of a consultant who gave a speech at a conference, but he unfortunately arrived about ten minutes late. There were about 600 people at the conference. That meant 6,000 minutes of their time or a little over four days that the country wasted in productive work time.

This is how the Japanese culture views lack of punctuality, which is rampant and accepted (sometimes even encouraged) in other countries. In some countries, being late is not important at all. In fact, it is a tradition or custom to make people wait as means of showing power or superiority. Yes, this is kind of twisted, but that is the way it is in some cultures. Many Asian and Latin American countries suffer from this detrimental syndrome. It might not be openly accepted, but that is exactly what takes place and repeats itself in many day-to-day actions, due to their type of business philosophy, which is different from North America. In Japanese society, lack of punctuality is considered to show total disrespect to others. It goes against not just their immediate way of thinking, but against their educational upbringing at school and at home.

Another fine Japanese ethic is that, if somebody in that country finds a book, a wallet, a pen, or a sweater, they immediately know that it belongs to somebody else, not to them. In many other countries (nowadays including even the United States and Canada), people do not necessarily follow this philosophy. In fact, there is an expression in the US and Canada that goes "finders, keepers." That is, if you find something, it is your "right" to just keep it.

**Respect and Work Ethic**

Respect is the ethical and polite way of treating others. Respect is in direct correlation with admiration. The more you admire somebody, the more respect you have for that person.

In Japan, the idea of respect is of utmost importance. In Mexico, the concept of respect is also very important. Benito Pablo Juárez Garcia, known at the time just as Benito Juárez (Mexican president from 1858 to 1872), used as his motto the phrase *El respeto al derecho ajeno es la paz* ("Respect for other's rights achieves peace"). The majority of children in

Mexico and Japan still respect their teachers, the young, the elderly, their parents, their flag, their national anthem etc., something that is disappearing at a consistent rate in other European countries and North America. Mexico is also starting to experience this slowly in the upper classes.

Not everything is milk and honey in Japan. There are serious problems in the country that are worth mentioning. Their culture is very strict and sometimes very unforgiving when it comes to social issues like when universities accept or reject students and the high degree of company loyalty while at work. Women remain professionally unequal, and extreme disciplined behaviors is expected from everyone. The younger generation is showing its frustration in many ways, such as rebelling against the existing strict order, having eccentric tastes, preferences, and activities, leaving their country for more equal professional opportunities abroad, and a considerable percentage are even committing suicide. Young Japanese women are not getting married as they used to because of the oppressive male-dominated culture. They are devoted more to their careers, to making money and having the freedom to choose their own course of action.

What is really important regarding Japan vs. Latin American countries (and also vs. many other countries in Europe, Africa, and in Middle East) is that, at work, their philosophy is to do things once and only once. They have a high degree of pride and respect for the work ethic. But to achieve this, they need to do things correctly the first time! Japanese seem to have an amazing ability to focus on doing things properly and correctly the first time. Why waste your time doing it again for the second or third occasion? In many other countries, this philosophy of doing things perfectly the first time does not exist. People do not realize (or do not care) that things that are not well done the first time will eventually come back to haunt them. That is a fact. In Mexico, there is an expression that goes "Ahi se va," which roughly means: "It is passable" or "Let It Go".

A very important factor that affects our North American society (contrary to that of Japan) is that the average individual does not seem to be happy with what they have and with what they have achieved. The Japanese, although not immune to this, seem to accept what they have much better than we do. It seems that in North America, we are never happy with what we have or what has been given to us, and therefore, there is a high degree of continued and relentless consumerism. We always compare ourselves with our neighbors. We always seem to want the newer and the better model or gadget. Okay, there is nothing wrong in wanting more or better things than what we possess at a given point, but to allow this to control our lives on a continuous and relentless basis and go into bigger and deeper debt to achieve it, is ludicrous.

At this point, it is important to emphasize that humans throughout history have never been happy with what they have, and they have always ventured to other places or regions around the world to get more and try to achieve happiness and fulfillment, usually with only a short-term level of satisfaction. Why? Because there is always something different and better out there and, in their archaic minds, they have to have it! That alone makes them insecure and unhappy in the long term.

According to Mr. Kasuga, there are two other very important aspects to the differences in education and professional attitudes between Japan and North American, Latin American, and European countries. One is their approach to how they practice their religion, and the other is the profit distribution within their companies. These two approaches are so strongly different in many aspects that they have made Japan a great industrialized country with amazing and very profitable multinationals compared to many other countries.

## Religious Approach

When a North American, European, or Latin American worker prays or goes to church, they usually ask God to help them to achieve a better job, better working environment, a better salary, more vacations, a better relationship with family members, for good health, strength of character, more benefits, better luck, etc. They tend to ask for material things. At least that is their main focus—immediate needs. Ask first and then offer something in exchange, if God grants it. When the Japanese pray, or go to church, they offer a lot more things instead of asking for things. They offer to focus and concentrate more at work, make fewer errors, be more productive, minimize obstacles, solve problems, be more honest, and so forth.

We all have heard the following saying: "Help yourself and God will help you." If there is really a God in every culture, regardless of your religion and the country you are living in, do you really think God would come down or send an angel and help you solve your surrounding issues and problems? He could have done that a long time ago all over the world. People need to believe in God, but it is my understanding that God wants you to believe in yourself and work hard, diligently and intelligently, for things to happen your way. It is not until then that God may show you the light, or that luck will show you the way. I am personally convinced that hard work and dedication come first, second, and third; then the rest follow.

Those who get up early to work hard in a diligent and intelligent manner are those who make it in this world. But do not forget; to succeed you also need discipline, stamina, persistence, and the right attitude. It is not easy. Otherwise everybody could do it, and everybody would be a boss. We all need to start by having faith not only in God but also in ourselves, in our own abilities, in our efforts, and in our future results. I personally believe we should start by praying less and being more proactive and responsible. We need to be productive and, yes, sacrifice ourselves for a few years before we can see the results of our sacrifices and efforts.

Gratification during the early stages of our efforts does not come easy or fast. But if your main goal is immediate gratification, most probably you will fail. Everything tends to take time and follow its own course, which usually is out of your complete control. A similar situation applies to another great country that we all know as Germany. Their culture is extremely disciplined, dedicated, and proud of what they do. Look at them now. Since the Second World War, when they were pretty much destroyed, they have now become the most powerful country in Europe.

Germans have been the pillars in bailing out other countries like Greece (who seem to also ask God for things in church, instead of offering a better side of themselves with better working ethics and attitude). Nowadays, as much as other countries envy them, Germany is among the three most advanced and efficient countries in the world, with brilliant people, an amazingly productive system, strong economy, and advanced technologies. Once again, what makes them number one are discipline, focus, cohesion, and a winning attitude. They have pride in whatever they do, and it shows. Everything made in Germany is usually very well made.

## Profit Distribution

The second aspect is that, in Japan (as in Germany, South Korea, and a few other countries), the owners and managers of Japanese companies have the attitude (similar to the one described in the previous paragraph) of taking serious care of their company before they get anything out of it. A company (according to Mr. Kasuga) is like a little baby. In the first three years of its life, the employees dedicate their time and efforts to keeping it alive, healthy, and productive. They do not expect anything more in return from the company than a decent salary and benefits. If they are lucky to have profits at the end of the year, it is reinvested instead of paying dividends to employees and shareholders. Why? Because they want to make the company grow stronger and be more productive.

They know that their future and that of their children depends on the success and strength (profitability) of that company. They need to allow it to grow and get well established. Therefore, it is not until the company is in its teens or even its twenties that employees start expecting better salaries and some dividend payments (profit shares). The bosses then start getting better offices, cars, desks, improved benefits, and more vacations, and that is also reflected down the ladder in all their employees.

In North America and in many other countries, we expect the

average company to pay us dividends and better salaries in the first two to four years of the company's life, so we go ahead and purchase a better car, a bigger house, a new boat, do more travelling, get a new computer, a new iPad, a better iPhone, etc. We are convinced we need these items (and more) and have to have them. Once again, immediate gratification. That may be the cause of an unhealthy company that a year later might go broke. This makes me sometimes doubt the integrity, the degree of responsibility, and the capacity of many CEOs. If we cannot wait patiently for our rewards, how can we expect our children to be any different? We convince ourselves that we deserve such things, because we only live once and need to enjoy the fruits of our efforts. We do not seem to realize that we need to put money aside for rainy days, which seem to come more and more often in our volatile financial markets.

The young generation in particular wants to live now and to the full extent of their possibilities. They have not lived through famine, starvation, war, and diseases during their lives. But I can guarantee these things will happen to them eventually, and I hope they are ready to deal with them. I am not being negative—it is the cruel reality of being human. We make the same mistakes generation after generation. Is this a responsible way of living and setting an example for our children? I highly doubt it.

## Children Learn What They Experience

"If humanity is to progress, Gandhi is inescapable. He lived, thought, acted and was inspired by the vision of humanity evolving toward a world of peace and harmony." – Dr. Martin Luther King, Jr.

Not every person who has contributed to the world is known as a sage. There are only a few examples of people who contributed in a certain form or shape to this world and, in fact, might even have some negativity attached to their reputations. Regardless of rumors, we need to acknowledge their contribution to our society, which they helped chisel. A good example was Michael Jackson, who was not just a gifted singer and dancer known worldwide, but also saw the world in a totally different, brilliant light. He had a passion for music and for many other artistic activities, including poetry and even philosophy. Among many thoughts, he shared with the world, he wrote two that caught my immediate attention:

- All of us are a product of our childhood.

- Human knowledge consists not only of libraries of parchment and ink – it is also comprised of the volumes of knowledge that are written on the human heart, chiseled on the human soul, and engraved on the human psyche.

Mr. Jackson could not have been more accurate. If we train and educate children in a certain way, they will always develop and act according to what they were taught during their upbringing. If we provide children with strong self-esteem, they will grow up to have self-confidence and be assertive. If we traumatize them, they will grow up to be insecure and afraid, with a low level of self-esteem.

A Jesuit acquaintance of mine once told me: "Give me a child from one to nine years old, and that child will always be mine." Even though he said it metaphorically speaking, his message was loud and clear to any good listener. Whatever we teach a child is what they will remember for the rest of their lives. If you support, train, and provide a good example to your children, they will grow up to be strong and ready for any challenge in life. But if you overprotect them and fail to train them with firm principles, good ethics, and a strong sense of responsibility, they will grow up to be weak and dependent on others.

Throughout history, humans have unconsciously or consciously (depending on time and place) set an example for the next generation. We all have read or heard, and therefore know, that children learn what they see and experience, especially during their early life. There is no doubt about it.

Dr. Dorothy Law Nolte, born and raised in the United States (1924 to 2005) was known to be a gifted writer with a clear mind and focus. She made it very clear that kids learn what they live. Even if we do not totally agree with some of her thoughts, I certainly back her overall approach: "Monkey see, monkey do." Children are like cute little monkeys (metaphorically speaking) regardless of their background, so whatever they see Mom and Dad doing, they will try to emulate. They are always looking for comprehension and appreciation from Mom and Dad, who are their idols and heroes. Dr. Nolte believed in positive youth development and insisted that children learn what they live. Therefore, as parents we need to provide them with a balanced view of life without going to extremes. Moderation, to my mind, is the key to bringing up children, that is, not too rigid and not too loose. What they do not learn at an early age, they might not learn ever. As parents, we need to keep that in mind.

Dr. Dorothy Law Nolte is very well known for the following

thoughts that she wrote in 1972:

> If children live with criticism, they learn to condemn
>
> If children live with hostility, they learn to fight
>
> If children live with fear, they learn to be apprehensive
>
> If children live with pity, they learn to feel sorry for themselves
>
> If children live with ridicule, they learn to feel shy
>
> If children live with jealousy, they learn to feel envy
>
> If children live with shame, they learn to feel guilty
>
> If children live with encouragement, they learn confidence
>
> If children live with tolerance, they learn patience
>
> If children live with praise, they learn appreciation
>
> If children live with acceptance, they learn to love
>
> If children live with approval, they learn to like themselves
>
> If children live with recognition, they learn it is good to have a goal
>
> If children live with sharing, they learn generosity
>
> If children live with honesty, they learn truthfulness
>
> If children live with fairness, they learn justice
>
> If children live with kindness and consideration, they learn respect
>
> If children live with security, they learn to have faith in themselves and in those around them
>
> If children live with friendliness, they learn the world is a nice place in which to live

Every person is born with a distinct personality, but strength of character is learned and worked upon. It is developed from the early stages of life. Strength of character helps control your personality. Character in people reveals their unique traits such as honesty, decency, friendliness, or kindness. Traits can be molded or guided, but personality is deeply imbedded by the way the individual has been raised, and it is extremely difficult to change or influence compared to the traits that constitute the character of a person.

It is the parents' responsibility to teach their children to adapt to change, not to provide whatever the children want at any specific moment. Parents give up too easily in their responsibility of being a responsible parent, that is, to be their children's mentors. They need to be determined and teach right from wrong, but they usually succumb to the irrational caprice and uneducated instincts of their children.

Parents tend to hide children's stubbornness, rudeness, and mistakes under the shadows of their "love for their kids" without grabbing the bull by the horns and teaching their kids the real value and facts of life from an early age. These are the reasons teenagers take things for granted that they should not take for granted. It is very easy to be a child's buddy, but it demands sacrifice, work, and discipline to be a parent. It also demands:

- Firm character.
- Determined attitude.
- Consistent behavior.
- Caring mindset.
- Understanding approach.
- Loving philosophy.

In summary: firmness, consistency, and determination again and again and again!

## The Swinging Pendulum

Throughout history, parents have swung from extreme to extreme like the pendulum in a grandfather's clock. They used to be very strict with their children, but this impeded the proper growth of their children's creativity, initiative, and inventiveness. Nowadays, parents are very easy-going with their children. From my personal point of view, they are too easy-going. They are "laissez-faire–laissez-passer." They let them do literally anything, and they fail to teach them the real value of, and respect for, things and for others. They teach them only a few manners and superficially, which children tend to forget quickly. It seems that North, Central, and South American children (from Patagonia in Argentina all the way to the north of Alaska) in general are now being pampered instead of being properly educated.

Let's look at this subject through three different examples:

1. How many times have you heard children saying: "I don't want this for breakfast, lunch, or dinner." It is very common that at supper time, for example, a child will prefer a hot dog to steak and potatoes with salad. Yes, it is easier to slam together bread, a steamed hot dog, ketchup, and mustard. Finito! But is that healthy, and are we teaching our children proper healthy eating? Why are Mom and Dad too lazy to prepare them a small steak, potatoes, and a salad? If it is a matter of money, then buy on sale, but take care of what your children eat. Above all, make an effort to avoid manufactured foods and fast foods, which are detrimental to their health.

 2. How many times have you heard Mom and Dad asking, "What would you like for breakfast, lunch, or dinner?" It is fine every now and then to ask them that question but not on a

daily basis. Many young men and women are very picky about food. When they go to social events where food is served, they put aside items they don't want to eat. This is not just rude (unless there is an allergy or medical condition), but we need to teach them that, in other parts of the world, many children will do anything to have something to eat during the day and especially at night before going to bed.

3. It is more common nowadays for children to eat supper while watching TV. This will certainly not help them to develop the proper etiquette for eating and behaving properly at the table. Knowing how to eat at the table is of extreme importance, because it will either assist or hinder their development and opportunities as professionals or simply socially as average human beings in the future. Nowadays, it is very common to see young people with really bad habits of eating. Many chew with their mouths open, so you can see what they are chewing, at the same time trying to speak while spreading particles of food and saliva on the table, which nobody wants to experience while eating.

It is very common to see children with no idea of how to hold their cutlery. Instead of properly cutting a piece of meat with good etiquette, they literally stab it with the fork in one hand, while the other hand holds the knife incorrectly with an aggressive and primitive Viking flare, as if they were stabbing somebody. It is also common to see young people with their elbows on the table, slouching with their heads literally on top of dishes and eating at the speed of light like a glutton, stuffing their mouths with food as if somebody was going to take away their plates and starve them to death.

Table manners are almost a thing of the past, and it is sad to see that newer generations do not even have a clue or care how they're behaving at the table. The great majority do not even know how to drink water properly. They tend to slurp or gulp quite loudly instead of drinking quietly and with proper etiquette. Sometimes it is like having a quasi-barbarian sitting with you at the table. It is extremely uncomfortable to those with good manners and education. Yes, people are free to act as they please within certain parameters in society, but why do the rest of us need to endure such painful sights and sounds while eating our food?

Where are the days when parents used to teach their children with good examples and daily efforts? Where are the days when parents used to explain concepts with sayings such as: "You should eat with the manners of a king when at home, so you can eat with the king as if you were at home." If children were taught how to properly eat at home from their early years, it would come easily and naturally to eat properly anywhere else. Guess what? It is true and it works!

Not too long ago, I was reading an interesting and inspiring book by Richard J. Lamoureux entitled Dummy, an excellent prose and poetry book published in 2013 with interesting stories and messages. In Chapter 2, he starts with a quote from American businessman Arnold Glasgow (1905-1998):

> Parents can tell but never teach,
> unless they practice what they preach.

Yes, children learn to behave in a similar manner and fashion as their elders. Traditions and ways of being are learned by example, by repetition. As we said before, children learn what they see. Even though children tend to emulate every move and expression of Mom and Dad, this does not last long, so parents should take advantage and teach them as much and as fast as they can through their own example. As soon as children reach their teens, they are on their own, with lots of negative peer pressure, so they need a strong and solid foundation to deal with the pressures without leaving the boundaries of good manners and etiquette.

In more advanced countries, the younger generation seems to be taking things for granted. They have never experienced scarcity in food or interruption of services such as water, gas, and electricity. It breaks my heart to see the new generation not appreciating fully what they have at home, at work, in their communities, and above all, on their plate on at the table. Children are used to wasting food almost every day, and their parents are allowing it. I have seen hundreds of children piling up their plates with food they do not eat. This happens often at social events, in schools, at home, on cruise ships, in all-inclusive hotels, at all-you-can eat brunches. It happens everywhere.

Children seem to be eating with their eyes, with absolute lack of consciousness, ethics, or common sense and with a selfish approach that is very sad to see. What's worse is that Mom and Dad allow this and fail to provide guidance by teaching children to eat everything they put on their plates.

Parents are not succeeding in teaching children the proper value of things and the high cost of living, while millions of other children around the world have almost nothing to eat every day. Why are parents like this? The answer is simple; either they were also brought up irresponsibly, or they are too lazy or weak in character to insist. It is not easy, but that is what a parent is there for. A parent should insist on positive and proper behaviors. When an average parent is teaching, and guiding their children, they are actually strengthening their children's character while providing them with a better chance to succeed in life.

It is heartbreaking to see so much food go to waste when children are starving in other countries. Wait, please stop reading for a second and make a real effort to think about the word STARVING. Do not just read it quickly and lightly.

Starving means when a person or animal severely suffers and dies from malnutrition, hunger, bad quality food, or no food at all. Some do not even have clean water to drink. They die with an empty stomach. If we make a conscious effort right now and try to remember how it really feels when we are very hungry after a busy day when we did not have time even for a snack, we know it feels extremely uncomfortable and even painful. We feel empty, dizzy and often have a headache or stomach ache. We feel weak, irritable, and desperate to eat or drink something.

Now imagine this going on for days on end and weeks on end. Imagine going to bed night after night with an empty stomach, feeling pain, weak and absolutely desperate. If you manage to fall asleep, it will be most likely because of weakness, from which some never wake up again. I know I might have gone on a bit about this, but I need to get the message across, because everybody understands it, but we have grown numb. Truthfully, the average North American has no clue what it really is to be hungry. We are very lucky!

## Lack of Manners

There is a lack of appropriate manners (in the context of common courtesy and consideration), not just in younger generations but in the older generations as well, who seem to be forgetting what they once learned and practiced daily. Not because they did not learn them properly, but either in reaction to the lack of manners of younger people or because they feel, in their weird and confused understanding, that they have "earned the right" to be selfish, rude, and careless to others. Sometimes, it is simply because they are lazy and have lost their self-esteem and self-respect. Some have simply given up and do not care anymore.

An example happened to me last weekend when I went to exercise in a local community club. I was getting dressed right after my shower, and the man beside me (about three to four feet away) passed wind so loudly that I turned around and said: "Wow, what was that?" Without even looking at me, he replied: "Oh, it is my age. I am getting old." He did not even excuse himself, and he was only around 60 years old. There were three boys present, about 12 or 13 years old, laughing discreetly but also paying attention and learning what they heard. Is that the example the older generation wants to provide? They then complain if the young do not know how to behave.

There is a very good definition of etiquette in the Oxford Dictionary, and it goes like this: "The customary code of polite behaviors in society or among members of a particular profession or group." For me, etiquette can be understood as behaviors that conforms to conventional standards within a specific social class or group in society.

When I was brought up in the 1970s and 80s, we were taught to say "Thank you," "Please," "You're welcome," "Good morning," "Excuse me," "Have a good evening," "Gesundheit (Bless you)", among many other polite phrases. Nowadays, younger people either do not know they should do this or just do not want to. Some feel shy to act properly, but they need to overcome this for their own good. Good manners will always be acknowledged and will never go out of style. They always create an atmosphere of good will. Only positive karma is generated while practicing them. This is totally contrary to when bad manners and lack of etiquette are predominant in a specific place or environment.

## Bring Back The Good Old Days

Some basic and more common codes of good behaviors that we have been losing over time and that would be nice to rescue are the following fifty-six ethical codes:

1. Do not laugh at and make fun of people, especially those with disadvantages.

2. Do not interrupt while others are talking.

3. Do not slam doors shut on people following behind you, pretending you did not see them coming. Open the door and hold it open for the next person coming, if the timing is right.

4. Do not intimidate, insult, or embarrass others, regardless of your position and power.

5. Look straight into the eyes of someone when talking to them and show interest in what is being said.

6. Validate and congratulate people for their good intentions, actions, results, and even the way they dress and look.

7. Try not to misuse the cutlery and dishes while at the table, but learn how to use them properly. Every piece of cutlery and dish is for a specific use and reason.

8. Avoid putting your elbows on the table or slouching.

9. Try not to stretch across the table or in front of the person seated beside you. If you want the salt or pepper (or anything else) that is slightly away from you, ask politely for it to be handed to you.

10. Pass dishes of food to others counterclockwise.

11. Take the time to eat slowly and courteously.

12. Speak politely and with the proper tone of voice according to your surroundings.

13. Ask to leave the table when done or if you need to go to the washroom.

14. Be punctual for any event and know when to leave. Try not to be the last guest to leave, unless you are family or a very close acquaintance.

15. Do not bring friends to an event who were not invited or that you were not asked to bring.

16. Always bring something for your host. It could be a bottle of wine, flowers, good bread, dessert, etc. This is a welcome

gesture of appreciation.

17. Let the host know if you are allergic to something.

18. Serve yourself only what you will be eating without leaving leftovers on your plate.

19. Make an effort to pay attention to the names of others and refer to them by their names.

20. When introducing two people to each other, refer to them by their names and explain what they do, so they can carry on an interesting conversation. Or let them know of a similar hobby, vacation, goal, or activity to help them break the ice.

21. At a party, do not just take off unexpectedly. Say goodbye before you leave to as many people as you can.

22. Let others talk and avoid trying to listen to yourself only. Be courteous in conversation with a group. Take turns and learn how to listen.

23. Make an effort to thank people for the meeting or party with a short and sweet text or e-mail message the following day.

24. Respect traffic policies, along with all pedestrians, cyclists, electric chairs for the handicapped, motorcycles, and scooters.

25. If you have to leave an office or meeting suddenly, always say "Excuse me."

26. Do not litter or spit in public places. Throwing gum, paper,

cans, or bottles on the ground denotes primitive behaviors penalized with a fine or jail in most countries. Why should others pick up your garbage? Would you like to pick up theirs?

27. Respect others' personal space by leaving a restaurant or a gathering of any kind if you need to answer your cell phone.

28. Respect other's creeds, traditions, and habits the same way you want yours to be acknowledged and respected.

29. Keep your habits and traditions within the boundaries of the society that welcomed you in.

30. Know how to answer properly in person or on the phone.

31. Avoid taking a gift given to you to another party or gathering. You risk bumping into the person who gave you that gift originally. Re-gifting, happens more often that it should.

32. Always show appreciation and gratitude if somebody compliments you, invites you to a party, gives you a gift, or recommends you.

33. In lines, wait for your turn and avoid trying to jump ahead regardless of any excuses you might have.

34. Maintain your own style of expressing yourself with courtesy and avoid foul words.

35. When you go out with friends for dinner or to a pub for a beer, ask for separate bills. Do not divide the account in half, because you might want to have something extra with its corresponding extra charge. Nobody wants to pay somebody

else's bills.

36. If you are invited for dinner, be cognizant and take heed of the other person's budget. Never ask for the most expensive dish to try to impress the other person. Yes, you will impress him or her, but from the wrong angle or perspective.

37. If possible, know the birth dates of your peers, family members, and friends. Send a short e-mail or card on their birthdays. This shows you care about them, which will only bring good personal feelings.

38. Try to avoid wearing flip-flops or sandals. They are far from being formal, and they also put you at risk while driving, walking, or going down the stairs. Sandals and flip-flops were originally invented for the beach or the shower. But if you must wear them, ensure that your feet and toes are groomed.

39. If you have small children in a public place, control them. If they cry, take them outside until they stop. If they throw a tantrum, control them. Others do not need to hear them. You are invading others' space.

40. Be civilized, and be an example of a well-behaved dad or mom at your children's games or events.

41. Be aware and careful of everybody else's feelings. Nobody can please everybody, but try doing your best.

42. Do not stare at people, especially those with a handicap, or make fun of them. This sounds obvious, but people still do it and seem not to care.

43. Avoid, at all costs, throwing garbage in public places (as mentioned above) but especially into rivers, lakes, or the ocean. It is not only uncivilized but is a very aggressive act toward our environment. Report all those who do this to the proper authorities.

44. Why go to work sick? You could be the cause of the next contagious flu.

45. If sneezing, do it as quietly as possible. Avoid sounding like a noisy hyena. Unfortunately, there are people who sneeze so loudly that it seems their lungs might spill out. Also, when sneezing, we should have the courtesy of properly covering our mouth by sneezing into the inside of our elbow and saying "excuse me" immediately thereafter.

46. When shaking hands do it firmly, looking straight into the eyes of the other person.

47. Show your children how to answer the phone properly. A plain "Yeah" is far from civilized. Compare it with: "Good morning, this is Johnny. Who is this?"

48. Accept things with enthusiasm and humility and always with a thank you.

49. When somebody else sneezes, the other person should say, "Gesundheit" (German for health) or "Bless you" or "Salud" (Spanish for health). It is just common courtesy and good manners.

50. Cover your mouth when yawning. In meetings and in conversations with other people, avoid yawning altogether if

you can. When yawning, nobody really wants to see how many cavities you have or if you brushed your teeth and tongue or not.

51. If you really need to burp or release gas, do it privately and silently. Nobody needs to know what you just did, much less be exposed to the hideous odor. It is just a civilized courtesy to others and to yourself. But the worst is that many people just find it funny, they brush it off and laugh about it.

52. Avoid abusing or bullying others at all costs. It is a coward's practice. Bullies do not fit into society and need to be severely punished. Those who succumb to peer pressure to bully and harass others need to learn their lesson and be sanctioned severely. If you witness abuse, have the courage and confidence to expose the abusers. Silence, at that moment or afterwards, makes you an accomplice and should be punishable. Remember, the bully is a bully until the coward decides otherwise.

53. Avoid putting your feet on desks and tables (or any kind of furniture, for that matter). Sometimes, when we go to public places such as malls and cafeterias, we see people placing their dirty feet on the benches or on the same table that somebody might be setting their drink and food on later. That attitude denotes lack of education and is extremely rude and selfish, and is even considered by many to be an act of aggression. It is an unhealthy habit in any case. These days, if you see this happen and dare to say something, you will most likely get a rude and aggressive answer, because people today have the distorted idea that they have the right to act any way they want, which sometimes includes behaving aggressively, stupidly, and even savagely. Just imagine the

amount of germs or bacteria on the bottom of your shoes, especially after leaving a public bathroom. Gross!

54. Dress according to the occasion, and be smart about it. Better to be overdressed than underdressed. More people are dressing beneath the code level they should dress for an event. Yes, we can go to the theatre with jeans and T-shirts. It is our right! But should we? People believe that anything goes, but guess what? Not anything goes, and not everybody has to accept others, if they dress sloppily or inappropriately, especially in certain places. You show your host how much or how little you respect them by the way you dress for their event. Again, always better to overdress. A proper dress code positions you at a higher level in your society. Whether we like it or not, our clothing makes a statement about who we really are. If you are sloppy, this might indicate you are careless or messy in other matters such as personal hygiene, feelings, behaviors, responsibilities, work ethic, money management, etc. Is that the image you want to portray?

55. Show respect in every one of your actions. Respect others the way you want others to respect you, which means treating others the way we want to be treated. Respect is an essential part of human behaviors. It is the pillar of good relations among people and between countries.

56. Sticking our fingers in our mouths in front of others while at the table or even in public is bad manners. Regardless of whether we are using the little pinky or not, it is plain rude and disgusting for others to see somebody using their little finger as toothpicks and, even worse, flinging the piece of food off their finger. The list could go on ….

## Civic Politeness – A Thing of The Past?

As positive as I want to be, I have to be realistic and therefore acknowledge that we are experiencing bad habits, poor manners, and lack of politeness and consideration almost everywhere and in various situations. The degree of civic politeness and consideration has diminished as our population grows and our overall level of education received at home and at school has declined.

This is happening all over the world, not just in North America. It is happening in some countries more than in others. It is unfortunate, but it is a fact of life. We experience it in almost every family and at all levels of education. It is alarming that it is happening more frequently and with absolute disregard for others, for their own reputation, and with no remorse or embarrassment at all. I now wonder, what does embarrassment really mean to the great majority?

When I was younger, public transit was my main means of transportation, and it was just a matter of courtesy to give up one's seat to an elderly person or a pregnant woman. You seldom see that today on public transit. Passengers all seem to pretend they are sleeping or not paying attention to their surroundings. I strongly encourage younger people to act considerately toward the elderly, the disabled, and pregnant women.

It is never too late to correct these patterns. So, let us start feeling pride now in what we do, while being a better person and a good example to others. It will bring satisfaction and good feelings to you, and the people around you will definitely notice it and appreciate it. The question is: Do you like behaving in a civilized manner and being appreciated?

## A True Valuable Story of Setting an Example

Public figures have even more responsibility to behave politely. The world is watching them, but they often fail profoundly, as Sasha, President Obama's daughter, has done a few times. For example, during her dad's inauguration speech, while seated beside her sister Malia and her mom Michelle Obama, she suddenly gave a prolonged, reflexive, and mighty yawn that attracted all the keen eyes and cameras around them. Did this show lack of proper education? Many people will say "Come on, she was only 11 years old" or "She is just a little girl," or "Oh, poor thing, she must have been very tired." Well, let me tell you that, since I was five years old, we knew that not covering our mouths was rude and unacceptable behaviors that could land us into trouble.

Now guess what? In 2008, Sasha was also caught giving a huge yawn at the Democratic National Convention. She was seven years old then. To me, it was understandable, as she was very young at the time, and she was bored and tired. But in my opinion the question remains that, if the Obamas do not seem to be concerned about how their children behave or act in public, what can we expect from the rest of the people, either in the US, Canada, or Mexico?

Is the lack of proper civil behaviors one of the reasons why people from the United States are not well liked or well-regarded and accepted around the world? People learn by example, and if we believe that bad manners and lack of politeness are cute or funny or not intentional, then we are definitely on the wrong track. Ask all around the world what locals think about the behaviors of the average American at an all-inclusive resort. They are tolerated for their money but not necessarily liked. This is sad, because not every person from the United States is like that. Please do not take me wrong. It is obvious there are good, decent and refined people in the United States too, but unfortunately, today they are most likely the minority. The same is true of Canadians and Mexicans.

We can always use excuses to justify any action, but the bottom line, as in the above example of Sasha Obama, is that she failed to cover her mouth due apparently to lack of proper education, even at 11 years old. My parents were there for my brothers and me every minute of the day while growing up. It should have been an automatic reflex for Sasha Obama to cover her mouth at that age. I repeat, an automatic reflex!

We all have to do our best to teach and guide our children better. On a daily basis if necessary. There are no limits to good education, and it is not limited to a specific age bracket. The younger children learn, the better.

Children need to develop instinctive habits that will allow them to perform the right courteous action without even thinking of it or realizing they are doing it. Being a parent is not always fun; it comes with serious responsibilities and sacrifices. We all must contribute to the enrichment of our societies through better manners, proper public respect, and politeness in all our actions.

## A New Generation of Parents

Education is transmitted through generations; that is what makes or breaks a country. It is passed on to the children first by their parents at home, then at school, and lastly through the media and the overall society in which they live. Unfortunately, in the last two generations (starting in the 1970s), the children have gained strength while parents have lost control. Parents have lost control over their children, who now seem to be dictating what goes on at home.

Let me explain. We are part of the first or second generation determined to not making the same mistakes our parents made with us. Unfortunately, we have been taking this too far and have not been able to negotiate a happy medium with our children. This is perhaps because of stronger peer pressure, our style of living, access to entertainment, the media, the high-tech life, etc., but there is no doubt that education levels have definitely been on the decline.

We have tried to solve the mistakes or abuses that happened in our past when we were growing up, in which the elderly (including parents) were too strict and, in many cases, even a bit abusive. The problem is that, in our efforts to correct those mistakes or abuses, we have tried to be too understanding and easy-going with our children and have ended up being the most insecure, weak, and tolerant parents in history. We have gone the extra mile to understand and be friends with our children and have extended our hands so far that our arms have been figuratively ripped from our bodies. Why?

Because as much as some parents fail to admit, instead of raising children, we have been raising capricious little monsters that always want their own way; they demand everything, they are irreverent, disrespectful, belligerent, and, worst of all, powerful in our society. They just need to scream wolf against Mom and Dad and the parents can be in serious trouble, with the local Child Service Society at their door.

Parents do not really have full control of their children at home for many reasons. It is like "seeing the geese fly by shooting the hunters instead of the hunters shooting the geese." We have gone to the other extreme from that of our parents. We are part of the last generation who were afraid of our parents and are now afraid of our children. We are the last generation that respects and takes care of our parents and grandparents (the elderly in general), and the first generation that does not have the luxury of owning the full respect of our own children.

We urgently need to return to a measured and balanced authoritarian parenting instead of cooperative or friendly parenting, to bounce back closer to what was before. Parents should stop asking their children and should start telling them what to do or not to do. We need to be emphatic, direct, assertive, and insistent with our children. With energy, determination, and firmness, parents can handle the resistance they will most certainly encounter and that is normal in any child.

Our parents were very strict and even quite tough on us during our upbringing. Respect, silence, good behaviors, obedience, and sometimes submission were enforced. We grew up almost hating it and promising to ourselves not to make the same mistakes with our kids, but we have gone too far. We have turned into very soft parents who think or believe that our children are the best behaved in the world. Family relationships have changed for good and for bad— unfortunately more towards the latter.

This is most obvious in European and North American societies. In the past, there was more authoritarianism, governed by the strict hand of the father. Unfortunately, mothers in many places would tend to follow, whether they liked it or not. Divorce was seen as an evil and bad thing. Things have changed radically in the past 30 to 40 years but unfortunately to the other extreme.

Parents nowadays have trouble differentiating between education and authoritarianism, between being a friend and being a mentor, between education and permissiveness. We all know that both too much control or too much freedom will transform into chaos sooner or later. People rebel, and that is just human nature.

The real challenge is to find a happy medium in which you show your children control and freedom at the same time. You teach them and explain to them the good and bad of both extremes until they understand and accept. But it is not easy. It is a continuous effort on a daily basis, and this is where the average parent fails. Parents themselves lack discipline, perseverance, and stamina to control, guide, and help their children to grow up physically and mentally healthy. It is much easier to say "Okay" and turn your head than to say "No" while upholding and explaining your decision. It is also important to keep in mind that there is nothing wrong with making a decision and not providing the child with a full explanation. We are adults, and they are children. We have the experience and brains; they do not. Their brains have not fully developed, so how can they properly evaluate the decisions of an adult?

In the 1960s and 1970s, good parents were those who had well-behaved children who respected them as well as their grandparents, their teachers, the elderly, the young, and everybody within their close-knit society. Children who were studious, polite, well-behaved, and who were involved in sports, music, or other constructive extracurricular activities and were well perceived in society.

Today, nobody seems to care. I have been asking myself what has been going on to get to this point, and I have researched and also exchanged ideas with other thinkers and friends of mine. I have come to the conclusion that one of the main causes is that the hierarchy has changed. Today parents do not control their children, and, consequently, they do not have their respect. Yes, they are still loved by their children, but with a low degree of respect and a high degree of entitlement. A high percentage of parents nowadays are hesitant, reluctant, or even afraid of demanding certain standards from their children.

Let me just give you one example. Parent-child relationships have developed serious issues in the past 20 years that are now getting out of control. Some of these problems come from the amount of electronic gadgetry parents provide their children without any control measures. An average middle-class child in North America has a cell phone, a tablet, a laptop, and a music system at a minimum. It is great if their parents can afford these electronics and provide them to their children, but the problem is that the average parent allows their children to use them without any measure of control. This disconnects the children from reality (and from Mom and Dad) and invites them into cyberspace and into cyber-relationships with others. This seriously impairs the youngsters' social skills.

Again, moderation in everything is the key. In today's society, children need to develop cybernetic skills but should not be limited to those, and Mom and Dad should interfere and guide their children at an early stage, when they still listen to their parents. One in every 10 children in the United States now has the behavioral disorder known as ADHD (attention deficit-hyperactivity disorder). Is it possible that children's cyber-dependency causes this? According to a Pennsylvania family physician and psychologist, Dr. Sax, children suffer serious sleep deprivation due to today's style of living (excess number of activities) and easy access to modern technology (iPhones, tablets, computers, etc.). The symptoms of sleep deprivation resemble those of ADHD, says Dr. Sax, and are a major obstacle for children's learning abilities at school.

Parents should discourage their children's continuous electronic connections and help them improve their social skills instead. A similar situation is happening in Canada and Mexico and all over the world in various proportions. The United States does more statistical analysis, which allows involved people to know where the situation is really standing and how to go about trying to solve it. Attention deficit hyperactivity disorder (ADHD) in children seems to be an epidemic, as obesity in the young is as well.

Margaret Rock wrote an article, "A nation of kids with gadgets and ADHD," for the health and science section of Time magazine, July 8, 2013. She raises the big question many scientists and authors have raised before her: Is technology to blame for the rise of behavioral disorders? She writes:

> The rise in ADHD has coincided with the rise of mobile devices. According to a report by the Kaiser Family Foundation, children on average spend nearly seven and a half hours each day staring at screens. That's up 20 per cent from just five years ago. Is there a relationship between the two?

She portrays the average child with head down, eyes focused on the screen, attention totally dedicated to cyberspace. The actions and development of such children will obviously be very different from those of other children running and playing around instead of being completely connected and absorbed by technology. Margaret Rock confirms that these children have strong and powerful attention skills but only if they receive continuous intermittent rewards, which does not happen in real life! This puts them at a disadvantage compared to other children who do not suffer from ADHD.

There is a good, concise article by Cathy Gulli in Maclean's magazine of January 18, 2016 entitled "The Collapse Of Parenting." She strongly encourages parents to stand up to their children, arguing that "treating children like adults does not help them succeed in life. New research shows this is making them anxious, depressed, overweight – and downright unlikable." Gulli based her conclusions on Dr. Leonard Sax's book The Collapse of Parenting: How We Hurt Our Kids When We Treat Them Like Grown-Ups. Sax argues that today's parents have given away their authority and have lost their own confidence, whether they accept this or not.

Parents negotiate with and bribe their children instead of telling them how to behave. Parents need to be more assertive in respecting their kids while being the ultimate deciders. But Gulli starts her article by noting that "if anyone can be called the boss in modern, anti-hierarchical parenthood, it's the children. It is time for parents to start being grown-ups again." As parents, we need to help our children by offering other activities (many of them outdoor activities) or different gadgets or items that are not screen-related, so they can move their heads (and attention spans) away from those screens. We need to keep the children from becoming what Geoffrey A. Fowler calls "iPad zombies" in his article published in the Wall Street Journal on December 16, 2014, "Tech Toys to Make Children Smarter." As an example, he wrote:

> Some of the smartest toys of 2014 are about building technology, not just consuming it. There's Kano, a $150 kit for piecing together a tiny computer that teaches programming. Modular Robotics makes two kinds of kits priced $150 and up, called Cube-lets and Moss, for creating small robots that respond to their surroundings. And a company called Little-Bits sells kits starting at $100 to make fun machines that snap together."

According to Fowler, with whom I completely concur, we need to inspire our children to be inventors rather than just users of technology. Through the use of new technological toys and gadgets that do not involve hypnotizing screens, the children can snap out of that lost mind state and not just create their own ideas but socialize and interact with others better. If there is a will, there is a way, and the parents who really care can help their children.

I found a wonderful poem on the web (at poetry.com). It is credited to Eden Andrades and is entitled: "Live Life the Real Way." There is also a YouTube video in which the poem is recited with very interesting images in the background. For more details visit: YouTube.com/embed/ut7IdSovP_E.

The poem is worth quoting in full:

> I have 763 friends, yet I am lonely.
> I speak to all of them every day, yet none of them really

know me.
The problem I have sits in the spaces between
Looking into their eyes or at a name on a screen.
I took a step back and opened my eyes,
I looked around and realized
That this media we call social is anything but,
When we open our computers and it's our doors we shut.
All this technology we have is just an illusion.
Community, companionship, a sense of inclusion.
Yet when you step away from this device of delusion,
You'll awaken to see a world of confusion.
A world where we're slaves to the technology we mastered,
Where information gets sold by some rich, greedy bastard.
A world of self-interest, self-image, self-promotion,
Where we all share our best bits, but leave out the emotion.
We're at our most happy with an experience we share,
But is it the same if no-one is there?
Be there for your friends, and they'll be there too,
But no one will be, if a group message will do.
We edit and exaggerate, crave adulation,
We pretend not to notice the social isolation.
We put our words into order until our lives are glistening,
We don't even know if anyone is listening.
Being alone isn't a problem, let me just emphasize
If you read a book, paint a picture, or do some exercise
You're being productive and present, not reserved and recluse,
You'll be awake and attentive and put your time to good use.

So, when you're in public and you start to feel alone,
Put your hands behind your head, step away from the phone.
You don't need to stare at your menu or your contact list,
Just talk to one another, learn to coexist.
I can't stand to hear the silence of a busy commuter train
Where no one wants to talk for the fear of looking insane.
We're becoming unsocial, it no longer satisfies
To engage with one another, and look into someone's eyes.
We're surrounded by children, who since they were born
Have watched us living like robots and think it's the norm.
It's not very likely you'll make "World's Greatest Dad"
If you can't entertain a child without your iPad.
When I was a child I'd never be home,
I'd be outside with my friends, on our bikes we would roam.
I'd get holes in my trainers and graze up my knees,
And we'd build our own clubhouse high up in the trees.
Now the park is so quiet it gives me a chill,
I see no children outside and the swings hanging still.
There's no skipping, no hopscotch, no church and no steeple,
We're a generation of idiots. Smartphones but dumb people.
So, look up from your phone, shut down the display,
Take in your surroundings, make the most of today.
Just one real connection is all it can take
To show you the difference that being there can make.

Be there in the moment as he gives you the look
That you'll remember as when love overtook.
The time he first held your hand or first kissed your lips,
The time you first disagreed but still love him to bits.
The time you don't have to tell hundreds what you've done,
Because you want to share this moment with just this one.
The time he sold his computer so he could buy you a ring,
The man of your dreams, who is now the real thing.
The time you want to start a family, and the moment when you first hold your little girl and get to fall in love again.
The time she keeps you up at night and all you want is rest,
And the time you wipe away the tears as your baby leaves the nest.
The time your baby girl returns, with a boy for you to hold,
And the time he calls you Grandma and makes you feel quite old.
The time you take in all you've made just by giving life attention,
And how you're glad you didn't waste it by looking down at some invention.
The time you hold your husband's hand, sit down beside his bed,
You tell him that you love him, lay a kiss upon his head.
He whispers to you quietly, as his heart gives a final beat,
That he's lucky he got stopped by that lost girl in the street.

But none of these times will ever happen, you'll never have any of this
If you're too busy looking down, you don't see the chances you miss.
So, look up from the phone, shut off those displays,
We have a finite existence, a set number of days.
Don't waste your life getting caught in the net,
Because when the end comes, there's nothing worse than regret.
I am guilty too of being part of this machine.
This digital world where we're heard but not seen,
Where we type as we talk and we read as we chat,
Where we spend hours together without making eye contact.
So, don't give into a life where you follow the hype,
Give people your love, don't give them a like.
Disconnect from the need to be heard and defined,
Go out into the world, leave distractions behind.
Look up from your phone, shut down that display,
Go out and enjoy, and live life the real way.

As mentioned previously in this book, children's manners need changing, and this applies worldwide, not just to North America. It is so important that I have decided to refer to an article I read not too long ago in the Financial Times. It was published on Dec 22, 2012 in the World News section and is about how a new School of Etiquette in China is pioneering a new Cultural Revolution in that country.

Asians in general are not known for quiet eating. For example, without sounding racist, because I am definitely not racist, the average Asian, while eating noodles, tends to slurp them in an acoustically high and rhythmical pitch while flinging drops from the soup or sauce around the table or on their clothes. I guess that happens to almost everybody while eating such food, if they do not use the proper silverware or do not know how to successfully master the chopsticks in co-ordination with good manners. Eating noodles properly or even spaghetti with either fork or spoon or both is not necessarily a common practice everywhere. But if there is a will, there is a way!

The article, by Patti Waldmeir in Shanghai, is entitled "Chinese Wannabes Rush To Learn Etiquette" Waldmeir writes:

> Like gunpowder and printing, China had etiquette before most of the rest of us. But Confucius has been dead a long time and Mao Zedong got rid of what remained, leaving the Chinese with a reputation around the world for having more money than manners.

Apparently, average people at higher professional levels in China need to take these etiquette courses to improve their behaviors while socializing among themselves and especially with foreigners. The new trend amounts to a cultural revolution in etiquette and decorum. While other countries in Europe and Latin America teach proper etiquette at home, countries like China do not, so many have to work at it later in life. Therefore, according to the reporter, social and business cross-cultural training courses are in great demand in China, and demand is expected to expand.

## Children's Rights, Vaccination, and Traditional Medicine

According to UNICEF, children's rights are defined and understood as follows: "Children's rights are the rights of children with particular attention to the rights of special protection and care afforded to minors." This applies to all children worldwide, regardless of gender, national origin, color, ethnicity, sexual orientation, race, or religion. Researchers, politicians, social workers, teachers, youth workers, and others throughout the world acknowledge that children need to be identified as valuable participants in every society and need safeguarding and security. Their rights, as well as their responsibilities, require recognition and protection at all times.

Therefore, what really blows my mind and seriously challenges my logic and understanding is the growing number of parents who dare challenge science, modern medicine, and proven medical results by risking the health of their own children and those attending the same school by not vaccinating their children. Vaccination protects against dangerous diseases such as measles, small pox, mumps, polio, tuberculosis, and others. It is well known that flu shots are not necessarily good or effective, but vaccination against major diseases and illnesses (like those mentioned above) in my view must be mandatory, regardless of people's knowledge, educational level, thoughts, or understanding.

The problem is so serious that it should be enforced regardless of people's religion. Otherwise, we would be placing religion over the well-being and safety of their own children and those of others. To my mind and logical understanding, if children are not vaccinated, it should be considered parental abuse and therefore a crime if parents fail to vaccinate their children and send them to school without vaccination, placing others in danger. Yes, and I repeat, the danger is that those parents are also putting all the other students at school at serious health risk.

Just look at what happened in late 2014 and early 2015 in the United States and Canada because of parents who did not vaccinate their children with the MMR vaccine against measles, mumps, and rubella, which had been suppressed by the vaccine for so many years. In both years, the United States experienced a multi-state outbreak. Over 380 cases in 2014 alone happened, primarily among unvaccinated Amish communities in Ohio alone (according to the Centers for Disease Control and Prevention). Allan Maki wrote in the Globe and Mail (Apr 07, 2014): "In Calgary, after two Western Canada High School students were stricken with measles, 100 unimmunized students at Western Canada were ordered to stay home until they could provide proof of vaccination."

Measles are potentially fatal and can also cause blindness and brain damage. To expose your children (and other children at their school) should be considered immoral and unlawful, regardless of what parents believe or hear, because the proof is in the pudding (as they say) regarding the 2014 and 2015 multi-state measles outbreak in the US, along with serious cases in Canada. Unfortunately, there are religious groups who actually promote anti-immunization due, in my opinion, to their obtuse and narrow-minded beliefs that go against professional worldwide scientific research and conclusive evidence. Remember the saying: "Help yourself first, then God will help you." Unfortunately, it sometimes falls on deaf ears, in ignorant people or with religious extremists.

Prime Minister Tony Abbot from Australia announced a policy by which Australia will deny benefits to families that reject vaccination and fail to immunize their children unless, of course, they are exempt due to religious or medical reasons. But the Australian government will make immunization a condition for medical benefits for Australian families. Unvaccinated children's families will not get welfare benefits or childcare funded by the federal government. This policy is known as "No Jab, No Pay."

In New Zealand, however, it was determined that the decision to vaccinate or not should remain with the parents and that removing the right to refuse medical treatment (for lack of immunization) would be "an unjustifiable breach of the New Zealand Bill of Rights Act."

In my eyes, a question immediately arises: What about the rights of the children who did get their shots? Their rights seem to be violated, because children who do not get vaccinated, at their parent's prerogative, are putting their classmates at risk. If this is not a violation of children's rights, what is it? Why does New Zealand seem to protect the rights of those families that do not follow social standards (the minority) above the rights of families that do follow these standards and behaviors (the majority)? Personally, I take my hat off to Australia's prime minister. Tough solutions to tough problems…simple as that!

A similar situation is happening in Africa, where governments are having to force families to vaccinate their children against polio. Parents were avoiding vaccines for various reasons such as religious beliefs, not trusting that the vaccine will work, thinking vaccines cause other medical problems, fearing their kids might have reactions to vaccines, hearing through the grapevine or Internet that vaccines don't work or have not been properly researched and tested, etc.

In some African countries, it is said that parents risk losing custody of their children if they do not vaccinate them per the law and per the instructions of their local ministry of health. Perhaps that approach should also be implemented in North America to protect both the children of irresponsible parents and the children of families who did vaccinate but who risk being infected at school by unvaccinated children.

There is an adamant anti-vaccine proponent in the US called Jenny McCarthy, who is also an actress and model and apparently has negatively influenced many people in the US who think her "university degree from Google" (as she stated on the Oprah Winfrey Show) is more accurate and reliable than scientific proof from medical institutions. It seems Jenny McCarthy provides no proper research or scientific proof at all about the dangers of vaccines. Go figure that out!

I strongly encourage you to read the following two links (and watch the associated YouTube videos) regarding Rex Murphy's commentary on anti-vacciners. He is a reporter for The National Post (and a well-known Canadian commentator on political and social matters) "Anti-vaxxers have the intellectual power of a dead tree stump," he says. "Only arrogant, selfish, and silly people can reject modern medicine. These people walk away from reason and medicine to their own self-absorbed and dangerous practices."

For more information, visit the following two links:

cbc.ca/thenational/content/analysis/rexmurphy/anti-vaccine_movement.html

huffingtonpost.ca/2015/02/06/rex-murphy-anti-vaccine_n_6631184.html

Then there are those parents who, for religious reasons, give their children traditional medicine instead of scientifically proven medical treatments and deny the children proven medical treatments, such as blood transfusions, because of their religious beliefs.

There was a famous case in Canada involving a First Nations girl diagnosed with lymphoblastic leukemia, a cancer that, in this case, would have had a very good chance of being cured with modern chemotherapy treatment. The daughter accepted chemotherapy, but her Mom and some family members didn't.

An article in the Globe and Mail (Saturday, April 25, 2015) reports that the mother of the girl initially accepted chemotherapy, but 10 days into the 32-day treatment, she pulled her daughter out of treatment, saying she would have her treated with holistic healing instead. She then took her to Florida to a place called the Hippocrates Health Institute. Apparently, the cancer went into remission but came back in March of 2015. The family then decided that chemotherapy, along with traditional Haudenosaunee medicine, would be the ideal treatment for J.J. (as the little girl was known).

Traditional healers practicing Haudenosaunee medicine rely on a combination of natural medicines and spiritual practices, which many people believe and trust blindly. Hopefully, by taking the chemotherapy treatment again along with traditional Haudenosaunee medicine, little J.J. will succeed in her battle against lymphoblastic leukemia.

Connie Walker from CBC News wrote an article published in the Analysis section of CBC News on January 22 of 2015 entitled "Makayla Sault's death shifts the spotlight to J.J's." She reports that since J.J.'s problem started, she has only eaten raw vegetables such as wheatgrass, kale, parsley, and celery, among many other natural foods. But what caught my attention in Connie Walker's article is that she writes about "a fierce love" that J.J.'s mother has for her daughter. In our society that "fierce love" is usually highly praised and admired, but it should also be feared in some cases.

A "fierce love" can also be blind, twisted, biased, and utterly wrong, because many only think with their hearts instead of a combination of heart and brain. In my personal opinion, it appears to me that J.J.'s mother was strongly influenced by her people's ancestry and native traditions. These traditions have been proven, in most situations, to be effective in treating some diseases and maintaining a healthy lifestyle, but that should not exclude the results of scientific research that have been proven to cure diseases such as the lymphoblastic leukemia that J.J. is going through. I personally believe that if J.J.'s mother would not have pulled her daughter out of the chemotherapy but instead applied the traditional medicines of her ancestors in addition to chemotherapy, J.J.'s cancer would most likely have already gone for good. But we will never know. That opportunity is gone.

Fortunately for J.J., it appears that her mother is now allowing her to receive the chemotherapy treatment along with traditional Haudenosaunee medicine. We hope and wish J.J. a quick and long-lasting recovery.

There is nothing wrong with "fierce love" as long as it goes in parallel with logic, understanding, appreciation, rationality, and acceptance of scientific solutions. Especially when an innocent life is at risk, we need to find the best balance among treatments and not be blinded by a personal point of view or limited to only one alternative, if we really possess that "fierce love" for somebody. At least, that is my opinion, and, with respect, I firmly stand by it.

According to an article by Tom Blackwell entitled "First Nations girl who used alternative treatment back on chemotherapy after leukemia returns" (National Post, April 25, 2015):

> Evidence suggests that between 70 and 90 per cent of child leukemia patients can be cured with conventional treatment that includes chemotherapy; without it, the disease is usually a death sentence, medical experts say.

Unfortunately, another aboriginal girl, Makayla Sault, from the neighboring Mississauga of the New Credit First Nation, died in February after similarly pulling out of chemotherapy for leukemia.

A lawyer and a columnist, Paul Hergott, whom I personally know and have a high regard and respect for, wrote an article in The Capital News on April 29, 2016 entitled "Criminal conviction for parents over death of a child." He starts by reporting: "David and Collet Stephan have been criminally convicted by a jury for causing the death of their 19-month-old son, Ezekiel, who they dearly loved and dotingly cared for." According to the prosecutor, the Stephan's loved their child dearly, but unfortunately love alone is not enough, one of various reasons the parents ended up being convicted.

Apparently, the parents had never taken their child to a registered medical doctor, which in my mind is an extreme, illogical, and unacceptable lack of action. Extreme actions, or lack thereof, are the cause of misunderstandings, big mistakes, and even deaths, as happened in this case. It seems to me that the parents failed profoundly in their excessive "love for their child," by not seeking help from a qualified medical doctor. Instead, as the article reports, they opted for natural remedies such as garlic, hot peppers, horseradish, and onions, hoping to boost the child's immune system.

Extremes almost always end up being bad strategies. Moderation is the key to a balanced outcome and success. That is a proven law of nature. If, at the very least, these parents had taken their child for a proper medical diagnostic, they would have known he had meningitis and that natural remedies would have not worked with that disease. Antibiotics would have given their child a better chance of survival, but Ezekiel was deprived of that chance. Was it negligence, natural healing beliefs, stubbornness, a know-it-all attitude, or religious faith that caused little Ezekiel to die, or simply the blinding and excessive love that some parents have for their children? I do not know, and I am certainly not accusing them of such actions, but these possibilities obviously crossed my mind and that of thousands of parents. It is very sad that they failed to realize that their son was suffering from bacterial meningitis, which as the article notes, "is a very serious illness."

I believe that loving your child dearly does not exempt a parent from acting responsibly for the benefit of the child. Excessive love does not mean a parent is always right. Reasoning, common sense, and proven science should always prevail.

Paul Hergott is well known in the community for his high values and persistent efforts to fight for justice. In his article, he reflects on the dilemma the case raises as follows:

> Criminal law experts could offer their opinions in answer to these questions [about the parents' options]. But in my view, these questions ought not to be answered on the basis of legal precedents that are built on Criminal Code offence that has largely remained as it was since being enacted in 1892.

He then asks, "what if they had sought medical attention but their child was still seriously damaged or died from the illness?" Well, Hergott certainly has a point here, but in the well-known and proven law of probabilities, the child would have had far better chances of survival with proper medical treatment. Parents are there to protect their children, and when they diminish their child's chances of survival through excessive love or a fascination for natural treatments, they should be evaluated under the Criminal Code. Sometimes, lack of proper action can constitute a serious offense. At least, that is my personal point of view.

A responsible parent will at least take a child to a registered medical doctor, listen to what he or she has to say, and then make an informed decision. What gives them the power of playing God with natural remedies and not even giving their beloved child the chance of at least being seen by a registered medical doctor for diagnosis? Nevertheless, I completely agree with Hergott that all these types of issues "ought to be discussed and debated with updated laws put into place under the leadership of our elected officials."

## CHAPTER FOUR: MISCONSTRUED LOVE AND OBESITY

### Children's Obesity Problems

Let us now talk about an issue that is affecting children in North America and, to my mind, is extremely important to bring to the attention of the reader. The problem is that a high percentage of children do not like or eat healthy foods and are naturally prone to eating unhealthy foods on a regular basis. In many instances, they are allowed to or, even worse, encouraged to do so by their parents.

Cathy Gulli's article in Maclean's that I referred to earlier, notes an alarming decline in children's fitness in North America. This contributes to serious weight gain in the younger generation. Gulli wrote, "There is even a medical term for it, 'deconditioning', which is described in The Collapse of Parenting as a euphemism for 'out of shape'."

In the summer of 2016, I personally asked 100 random children at two local community centres and the local mall what they would prefer to have more often for lunch between the following two choices:

Lunch A.  A slice of pizza, a hot dog, some French fries, a can of soda, and ice-cream for dessert.

Lunch B.   Chicken, vegetables, rice, corn, homemade lemonade and strawberries with a dash of whipped cream for dessert.

My goal was simply to see what approximate percentage of children would choose lunch A over lunch B.

Answer: Eighty-four out of 100 children chose alternative A. But that is not really the problem. It is normal for a kid to choose what they like best, not what is better for them. The real problem is that the parents allow them to do it, and this is the reason malnourishment and obesity are so rampant among children nowadays. When I was growing up, there was always the "fat" boy or the "fat" girl or, to speak properly, the overweight child. But they were only one or two in an average class of 30 to 35 students. Nowadays over 30 per cent of the average class is seriously overweight, and the percentage is increasing. Child obesity is becoming an epidemic, and it is not the children's fault. It is the fault of parents who are not taking parenthood and its responsibilities seriously, especially when feeding their children.

Note:

In the BC Medical Journal, July-August 2015, page 239, there is an article written by six doctors (Dr. B Matthew, Dr. M Flesher, Dr. S Sampath, Dr. N Nguyen, Dr. N Alizadeh-Pasdar, and Dr. K Barclay) in which they report that "in British Columbia (Canada) alone, 59 per cent of the population of adults is overweight and 20 per cent of these are obese." If that is the case in July 2015, imagine how it is going to be by 2025 or 2050 if we do not educate our children in better eating habits while giving them a bad example ourselves!

I was in the food court not too long ago and at the next table was a family of five (Mom, Dad, two daughters, and a son) sitting down to have dinner. It was about 6 pm. They each had something different, which is normal because they were in the mall and could enjoy whatever they preferred. But all had very unhealthy foods, even though there were other healthy alternatives. Four out of the five family members were seriously and grossly overweight, so much so that they even walked as if deformed, with open legs, most likely from joint issues. Mom ate two hot dogs, poutine (fries with cheese curds and heavy-duty gravy) and a soda; Dad had a Big Mac with fries and a soda; the younger daughter (around 15) had a large slice of pizza with a soda; the son (about 18 years old) had pasta, garlic bread, French fries, and soda; and the older daughter (around 19) had a tossed salad, a piece of fish and fries, and a glass of ice water. She was the only one in the family with a healthy, slim body. When they all got up and left, everybody left a mess behind except for the older daughter, who picked up her tray and placed it at the bussing station after putting her trash in the bin.

I was sad that day, but at the same time, it confirmed my observation that you are what you eat, and that people with self-control, self-esteem and self-respect tend to be healthier, cleaner and more organized than those who lack those positive attributes. Being overweight is not always an inherited problem within the genes. It has a lot to do with the type of food people put in their mouths.

Yes, there are people with a genetic issue who cannot do much about their weight. I absolutely understand and respect that, and truly feel for their situation. I wish there were a magic pill to help them. But most overweight people are overweight for one or more of the following simple reasons, which have been proven accurate throughout time:

- They are simply eating too much, that is, more than what the body really requires to keep in good condition.
- They eat lots of candies and unhealthy snacks (e.g. chips, cookies, ice-creams, etc.).
- They eat more processed, packaged, and fast foods than they should.
- They tend to be sedentary people who do not practice any sport or exercise. A sedentary style of life is detrimental to health and fitness.
- If they do some kind of exercise, many still eat more than what they should or do not eat healthily. They consume more calories than those they burn with exercise.
- Many fool themselves into believing they are exercising when they are just pretending to exercise, because they do not even break a drop of sweat.
- They lack either common sense or the discipline to find the right balance between good and bad calories eaten and calories burned. Calories consumed and calories burned need to be carefully evaluated based on the type of calorie intake, not necessarily based on the amount of calories consumed.
- Some have no idea that the food they are eating has chemicals that reduce their body's ability to burn calories.
- Their body is naturally chubby regardless of what they do.
- There is a new theory about the bacteria in people's guts, which says it influences people's craving and hunger. There are good and bad bacteria that need to be fed different types of food. If the wrong food is fed to the bad bacteria, people will gain weight. The opposite will happen by feeding the right food to the bacteria.

<u>Note</u>:

Yes, there are indeed overweight people who have a medical condition that compromises their health and causes many physical problems. Their challenge to lose weight is overwhelming; it is like climbing Mount Everest. Not everybody can climb it. Likewise, not everybody can lose weight. Again, I truly feel sorry and, from the depth of my heart, sincerely wish I could help them. But I also encourage these people to read the next section of this book for potential solutions and to do their own further research for specific and custom-made alternatives. Some of these people actually need to see their doctor and a specialized nutritionist and exercise coach, if they really want to lose or at least to control their weight, with adequate team support.

Everybody should stand in front of a mirror, be honest with themselves, and evaluate each of the twelve points mentioned previously. I would love to have a six-pack at age 57, but I would need to continue doing exercise the way I once did and definitely cut down my intake of sugary treats. That is the only way I could get rid of that little thin layer covering my six-pack. Yes, it is hiding under that thin layer. At my age, I do not burn calories as I used to. It is harder now. Age definitely matters.

Therefore, I must either eat fewer sweets (my real weakness) than before or do twice as much exercise, for which I do not have the time nor the inclination. Therefore, I choose moderation, somewhere in between, and it seems to be working just fine. I made a compromise with myself to feel healthy and to look relatively slim and fit since I was in my teenage years. I am now, and have been for the past 30 years, 5'10" (1.79 m) in height and 175 lbs. (79 kg) in weight.

How have I managed to keep this way without sacrifices and relatively easily, while having just an average metabolism? Nothing special. I am just another average individual with the same strengths and weaknesses as 80 per cent or more of the population.

I am about to share what I was taught by my parents, and their parents before them, and their parents before them, and so on. This has been passed on through many previous generations. For two reasons, I do not want to get scientific in the matter of losing weight and being fit. First, I am not a qualified nutritionist, training coach, or doctor. Second, there are hundreds of good, reliable books out there that have proven research behind them. Not all diets or techniques are good for everybody. We need to research and find the right approach for each of us.

## Malnutrition vs. Obesity vs. Starvation

The BBC News published an article written by Tulip Mazumdar (Global Health Reporter) in June 14, 2016 entitled "Obesity boom fueling rise of malnutrition". Mazumdar says that the 2016 Global Nutrition Report acknowledges that 44 per cent of countries are suffering extreme levels of undernourishment population and obesity. The report confirms that in at least 129 countries being malnourished and ultimately obese are "the new normal."

There is no doubt that in the 21$^{st}$ century what is mainly making us unhealthy and ill is too much food, bad quality food, too many synthetic chemical agents and sugar in our food, lack of self-control and a passive lifestyle. Worldwide, one out of three people eat poorly and therefore suffer malnutrition.

This is an alarming proportion that is bound to get even worse if we do not pay adequate attention and implement drastic measures.

Twenty or more years ago, malnutrition was mainly a matter of not having enough food. Nowadays it is the excess of unhealthy food that is the main cause of both malnutrition and obesity. According to Mazumdar, the report confirms the following: "hundreds of millions of people are malnourished because they are overweight as well as having too much sugar, salt or cholesterol in their blood."

On Thursday 28, 2016 The Telegraph published an article by Stephen Adams (medical correspondent) entitled "Obesity killing three times as many as malnutrition." According to Adams, "obesity is now killing triple the number of people who die from malnutrition, as it claims more than three million lives a year worldwide, according to a landmark study".

For the first time in history eating too much is a global health issue. Eating poorly and in large quantities causes not just obesity, but it unquestionably affects people's overall health and represents a continuously expanding worldwide problem, with a few geographical exceptions, of course. Adams insists that increasing prosperity worldwide is not just "expanding our waistlines" but causing the deaths of many people.


**Children's and Parent's Addiction**

Questions: Are parents really taking care of their children? Do they truly care about their children's health? Is the average parent ignorant, careless, selfish, weak or dumb? Or are the social pressures with which they live so strong that the average parent simply cannot handle it anymore?

Answer: It is obvious that the average parent loves and cares for their children. That is a given. They all strive to provide for their children as best they can. Unfortunately, the cruel reality is that some cannot and will never achieve their goals, because they themselves are victims of addiction. They themselves suffer from obesity, lack of energy, lack of faith, and, a very strong addiction to processed foods, fast foods and the main culprit of all evils: they are addicted to sugar!

Did you know that sugar is about eight times more addictive than heroin and cocaine according to numerous laboratory studies? There is an article written by Alanna Ketler that caught my attention. It was published on October 14, 2013 and was entitled "Sugar is as Addictive as Heroin, Says Study". Ketler reports that a Dr. Leri, Associate Professor of Neuroscience and Applied Cognitive Science at the University of Guelph, Ontario, Canada, conducted a study that clearly linked behavioral reactions in rats that were fed sugar to the same problems produced by addictive drugs. Dr. Leri concluded that "addiction to unhealthy foods could help explain the global obesity epidemic" and also noted that "we have evidence in laboratory animals of a shared vulnerability to develop preferences for sweet foods and for cocaine." David Kessler a former head of the Food and Drug Administration, believes that sugar is just as addictive as cigarettes; it is "highly pleasurable, it gives you this momentary bliss. When you're eating food that is highly hedonic, it sort of takes over your brain." Unfortunately, these findings are unknown or rejected by many people.

According to The US National Library of Medicine, other

studies discovered that rats in lab tests were very motivated to consume cocaine, amphetamines and even alcohol in considerable amounts. They would obviously become addicted to any of those substances, but if they were given the choice between these substances and sugar, over 90 per cent of rats chose sugar over anything else. If the same choice was given to already cross-addicted rats, they always chose sugar. Sugar is extremely addictive, and there is no doubt that sugar consumption causes neurochemical changes in people's brains in much the same way as other addictive drugs, such as caffeine, nicotine, cannabis, ecstasy, morphine, heroin, and cocaine.

Why? Because sugar also releases dopamine and opioids (neurotransmitters), which then cause addiction to processed foods and fast foods rich in sugar and or sugar derivatives. These foods open the pathways that allow the brain to immediately respond to natural feeling rewards. Addictive drugs such as cocaine and heroin also activate this brain pathway.

Are fat and obese people just meant to be fat and obese? Certainly not, regardless of what some people might believe. Is every fat and obese person voracious, lazy, and lacking willpower? Although I want to believe they are not, I have no doubt that the great majority suffer some of these symptoms.

Why? Is it because they eat a lot and do not exercise? Definitely not. You can eat moderately, do a lot of exercise, and still not lose weight. If we practice the modern and widely accepted principle of 'energy-balance consumption', will we lose weight? Not necessarily. We may even gain, if we do not change our diets. Why? Because if you eat a healthy diet with no processed or fast foods but heavy on vegetables and fruits, then yes, you will lose weight, but if you keep on eating foods heavy in sugar content (such as processed foods and fast foods) you will never lose weight (in fact you might gain) regardless of whether you exercise and burn more calories than your daily intake. As a result of my research, and contrary to what many think, there is no doubt in my mind that "we are what we eat" regardless of exercise. We cannot cover our eyes any longer and pretend we do not know.

## Are all calories the same?

Not all calories are the same. Why? Because if we consume 100 calories of chocolate, bread, rice, pasta, etc. compared to 100 calories of nuts, fruits, or vegetables, we will burn them at a totally different rate. We will need to exercise two or three times as much if we consume 100 calories of the processed foods listed above compared to the same 100 calories of healthy food.

The fiber in healthy food slows down the sugar impact and will not be assimilated at the same speed as the sugar coming from the processed food. Therefore, our liver will work a lot less. The rise of sugar in our system will be far slower and will last longer. The liver does not need support from the pancreas to produce insulin at high amounts to store the energy as fat. With processed foods, there is simply a lot less fiber (or none), which leads to quicker absorption, causing the rise of sugar to be faster and the energy to be less long-lasting. This spike in sugar is going to force the liver to work harder and the pancreas to produce more insulin at such a fast rate that it is forced to turn so much sudden energy into fat. This fat needs to be stored somewhere.

The question remains: Is it the parents' fault that one out of five children are now obese (not just overweight)? Definitely yes, but they are not 100 per cent at fault. There is a darker side to our society that pushes parents to keep feeding their children junk food. There is an "invisible hand" that pushes families into unhealthy eating habits. My third book (Our Runaway Rights) will uncover the tragedy in our modern society and its dark accomplice, which, almost at gunpoint, are forcing parents to feed their children unhealthy, addicting food.

Is there a solution? Absolutely yes, but we all need to be willing and able to use it as soon as yesterday! A large proportion of our population cannot resist, or do not even want to resist, processed and fast foods, due to tastes, preferences, values, opportunities or psychological issues. But human history has proven that "if there is a will, there is a way." We all need to love and care for our children and ourselves a wee bit more. First of all, we need to acknowledge that sugar is addictive and that we might already be addicted. We need to pay attention to what we eat, understand the labels of processed food products (candies, cookies, cereals, canned soups, dressings, etc.) and make a strong effort to slowly but surely reduce the amounts of food we normally eat. Yes, we can totally cut out sugar consumption for a period of time in order to detox, but almost everybody goes back to old habits afterwards. However, if we approach the reduction of sugar consumption with a long-term rigorous but achievable plan, there is no doubt the average person can stay out of the "sugar bowl."

## The truth about "healthy" obesity

Healthy obesity describes a sector of our population that looks and feels healthy, regardless of their obesity. The truth is that there is proof that as time goes by, their looks and healthy feelings, take a drastic turn to the opposite, which means that their metabolic risk factors takes a turn for the worst. The Department of Epidemiology and Public Health at University College London England did a 20-year study with over 2,500 women and men between 39 and 62 years of age in relation to: body mass index (BMI), blood pressure, insulin resistance, cholesterol and fasting plasma glucose. This research was formerly published by the Journal of the American College of Cardiology. It concludes that only 11 per cent actually lost weight and kept their metabolic risk factors under strict control. For more information, please refer to an article by Dr. Marla Shapiro on January 06, 2015 for CTV News-Health entitled: "The myth of 'healthy' obesity."

Dr. Shapiro says that healthy obesity will be considered valid if it remains stable over time, but all her research has indicated that it is often just a phase in people's life. Obese people ultimately are prone to suffer any of the main following health issues: musculoskeletal issues, heart disease and stroke, cardiovascular diseases, diabetes, and some type of cancer (the most common being colon, endometrial and breast cancers).

An article in Time Magazine-Health by Alexandra Sifferlin on April 30, 2014 entitled: "There's No Such Thing as Healthy Obesity," Sifferlin says that for many years there were controversial opinions about whether obese people were considered healthy or unhealthy. There is a strong tide proving that there is no such thing as healthy obesity. She wrote:

Researchers at Mount Sinai Hospital in Toronto, however, reviewed studies dating back to the 1950s, and concluded that people cannot be both overweight and healthy. They found that people who had a high body mass index (BMI) but whose cholesterol or blood pressure were normal for example, were still at a higher risk of dying from heart disease. "This concept of healthy obesity came in the last 10 years,"

Sifferlin quotes Dr. David Katz (Yale University Prevention Research Center) who insists: "The things we recommend for people to be fit are the very things we are recommending for people to not be fat." But Dr. Katz tells all his patients that the idea to be healthy is to have a good life, but if to achieve the good life they need to lose weight, and that makes them miserable, then it is not worth trying, Sifferlin confirms.

I invite the reader to visit *smartbmicalculator.com* to find how to calculate your BMI and evaluate through your weight and age, regardless if you have a health risk factor or not.

**New theory about chemical agents making us fat**

According to David Suzuki on "The Nature of Things," certain man-made chemicals may be making us fat. He suggests that modern chemicals are the "invisible culprits" making us gain weight. In his research, he found that scientists around the world are arriving at the conclusion that, from the womb, modern chemicals hidden in our food and overall environment are affecting our metabolism and causing us to gain weight.

Apparently, endocrine-disruptive chemicals are now found everywhere, even in the water and food we consume. According to Suzuki, they are not supposed to be absorbed by our bodies, but it is happening. This will definitely cause serious health problems in future generations, but scientists are still evaluating this theory in laboratories using animal trials. The findings of current research are not good, however, and if these findings are confirmed, we are in for an alarming worldwide health problem in the future.

## Technique and Philosophy that Guarantee Losing Weight

From research and longtime observations, I have identified three main types of overweight people:

1. Those who want to lose weight but have either a physical problem or a specific health issue, such as high insulin levels, hypothyroidism, Cushing's Syndrome (glands not working properly), and so on.

2. Those with a psychological problem or mental disorder such as depression, trauma, stress, addictions, bipolar disorders, personal insecurities, etc.

3. Those who simply have the wrong attitude or wrong disposition and do not suffer from a physical problem, a specific health issue, or a psychological problem or mental disorder.

The third group belongs to what I call the general population. I am a member of this population, an average individual, but the difference is that I care, and I try every day to have the right attitude. I try very hard, and let me emphasize - it does not come easy.

This book will not evaluate or consider categories one and

two. It will only evaluate and recommend solutions for the third category, which represents the general population of our planet, the average individual.

The technique and philosophy I recommend for all those people in category three works for a high percentage and it is straightforward to follow. The most important thing is that the person really wants and needs to change. For myself, I will only bring to the table what matters to me the most and what makes the biggest difference to me regarding medium and long-term goals, like the average Joe and Mary would do.

I never make big sacrifices, so I can stick to the plan for life. Yes, it is a personal challenge, but in life everything is a personal challenge. Let's face it; our overall well-being, our physical and mental health, our proper balance of feelings and emotions, and our physical appearance are (or should be) the most important goals in life. Taking good care of ourselves physically enriches our soul and spirit, which ultimately benefits our overall well-being. Some might classify this as narcissistic. Controlled narcissism is good. In my opinion, those who criticize vanity, self-love, and conceit have already given up. Why? Because a reasonable and healthy amount of narcissism should be taught early in life and never forgotten.

The reason why the Greeks and Romans created so many sculptures depicting the human body is because, in a state of health and fitness, it is a beautiful thing. The same reasoning applies to animals when you see them in their natural state running, swimming, and flying. In a fit and active state, every species is a thing of beauty to be admired.

In terms of attracting and being attracted to the opposite sex, a fit body has proven throughout history to be the most desirable. No question about it. That does not necessarily mean a perfect body, but a body that is at the right weight (in relation to height), and certainly not obese.

Throughout the years, my close family members, friends, and I, with only a couple of exceptions, have chosen the following activities to be as slim and healthy as we can be. The framework we followed to successfully feel healthy and look good include mainly twenty-two components, which are:

1. To exercise at least three to four times a week (ideally four to five times)

2. When we do exercise, we must avoid fooling around and stop pretending, as so many do. We should try our best to finish with at least some degree of sweat as our ultimate goal, which means that you made an extra effort during your routines. I personally exercise hard between 45 to 75 minutes (time permitting). I try my best to put my heart into it; otherwise why spend my time?

3. Have four different exercise routines. Four different routines will help us move every part of our body in a more systematic and efficient manner. Alternate those routines on a daily basis to allow rest and recovery of muscles.

4. Stay slim. Even though we do not really need more than one hour a day of exercise, we do need to be persistent and consistent along with a proper (moderate and balanced) food intake.

5. Have a decent but healthy breakfast. Leave behind the

typical North American breakfast of two eggs with bacon or sausage, hash brown potatoes, and two slices of toast with butter. *Deeelicious*, but definitely not healthy, and fattening. Eggs are fine, but the rest? Why put that junk in our bodies?

6. Smarter breakfast alternatives include oatmeal, bran cereals, fruit, soya milk, yoghurt, nuts, hard-boiled eggs, one slice of toast (not two), and ham, but no butter. There are many other healthy alternatives. Do your research. There is no excuse not to have a healthier breakfast with the same budget. Remember, you can always buy in bulk to safeguard the monthly family budget. Always try eating food in its original state, always!

7. Get used to having two full glasses of water first thing in the morning. If possible, add lime juice and warm up the water. It will improve your digestive system and help you eliminate toxins.

8. Have a light lunch. Good alternatives are soup and salad or nuts and fruit and vegetables or whatever you fancy that you know is healthy, but above all, have a light lunch!

9. Make an effort to go for a short walk during your lunch time. But walk at a slightly faster pace than normal.

10. Use any excuse to stand up from your chair and desk when at work. For example, stand up every time you are on the phone. The same thing applies when watching TV at home at night. Do not just sit down there for hours. Get up and roam around your house or, between programs, do some squats, a few push-ups, go up and down the stairs several times.

We do not need to listen to so much advertising, which only irritates us. Get up and move that butt while the ads are being played, unless it is during the Super Bowl game, because those ads are pretty good, at least for my taste.

11. Have a healthy vegetable and fruit shake or smoothie every day before dinner. I semi-fill up my stomach with the shake or smoothie and tend to eat half of what I would have eaten if I had not consumed that shake or smoothie.

12. Develop the habit of eating as healthfully as possible and, above all, in moderation. There is no need to overeat and feel full and bloated.

13. Do not eat processed foods and fast foods. At least have them as infrequently as possible with the honest goal of striving hard to push them off your table completely. Instead, bring fresh, healthy foods to your table. Give yourselves some time to make the transition. Set up achievable goals that you can follow and stick to.

14. Eat slowly. Chew the food more and take your time to eat, so that you achieve a better digestion and so that the stomach can send the signal to the brain that hunger is not an issue anymore. That will automatically slow down our food intake.

15. Reduce the size of your stomach without the need for bariatric surgery. Eat less, but do so gradually in combination with consuming more protein and fiber. Do not just suddenly cut your food intake by half. That does not work in the medium and long term.

16. Avoid any type of surgery to reduce stomach size. Many

say that adults cannot reduce the size of the stomach without surgery. But the less food you eat, the more you will reduce your appetite and change your metabolism. Try using smaller plates or eating a spoonful or two less food every day until you reach the right amount for your metabolism. We need to do this gradually, so we can stick to the plan and actually change our eating patterns and defeat the *psychological* need for more food. Eating less will assist you to reset what Dr. Mark Moyad calls your "appetite thermostat." Dr. Moyad wrote an article about this, "Nine surprising facts about our stomach." For more information, please refer to:

(webmd.com/women/features/stomach-problems).

17. Avoid sodas as much as possible, with the ultimate goal of getting rid of them from your daily menu completely.

18. Unless it is freshly made, do not drink fruit juices straight. Dilute them with 30 to 50 per cent water. You will consume less sugar for the same thirst-quenching feeling.

19. Do not snack while watching TV, working on the computer, or reading on your sofa, or at least be smart and disciplined about what you choose to snack on.

20. Have healthy snacks throughout the day between breakfast and lunch and between lunch and dinner. Magnificent snack alternatives include nuts, fruits, vegetables, and dates, among many others. Easy to carry and easy to snack on. Choose what you like for a snack, but do your research, be honest about it, and stick to it.

21. Get enough sleep every night. Lack of sleep affects your metabolism and your attitude.

22. Walk with a straight posture, and feel good about it.

Note:

Points 14 to 20 are well known, but the average person is still not complying. Therefore, it might sound redundant or even annoying to remind some people of these seven important points. But guess why I insist? Because we will never be better off unless we are willing to change our habits.

Things do not change magically. We need to make them change by putting in a conscious effort to promote change and sticking to it, until it becomes a habit and it is not an effort anymore to maintain it. In the medium-term and long term, it will end up becoming natural and easy.

Remember, *we are what we eat*, whether we like it or not. And it shows, plain and simple. If we eat healthy food, we will tend to have a healthy and slim body, but if we eat junk food we will have an unhealthy and overweight body.

Just think about it. When you feed yourself with vegetables, fruit grains, water, soya milk, etc., your molecular structure will be much healthier due to the nutritional values of those natural products. But if we feed ourselves with French fries, greasy burgers, hot-dogs, chocolates, chips, beer, soda, etc., our bodies' molecules cannot absorb the amounts of grease, sugar, and synthetic, man-made ingredients. Our bodies will end up storing them in the form of fat.

## Well Known vs. Forgotten Secrets for Losing Weight

Nina Teicholz wrote a book entitled "The Big Fat Surprise," which was used as a point of reference (along with other researchers, authors, and scientists) by Cheryl Chan in an article entitled "We Should Be Eating More Fat" in The Province newspaper, April 3, 2016. According to Chan, Canada's Food Guide has failed profoundly to help us keep our weight down and our bodies healthy.

Even though all the sources of information used by Canada's Food Guide seem to have good research and scientific backup and support, in reality, not all studies have been totally accurate. Additionally, some of Teicholz's conclusions and suggestions have been known and practiced for hundreds of years. But let's face it with honesty, looking at ourselves in the mirror. The average person needs to be told what to do, what to eat, and what not to eat, but, with a little bit of research, common sense, and discipline, anybody should be able to develop proper eating habits. Anybody can have a healthy body and proper weight within their specific budget. Let me explain.

It is common knowledge and has been proven over many generations, and especially throughout the twenty-first century, that we need to abide by seven crucial points:

1. Avoid as much as possible consuming processed fats. Eat natural fats instead, though in moderation. Saturated fat is good for the body in moderate amounts. Definitely stay away from hydrogenated fats. The body needs its doses of natural fat to help it fight many diseases. According to Ms. Teicholz' research, higher-fat diets based on natural fats are better for your health than low-fat diets. Even the Romans and Greeks

new that a high-fat diet was good for you. They never had any issues with saturated fat in their meats. Why is it that many people suddenly want to avoid it nowadays?

2. Reduce the consumption of dairy products, because we all know milk is not meant for humans. In my opinion it has been marketed for humans along with thousands of products made from milk, from ice cream to all sort of cheeses and more. Even though this is a well-known fact, people like to gorge on milk products because they taste delicious, and moderation is not necessarily a word found in their "dictionary."

3. Reduce the consumption of red meat, which can easily be substituted by grains and fish, for example. Beans, as well, are one of the best foods anybody can eat. They contain protein, folate, soluble fiber, lectins, iron, and carbohydrates. They are tasty, nice to chew, and quite filling as well.

4. Stay away from high-carb foods such as white pasta, rice, pizzas, and all sorts of breads, among many others. Just follow the advice of our great-grandparents and their great-grandparents before them: "eat with moderation." Personally, while at the table, I focus on three basic golden rules: I serve myself smaller amounts instead of gorging on a big plate, I chew what I put in my mouth very well, and I take my time to enjoy my food by eating slowly, and if possible, very slowly. I guarantee the reader that, by following these three basic and well-known golden rules, almost anyone can achieve a healthier body in the long term.

5. If possible, consume whole foods only. Like a rabid dog avoids water, we humans should stay away from refined and processed foods as much as possible. Nowadays everybody

knows this, but the average person keeps on consuming them.

6. Avoid overconsumption of eggs and butter, which are definitely not good for your cholesterol levels and other health issues.

7. Stay away from over consumption of sweets and sugars (in every shape, form, and name), which are very well known to be damaging to our body, especially in children. Soft drinks, for example, are extremely damaging to people's health. Packaged juices are also very bad due to their high sugar content. But the average person eats and drinks them with joy, madness, and frenzy, and with absolute disregard for their health and weight. They seem to only care about the "yummy" feeling at the moment. Go figure!

In summary, who does not know that the best foods for you are vegetables and fruits? You would literally have to be an alien not to know and understand that concept. Anything that Mother Nature offers is the best thing for human consumption. In my personal opinion, few will benefit from following any of the fad diets that have been so widely promoted in recent years. Why? For two main reasons:

First, many of these diets are based on weak, incomplete, or biased research, or they are suitable only for certain types of people.

Second, the research is influenced by the strong economic interests of many private food processors in promoting their processed and manufactured foods. In my opinion, the milk industry is a very good example as well as all those canned soups that are full of sodium, preservatives, and all kinds of junky chemicals. People should read the labels and if an ingredient is listed that you do not have in your pantry on a regular basis, do not buy it, much less eat it!

The diet that we all should follow is one for which we have personally done our own research and that suits our body, lifestyle, and daily needs. But we need to be honest with ourselves and feel truly passionate about it. We should get naked in front of a mirror and ask ourselves:

- Do I truly like what I see?
- Do I feel comfortable and healthy the way I am?
- Do I feel proud of myself?
- Can I benefit by improving the image reflected in the mirror?
- Do I have a physical or physiological problem?
- Can I overcome my problem, or do I need help from others?

I humbly believe that we need to acknowledge that obesity is mainly due to inherited or created psychological issues. The average person is self-indulgent and does not want to draw the line between wants and shoulds. Psychological problems or lack of will, strength, and character are the main obstacles.

Such people need help from professionals to overcome their problems and frustrations. They need to approach life differently and start by confronting something that I call "the double challenge", which goes like this:

1. Start with a simple set of rules or activities that only you can do for yourself, such as:

- Stop self-punishment.
- Love yourself with respect and discipline.
- Engage in more productive activities.
- Leave your self-physiological abuse behind bars.
- Stop blaming others and, instead, accept responsibility.
- Watch less TV.
- Play less computer games.
- Spend less time in front of the computer.
- Give your cell phone a rest several times a day.
- Take more showers, comb your hair, and dress with pride and enthusiasm.
- Get enough sleep, eat healthily, and be physically active.

2. The second set of rules requires honesty with yourself and determination in trying to solve your personal deficiencies, guided by someone I consider one of the best-ever researchers, the psychologist, speaker, and writer Dr. Phillip Calvin McGraw, known simply as Dr. Phil. He has written several books, and they are all "right on the money."

Yes, down to earth and to the point. He does not fool around but says things the way they are, whether some like it or not. He has the academic and professional background to back up all his theories and solutions. Aside from my research, I am a practical and down-to-earth world observer with a lot of experience in real-life human behaviors in various countries, but I am certainly not a specialist like Dr. Phil, who has devoted all his life to studying and analyzing human nature.

Every book of his is a challenge to his readers written in black and white. No hidden shadows to avoid misunderstandings. The reader gets the "bull by the horns," with advice on how to stop fooling around and go all the way to solve problems from the root. Among Dr. Phil's books that I recommend people to read for losing weight and gaining self-confidence are:

- The 20/20 Diet.
- The Ultimate Weight Solution.
- The Ultimate Weight Solution Food Guide.
- Ultimate Weight Solution Cookbook.
- Self-Matters.
- The New Rules For Winning In The Real World.
- Life Strategies.

The human race is interesting but frustrating to decipher properly. One thing is sure, however; every second generation, we seem to adopt different values and habits. We behave like a pendulum swinging from one extreme to the other.

For example, this generation dresses sloppily and seems not to like wearing proper shoes for the occasion, much less struggling with tying their shoelaces. An increasingly high percentage of the North American younger population wears loose sandals or flip-flops, and they tend to be so lazy while walking that they drag their feet instead of stepping forward. In my opinion, and with total respect, this generation is going to go into the history books as the generation of the flip-floppers, the tattooers, the obese, and the disheveled (scruffy, messy, untidy, and badly dressed). I truly do not know what is worse, the stiffness and pomposity of the old "British" generation or the sloppiness of today's generation, but they are certainly the very opposite sides of the pendulum, aren't they? Why can't the average person just be "normal" and position themselves somewhere in the middle of the swinging of the pendulum? It is very hard to understand, but, as many say, that is the beauty of this world. "It is what it is," whether we agree or not.

## Holding Your Health in Your Own Hands

They say that "aging is not for sissies." Aging alone is difficult, even cruel, but if we coast along on the shoulders of our youth without caring for ourselves and then gain a lot of weight, we will certainly regret it. Allow me to express myself in black and white and go straight to the point. All this is written without prejudice and with absolute respect, but I need to be straightforward and honest. As bad as it sounds, and against politically correct books, the reality is that beneath the skin of those obese people with bad eating habits and lack of exercise, there are more and more accumulated, thick layers of unhealthy white fat instead of healthy lean and clean muscle. That is one of the main reasons why obese people feel tired, sluggish, and lazy, sweat a lot more, cannot reach to wash themselves properly, have high blood pressure, strong body odors, and many other physical and medical problems.

The average obese person (not necessarily the merely overweight) tends to have less self-esteem, less self-respect, and definitely less self-control. They do not care about their looks anymore and dress inappropriately in public. They tend to act more slowly, physically and even mentally, and get sick more often. They attend the doctor's office a lot more and cost society more in health-related issues such as diabetes and cardiovascular disease, among many others.

Again, I write this openly, without prejudice and with respect, but I need to make myself crystal clear and transmit my message with some hope of having a positive impact, unlike authors who are afraid of speaking the truth in case they hurt people's feelings. This is not about hurting or sparing people's feelings; it is about the alarming obesity epidemic now being suffered by children as young as five or six years old. Again, in my dictionary, that is child abuse and should almost be considered a criminal act by the parents, who should perhaps lose their children to Child Services. They are overfeeding and fattening their children while traumatizing them for the rest of their lives, limiting their future to achieve success and happiness. But, that is just me!

The great majority of obese people are definitely less happy with themselves and the society in which they live, whether they admit it or not. In fact, some of them really suffer and need help, which they should receive.

Important Note: This is not an absolute rule, but healthier people tend to be more active and take better care of themselves. The great majority are happier than their overweight counterparts and need less help from others to cheer up and to have a more positive view of themselves and the society in which they live.

Above all, we need to keep in mind that the quantity and quality of the food people eat has a huge impact on their bodies, regardless of how much exercise they do. We need to eat in a rational manner, that is, with self-restraint. The more we eat, the more we will need to eat to feel full. We should all eat only until satisfied, *not until we are full.*

Our eating habits reflect not just on our bodies in the short and medium term, but also reflect how we feel emotionally, physically, and spiritually. If we have a heavy lunch and go back to work, the odds are we will be unproductive, sluggish, and sleepy, contrary to how we would feel if we had a light lunch (a smoothie for example), or some healthy snacks throughout the day and even skipped lunch.

It is important to keep in mind that, even if we do a lot of exercise, but eat unhealthily, we may look okay on the outside for a while, but the inside of our body will not be as healthy in the medium and long term, unless we feed ourselves with fresh, nutritious foods.

Fortunately, or unfortunately, the solution for over 90 per cent of obese and even overweight people is in their own hands. Why fortunately? Because if they really want, they can have an amazing positive impact on their own bodies, but they need motivation, strength of character, determination, discipline, patience, the right attitude, and adequate help or true, unrestricted assistance. Now why unfortunately? For the same reasons. It is not easy to develop the above attributes, though anybody can do so if they really want to. If they surround themselves with the right friends, with the right influences, and the right activities, they will certainly succeed. But do not jump into this abruptly or blindly; do it slowly, at a steady and determined pace. The odds of succeeding will be higher.

The main problem remains the fact that parents are not really teaching their children to be disciplined with themselves. Discipline, though challenging, is everything. All the evidence indicates that parents are not strict enough about their children's manners, eating habits, self-esteem, self-control, and self-respect. This is an epidemic that needs to be corrected as soon as possible. But the question is: Is it more of a mental or a physical problem?

Again, it comes down to denying ourselves something we want. Sure, we all want to get whatever we want, but we have to use our logic, common sense, and knowledge to say:

"I want it, but I choose not to have it."

It is not a matter of focusing on the fact that you cannot have something. This will only make you feel deprived and miserable, which is not the goal. The goal is to feel good and positive about having made the right decision for ourselves, which nobody else can do for us. Positive feelings go further than negative feelings, so we need to focus on the ultimate goal, which is to be positive and to eat and be healthy.

Adults who cannot or do not want to develop the strength of character to eat more healthfully and exercise but are desperate to lose weight, will be forced (if they have the money and the guts to do it) to resort to the following alternatives:

- Bariatric surgery.
- Liposculpture Suction Lipectomy.
- AspireAssist.

Bariatric surgery reduces the size of the stomach with a gastric band or by actually removing part of the stomach, reducing its intake capacity. Sometimes the small intestine is also reset or rerouted to make a small stomach pouch. This is known as gastric bypass surgery. These are serious interventions, and their effectiveness is the result of creating something known as a psychological condition of malabsorption, which ultimately can lead to anemia, malnutrition, and overall health deficiencies. Nevertheless, according to the article in the BC Medical Journal by Dr. B Matthew et al. referred to earlier:

An estimated 1.7 billion people worldwide are affected by

obesity-related comorbidities such as cardiovascular diseases and diabetes. Bariatric surgery is recognized as an effective treatment for morbid obesity. A study of patients at a BC clinic was undertaken to determine if combining bariatric surgery with comprehensive care provided by a multidisciplinary team improves postoperative outcomes. Many patients experience improvements in obesity-related comorbidities: 34 of 35 patients with type 2 diabetes were able to reduce or cease treatment, and 27 out of 44 patients with hypertension were able to reduce or cease treatment. Responses to the Impact on Weight on Quality of Life questionnaire showed significant postoperative improvement on patient quality of life.

This is fine and dandy, but imagine the cost to society compared with a proper preventive educational program at an early stage of children's lives, starting at home, and continuing at school and throughout their professional life.

Liposculpture suction lipectomy, more often known simply as liposuction, is a suction-assisted fat removal procedure from various parts of the human body. It is more of a cosmetic surgery to start with, and very costly. The doctors literally vacuum the patient's excess fat in specific locations. Regardless of what is done to the body, liposuction alone is not necessarily a solution for keeping weight off. Patients can eat their weight back, and many do.

AspireAssist is a relatively new weight loss solution for people desperate to lose weight. This method is based on a small, invasive, and reversible procedure. Though accepted in Europe, it is in clinical trial in the United States. There is a well-known website, aspirebariatrics.com, which explains the AspireAssist device and procedure as follows:

> To begin therapy, a specially designed tube is placed in the stomach. The A-Tube is a thin tube that connects the inside of the stomach directly to a discreet, poker-chip sized Skin-Port on the outside of the abdomen. The Skin-Port has a valve that can be opened or closed to control the flow of stomach contents. The patient empties a portion of stomach contents into the toilet after each meal through this tube by connecting a small, handheld device to the Skin-Port. The aspiration process is performed about 20 minutes after the entire meal is consumed and takes 5 to 10 minutes to complete. The process is performed in the privacy of the restroom, and the food is drained directly into the toilet. Aspiration only removes a third of the food, the body still receives the calories it needs to function.

Is AspireAssist for every obese person? Certainly not, but it is an alternative if you have the need and the courage to do it. It seems to be working for many people in Europe and in the US trials now underway. Anybody can watch a YouTube video for more details to evaluate if it is appropriate for them or not.

People say it is more expensive to eat healthily than to eat fast food. This is a myth and a distortion of the truth. If a person really cares about their health and overall well-being, they can save money by shopping carefully. But the average person is usually too lazy and disorganized to do so, or they simply like what they are eating and use the myth as an excuse. I could list lots of foods and drinks that are affordable, healthy, and tasty for the reader who is really interested, but every person needs to do their own research about this and find out where to get such products at their local markets.

It is not for me to make the reader feel uncomfortable about the dietary changes they should make, but, statistically speaking, the following have been proven over the years to be some of the most common and effective healthful alternatives that can be practiced by virtually anyone:

- Drink more water or homemade orangeade or lemonade instead of so much soda.

- If you cannot get away from milk, drink 2 per cent or skim milk instead of regular whole milk or chocolate milk. Soya milk with no added sugar is the best alternative.

- Eat very limited amounts of processed foods (avoid them at all if you can) and cook fresh instead.

- Avoid all fried foods and commercially prepared baked goods such as pizza, donuts, chips, white bread, and cookies. Substitute with vegetables and fruit in season

- If possible, snack four times a day on fruits, vegetables, and/or nuts.

- Bake home-made bread or cookies with less sugar, less fat, and at a cheaper cost.

- Eat more soluble fiber such as oats, beans, and rice, which are healthy and affordable.

- At all costs, avoid eating late at night while watching TV, reading, or in front of the computer.

If we succeed in developing better eating habits, our chances of developing heart disease, high cholesterol, and even cancer will be drastically reduced. And overall, we will be happier with our ourselves and surroundings.

Note:

Some people simply fall into the category of "I don't care; I like the way I am, feel, and look." As valid as that sounds, obesity comes with high health risks and, in the majority of cases, with a big sense of personal, even if hidden, dissatisfaction and frustration. Such is not the case with a lady called Mikel Ruffinelli, who has decided she is happy and does not want to lose weight, at 41 years of age and 5'4" in height, with hips eight feet in circumference and a weight of 420 pounds. She is referred to in an article as "Bootylicious." She is a mother of four and lives with her husband, Reggie Brooks, who loves her the way she is. They are a happy couple who like each other just the way they are. They do not seem to have any health issues or concerns and are happy living a normal life.

However, Mikel is the exception, and indeed unique. She holds the world record for the biggest hips and is happy posing as a model for Big Beautiful Woman website for $1,000 per shoot, according to the MailOnLine. For more information, Google her name or refer to an article at MailOnLine (.dailymail.co.uk) by David McCormack from January, 2013.

The attitude of "I do not care; I like the way I am" is growing in North America. Whether people really are happy the way they are or just lack will and focus is not my business, but I truly wish people would take care of themselves, have more pride in the way they feel and look, and serve as examples for younger children. Why? Because, aside from the health risks and high medical costs for society, obesity is not just demotivating and unpleasant but also alarming when, for example, you open a magazine and suddenly see pictures like the one on pages 6 and 7 of the October 2014 issue of the magazine Update published by the British Columbia Nurses Union.

Of course, this is just my personal opinion and is pointed out without prejudice and with respect, just as an example of what I am trying to explain. The picture shows ten female nurses and council members. In my view, one looks normal and nice for her age, three are quite overweight, and the remaining six are simply obese. I mention this example with no disrespect at all. It is just to show what is the norm nowadays in North America, which you would not have experienced 30, 40, or 50 years ago.

In my opinion, this trend has serious and negative medical, social, and cultural impacts on our communities and needs serious attention from the ground up. Some sources call it the obesity epidemic, and it is definitely a major public health crisis in North America and many other countries, such as South Africa. Unfortunately, nowadays you even see obese children as young as five or six. At this age, there is no excuse for being obese, unless they have a serious medical condition. But hey, that is just my opinion!

## Budgeting

The most important tips for buying healthy food without stretching the budget are:

- Have more meals at home and fewer outside. Eating at home costs a fraction of eating in restaurants, even if we consider fast food outlets. It is also healthier, because we know exactly the ingredients we are cooking with. Another advantage is that we can cook once for two or three days and eat leftovers on the following days. Nothing goes to waste if we do not want it to. In fact, leftovers are usually tastier than food that is eaten the day it was made.

- Select a store that suits your budget. Prices are not the same at Urban Fair or Save-On Foods compared to Superstore or Wal-Mart. At the latter, we may get more for our dollar, although not necessarily the same variety of products.

- Make a detailed shopping list before going to the grocery store so as to be able to stick to a predetermined budget.

- Try buying "no name" brands or store brands. You can save quite a bit by purchasing this way. But be sure to compare ingredient and nutritional information first.

- Never shop for food when hungry. We buy more when we are hungry. Have something to eat before going shopping.

- Make an effort to purchase more products in the bulk section of the stores, or go to specialized bulk stores in your area where you can get more for your money.

- Look for store specials and be diligent in watching for products on sale, which every store has every day of the week. They continuously change the products on sale, so keep an eye on that.

- Grow your own vegetables whenever possible. Even in a couple of pots on your deck or balcony, you can grow tomatoes, lettuce, herbs, and many other edibles. You do not need a big garden to do this, though it will always be easier and more productive if you have one.

- Consume less meat (beef, chicken, veal, etc.). We don't need to eat as much as we currently do, but we do need to increase our vegetable and grain intake. This will be healthier both for us and for the environment.

I really feel for those people who make an effort to lose weight and do not succeed, even though they do their best. They have my absolute respect. It must be very frustrating to try hard yet not achieve the desired results. In such a case, please get professional advice to help establish a specific plan and routine, and stick to the plan. Do not deviate. Persistence always pays, always! Remember, nothing good comes easily. I had a coach when I was a teen-ager who always said: "Try harder. Excuses are not allowed, though I wish you the best!"

## Temperament and Parenting

Nowadays the relationship between parents and children has reached an extreme in which children seem to have their parents by the neck. As parents, we need to be stronger and more determined when instilling a good example through our own positive behaviors. Our children will learn best from this.

We know that children need boundaries and require being taught that for every action, there is a reaction of the same force and sometimes even of a stronger magnitude. It is our responsibility to protect our children from harm, while teaching them to make proper decisions in life. We need to stop overprotecting our children and instead equip them, in a positive manner, to face the tough realities of life.

Our actions should always be geared towards the children's safety and overall well-being, regardless of how difficult it may be for us (as parents) to enforce or secure this for them. Not too long ago, a two-year-old fell inside the pen of African wild dogs at the Pittsburgh Zoo and was mauled to death in less than 60 seconds. I don't know if the real truth of what happened has been published, because there were a few different versions, but the end result is that the child was apparently in a position of danger and, unfortunately, disaster struck. Regardless of the specific situation that day, I have many times personally seen parents allowing their children to get too close to danger either because the children insist or because parents lack self-discipline or fail to realize what can happen and, therefore, unknowingly put their kids at risk.

The same things happen when young teenagers want to drive as they please without having enough experience or when parents know very well that their son or daughter still lacks maturity (self-discipline or self-control). We have all heard or read many times of teenagers being killed due to excessive speed or reckless driving. Some have been victims of other drivers, which is horribly sad, but the majority of their accidents are due to lack of experience and self-control. A truly responsible parent will say "No, it is not safe, so you cannot have the car keys." But a weak or "friendly" parent tends to make the mistake of giving into their children's pressure and guilt trips and provides them with what they want regardless of the end results.

I remember when Mom or Dad said "No" to something we wanted. If we insisted, we were sent to our rooms, where we did not have Nintendos, computers, iPads, iPhones, iPods, or TVs. We only had a couple of mechanical toys, a few books, some marbles, and perhaps a yo-yo. Nowadays kids have Disneyland-style bedrooms, so sending them to their room is close to a gift and a thank-you for their actions. If we were outside in a mall or somebody else's house, and we insisted on something when Mom and Dad said "No," they would only look at us with "that look" that meant: "Wait until we get home!" It did not matter if we only got home three or four hours later, Mom and Dad would have the discipline to punish us for what we did or did not do when we were out. As my grandfather used to say, "For tough problems, tough solutions."

We all know (or should know) that parents are there to safeguard their children at all times, even if the children get upset by not getting their way. They will understand and appreciate the tough love as the years go by. Today's parents mistakenly want only to keep their children at ease and happy, ignoring the potential risks in which they are placing them. Once again, parents should not be "buddies." They should be parents first, second, and third. In the future, when the children are grown and mature, they can be their friends if they want.

Dr. Phil uses an expression that I completely concur with: "commando parenting." I strongly encourage the reader to get Dr. Phil's' books and study them. He is extraordinary, yet thousands of parents do not agree with him and find him too tough. Well, toughen up, because that is the best way to save your children.

Below I cite five of Dr. Phil's key points that I like best and totally agree with. They come from his books Parenting With Change (2005) and Family First: Your Step-by-Step Plan for Creating a Phenomenal Family (2013), and are all about parents failing to comply with tough parenting standards to the detriment of their children's future.

## 1. Commando Parenting

"You must be willing to adopt what I call 'commando parenting.' If you don't commit to immersing yourself totally in the plan, you'll sabotage your child's chance to change, which may, in turn, sabotage your family's future. It's time for commando parenting. You have to do whatever it takes to stop that behaviors, even if it means you have to be late for work, take time off from work, or stay in for the weekend to address it. You need to withdraw any positive attention, introduce a negative consequence immediately, like a time-out without any distractions, and you've got to see it through."

## 2. Get Back to Basics

"An example of commando parenting is stripping everything from your child's room. Take away everything they love and enjoy. This means all toys, games, posters, and entertainment. Strip their bedroom of everything except a mattress, a blanket, and a pillow. Then make them earn it all back one item at a time. There's a sense of entitlement with spoiled children and they need to learn that their toys and games are privileges."

## 3. Be Prepared for War

"Your child will often revert to primitive behaviors, such as screaming, stomping around, wetting the bed, gagging, vomiting, throwing tantrums, and other disruptive behaviors. Be prepared to tough it out. Think ahead and make a list of your child's most probable power plays and plan a reaction to each. When they have ultimately calmed down, explain to them in detail that they haven't been behaving well and they will not be seeing any of their things until they have earned them back.

Be specific about what they need to do to earn them back: Play nicely with others, use a pleasant voice when asking for something, don't scream at Mom and Dad, etc."

## 4. Time-outs

"When it comes to putting your child in a time-out, choose a 'boring' location devoid of stimulation. A corner, an empty room, wherever you choose the time-out to be, make sure there's absolutely nothing there to entertain them. If you have trouble keeping them in a room, lock the door. If you have to get a nanny cam or cut the door in half so you can monitor them, do so. Time-outs should last no longer than five minutes. One minute per year of life is a good rule of thumb. Explain to your child that the time-out doesn't start until they are quiet and behaving. If they're quiet for four minutes and forty-five seconds and then they start screaming, start the time over."

## 5. Reward Good Behavior

"The other step of commando parenting and reshaping your child's behaviors is catching them doing something good. When you do, scoop them up in your arms and tell them how good they're being and thank them for being such a good kid. Then you can begin by giving them back a toy. If they revert to their previous behaviors, don't be afraid to start all over again. Your child will learn and soon you'll have a much happier, healthier family."

Children do not have a true concept of reality. Many parents let children make decisions as though they were small adults. Guess what? They are not small adults. Face it. They do not and cannot understand what is really going on. How can they, when they are just five, 10, or 15 years old?

We all need to keep in mind that parents are there to hold their children's hands and guide them securely, comfortably, and happily to adulthood. Parents are not there to carry them on their backs and fail to teach them how to walk by themselves. In fact, they need to teach them how to securely walk on the roughest terrains, because real life is not easy. Failing to do so will only make them insecure, uncomfortable, capricious, and weak when they're adults. Children are difficult to guide and control. Some are rude and challenging towards their parents on a continuous and relentless basis.

When Mom and Dad pass away, these children (now adults) will most likely feel a bit lost and insecure about their future. I have met several people like that in my life. They develop deep levels of frustration and unhappiness. Children who were held by a loving and firm hand and guided properly by their parents will feel sad when Mom and Dad pass away, but they will be secure and confident of their own future. They will be mature grown-ups and productive in society, not dependent on it. They will deal with their new reality in a professional and mature manner. Why? Because they were taught correctly how to walk on rough and treacherous life terrain. They were taught how to fly alone through both good, peaceful, sunny weather and dark, windy, stormy weather. The children who were carried by Mom and Dad had everything done for them. Their parents confronted and solved all their problems without allowing them to develop their own survival skills. In fact, the parents showed them the shortcuts, which usually are a short-term solution and not an efficient, long-term one.

One of the worst mistakes parents can make is to empower their children's controlling attitude by not stopping them in their tracks and say "No" or "punish" when required.

Many parents need to get it into their thick skulls, or into their 'know-it-all' attitudes, that children and even some young teenagers can end up being dangerous to themselves and others if they are allowed to feel entitled to control their lives and claim their "rights" at too young an age or at an immature stage of their development. But do not get me wrong; not all teenagers should be measured with the same ruler. Some are indeed mature and responsible for their age, but parents know better, right?

Therefore, the big question arises: Are you being a truly responsible parent (as everybody should be) or simply a really "cool" friend of your children? Many parents who "carry" their children (overprotecting them) will not agree with me. But I am sure they will see more clearly in the future.

The problem is that such parents mistakenly believe their children "belong" to them. However, we all need to be conscious of the fact that we are just our children's guardians. They should, and will, have a life of their own, guided by their assertiveness or their mistakes, and they will be guided by what they learned at home and then at school. If, as a parent, you teach them well, they will certainly be assertive and positive and achieve great things in life. Our children will become an integral part of, and contributors to, society.

We are already seeing the results of the influx of these spoiled, self-centered young people. They believe they know everything and refuse to listen to those with more experience, because they have been brought up thinking that their opinion is just as valuable as that of someone with far superior experience and knowledge. If, as a parent, you only pampered and overprotected them from everything throughout their infancy and teenage years, they will most likely be less assertive, less successful, and less prepared to defend themselves. Is that what you want for your children? I do not think so. Buckle up and learn how to say "No" and maintain your position.

In fact, if we study the statistical data of independent youngsters nowadays, we realize that, as the years go by, more and more young people between the ages of 20 and 29 are not properly equipped to live independently and are remaining at home with their parents. Statistics Canada confirms this:

> The 2011 Census of Population showed that 42.3% of the 4,318,400 young adults aged 20 to 29 lived in the parental home, either because they never left it or because they returned home after living elsewhere. This proportion changed little from 2006 (42.5%). However, it was higher than in preceding decades: 32.1% in 1991 and 26.9% in 1981.

In the United States, according to Gallup Daily tracking interviews conducted from August to December, 2013, 14 per cent of adults between 24 and 34 years old were still living at Mom and Dad's.

The forecast is for these percentages to get even higher, but why the apparent disparity between the US and Canada? Based on reports from Statistics Canada, applications for employment insurance shot up to the highest levels in several years in March of 2013, while in the United States the applications for employment insurance were less for the same period. In January 2014, the Canadian unemployment rate was 7 per cent and for June of 2015 it was still 6.8 per cent, the main reason why more young adults are still living with their parents in Canada. The other main reason is the high cost of housing (both buying and renting). The inflation rate of general goods and services is way higher than the official Consumer Price Index of 2.1 per cent, which is based on a "Basic Basket of Goods" such as bread, milk, eggs, and other basic items. For June 2015, the inflation rate acknowledged by the Consumer Price Index in Canada was only one per cent, but most non-basic goods and services have gone up much more than this. Who is the government kidding? Mexico is also suffering the same situation, though it lacks confirmed research and statistical analysis.

Obviously, the cost of living has a heavy bearing on the situation of young adults, but younger people are also not willing to sacrifice their comforts and confront reality. They have not been well prepared mentally and psychologically to sacrifice for a better, more independent future.

I trust that almost every reader has read or heard about the great Lebanese poet, philosopher, and artist Khalil Gibran. His work has been translated into over 20 languages, and his fame is worldwide. Why? Because he had a profound knowledge and understanding of human behaviors and its realities in society. Among the many wise things he wrote, I want to put special emphasis on the following statement from Chapter 4 (page 18) of his book The Prophet, published in 1992. Khalil Gibran wrote this about children:

> Your children are not your children. They are the sons and daughters of life's longing for itself. They come through you, but not from you, and though they are with you, yet they belong not to you. You give them your love, but not your thoughts. For they have their own thoughts. You may house their bodies, but not their souls, for their souls dwell in the house of tomorrow, which you cannot visit, not even in your dreams.

> You may strive to be like them, but seek not to make them like you, for life goes not backwards nor tarries with yesterday. You are the bow from which your children as living arrows are sent forth. The archer sees the mark upon the path of the infinite, and He bends you with His might that His arrows may go swift and far. Let your bending in the archer's hand be for gladness; for even as he loves the arrow that flies, so He loves also the bow that is stable.

Khalil Gibran was born in 1883 and died in 1931. His philosophy has been accepted and followed for over a hundred years by many cultures for a good reason. Why do people follow and keep following him? Because his deep reasoning and clear and reasonable logic and common sense were always based on true, practical, and down-to-earth observations throughout generations and transcend any border, culture, and society.

If we want success and happiness in the future for our children, we need to train them well, contrary to today's philosophies that challenge the proven past. Remember, if there is no pain, there is no gain. It is not easy to raise and teach a child. In fact, it is very difficult. If you think that your work is difficult, walking your dog is difficult, or even climbing Mount Everest is difficult, then you are in for a big surprise. Just wait until you try to educate a child. I mean educate, not just feed, dress, provide a roof, and send the child to school. It takes persistence, dedication, sacrifice, a firm hand, lots of love, understanding, respect, tenderness, and a tremendous amount of patience. It is a beautiful entanglement of actions from different disciplines simultaneously.

As parents, we need to learn through books, magazines, courses, and personal experiences, and apply them all. If there is a will, there is a way. If others have succeeded in the past, why shouldn't we? It is for our children's benefit, strength, stability, success, and a respectful place in society, while following the path for ultimate happiness.

## Mean and Abusive Parents

A while ago I read a very interesting essay on "mean and abusive parents" by Dr. Carlos Hecktheuer, a Brazilian psychiatrist. I read it in Portuguese but I am not an accurate translator from Portuguese to English, so I will express in my own words some of his thoughts while trying to honor his wise, down-to-earth, powerful, and positive philosophy. For

Hecktheuer's writings in Portuguese, please see:

cadernodemensagens.net/node/2183  or
pensador.uol.com.br/frase/Mzk5NzAx/

Dr. Hecktheuer wrote that one day, when his children were old enough to understand, he would have a serious conversation with them and tell them the following very important things that he held precious and firm in his mind:

I loved you enough to always ask where you were going, who you were going with, and when you would be back.

I loved you enough not to remain quiet and to let you know (whether you like it, you agree, or you don't) that your new friend was not a good influence for you and not even good company.

I loved you enough to force you to go to the store and pay for the candies and other things you took from the storeowner without his knowledge. I loved you sufficiently to go with you and tell that owner of the store that here was the money for those things you took away the day before without his consent.

I loved you enough to be standing in your room for two hours while you cleaned it up and organized everything, when I could have done it in less than 15 minutes.

I loved you enough to show you that, aside from the deep love and pride I felt and had for you (my children), the disappointment and deception I sometimes felt because you would occasionally bring tears to my eyes.

I loved you enough to allow you to be responsible for your own actions, even though the penalties were sometimes difficult and harsh enough to break my heart.

But above all, I loved you enough to say 'No' when I knew that, due to the use of that properly reasoned word, you would have feelings of hatred towards me (and I am sure you hated me many times).

Those were some of the most difficult battles that I remember right now, but I am very happy because I was firm and determined, and I won at the time, but you actually won in the long run! Yes, I won at the time when these things were happening, but you won bigger for the rest of your days.

Dr. Hecktheuer also wrote about what he thinks his children will tell their own children if their children ever ask them whether their parents had been mean or abusive. He believes his children will say:

Yes, my parents were the meanest parents in the world, because, while the other kids ate goodies and cookies for breakfast, we had to eat oatmeal, cereal, eggs, and toast. The other kids drank sodas, undiluted processed juices, chips, and ice cream for lunch. We were forced to eat rice, beans, meats, and fruits.

My parents required us to tell them exactly who our friends were. At all times, they insisted on knowing where we were going and whom we were going with, whether it was for three hours or for only half an hour. They always insisted we tell them the truth and only the truth. We expected the same from them.

When we were teenagers, they even developed the skill of almost reading our minds. Our life was really difficult!

My parents would not even allow our friends to honk their horns when they wanted us to come out. They insisted they ring the bell and come in, so they could meet them.

At 12 years old, my friends could return to their home late and after dark, but we were only allowed to do that at about 16 years old. My parents even got out of bed to ask if the party was fun or not, when in reality we knew they were just checking on our condition and whether we were making sense or not.

Because of Mom and Dad, we missed big experiences in our teenage years such as drug problems, property violations, car crashes, vandalism, robberies, and even the chance to go to jail after breaking some law.

There is only one thing about which I do not agree with Dr. Hecktheuer. That is when he says: "Those who are already parents, do not feel guilty, and for those who will be parents, I trust this will guide you and assist you in being alert."

I do not agree completely with this statement, because, while growing up, we were all taught to be 100 per cent responsible for our own actions (or lack of action). If we did something wrong or failed to do something right, then we *should* be held responsible and feel guilty, so as never to do it again. We were taught to deal with guilt in a healthy, positive, and productive manner.

As parents, we need to acknowledge our mistakes, we are able to try and mend what we did. Better to try and correct even 20 or 30 per cent than nothing at all. It is never too late, unless we give up, but parents should never, but never, give up! Never drown in our own guilt—instead, change, adapt, and learn from our mistakes.

We need to also understand, evaluate, and fully comprehend what the average kid needs their parents to know about them. The concerned and above-average parent says things like: "Be respectful with others, grow up to be professional, strive to be successful, make a sincere effort to be responsible, be a team player."

When children are smaller, they are constantly told to wash the dishes, cut the grass, clean the floors, organize their room, dust the house, respect their brothers and sisters, and so on. Parents expect lots of things from their children. But what is it that the children expect from their parents?

There is an interesting answer to this question from a famous writer called José Saramago, who was the recipient of the Nobel Prize in Literature in 1998. Born in Portugal, he was known to many as the greatest living novelist at the time. He once wrote about the importance and courage required in being a parent. He stated that God lends the children to us, so that we can go through an intensive course in learning how to love somebody and how to change our worse defects in order to provide the best example for our children. But he argued emphatically that to achieve this, we need to develop a lot of courage and focus, which are not easy to attain. It requires discipline, strong will, and love. Those children ("our" children) are only in our custody until the day they can depend on themselves to survive, because they do not belong to us. They belong to life itself, to destiny, and to their own future families. He said, "God, please bless our children as you blessed us with them."

The message here is the courage parents need to develop themselves in order to educate their children properly, so that the children can grow strong and follow a straight path in life. But this definitely depends on the example given to the children by their parents, because children copy and learn first from Mom and Dad.

## What Teenagers Want From Mom and Dad

After extensive research, I have compiled a selection of what I believe teenagers really want from their parents. The sources are cited following the list.

- We teenagers ask for understanding and appreciation. We are young, and we are very busy with our main responsibility, which is to study. We know you are busy, too and work all day. When you come home, you need to relax, and we do, too. We require privacy in our room. We are different from others and way different from you when you were our age. It is like living in different time zones with different priorities, responsibilities, and interests in life. We think differently, and we definitely have different goals and methods to achieve them. Please understand that we are different and always will be different. Your support and understanding will help us to get along better.

- We teenagers want our parents to be happy, content, and proud of us. We are very interested in the impression you have of us. We are interested in what you really think about us. But respect us, just as you want us to respect you. We are not perfect, nor are you. Let us accept each other as we are. Let us not try to change each other. Let us guide each other but allow freedom of action according to our own preferences and priorities. Yes, suggest to me what to do, but do not tell me what to do. We do not need the latter, though we are starving for proper guidance. We actually do care about what Mom and Dad think about us, and, believe it or not, deep within ourselves, we do want to please you and want you both to feel proud and happy.

- We teenagers ask for esteem, respect, and civility. We do not want to experience our parents fighting and discussing matters in front of us. Do this quietly, if you must, and behind closed doors. You are setting a bad example if you do not. We sincerely need peace, quiet, and harmony at home. Kindly make an effort to provide us with those. Home is also our sanctuary; let us all treat it as such. This will be good for everyone, not just for us. We need Mom and Dad to respect and understand our decisions, our opinions, our mistakes, our assertiveness, our preferences, our privacy, our secrets, our dreams, our goals, our objectives, our overall ways of being, both as humans and as your children.

- We teenagers ask for encouragement, support, and reassurance. Yes, we need your understanding and support to give us confidence in trying to achieve our dreams, our goals, and our daily desires. We need support in the friends we have chosen and the girlfriends or boyfriends we choose, because they are all important to us, very important. We definitely need your support in the sports we choose to practice, the music we want to listen to, the movies we want to go and see, the hobbies we select, and in the overall decisions and preferences we decide to fight for on a daily basis, because all these are very important to us. We need your support to make it easier to commit ourselves to achieving success, regardless of the route we choose to take. We do not want to be treated as kids, or you will continue pushing us to act as such.

- We teenagers ask to be understood, heeded, and listened to. We do not just want to be heard; that is not enough. We do not like it when you just listen to yourself and disregard our thoughts. Mom and Dad ought to listen to our stories and show sincere interest in trying to understand them. Pay attention to and understand our problems and our desires. Listen to our claims and our aspirations. Do not yell or raise your voice at us, because that just shuts us down and pushes us into our own world, our own bubble. We want Mom and Dad to listen to our deep desires, because you might just learn something new. They might be insignificant to you, but they are certainly significant to us and can mark our lives for bad or good. We teenagers need to listen to our internal frustrations and silent screams and attend to them with speed and accuracy. Yes, we are screaming inside, but you fail to listen. It is breaking our hearts, and we sometimes do not know what to do. Please listen to us, because as much as we hate sometimes to admit it, we need you both!

- We teenagers ask for our parents' counsel, direction, and guidance. We need these all the time, and we need you to repeat it as much as required. We do not learn immediately, so please remind us gently and with care, but decisively. Yes, sometimes we fail to do as we are told, but instead of getting mad, just remind us, with firmness, focus, and gentleness.

- Parents should choose their words wisely; they cannot take them back. Uncalculated and unreasonable words or expressions hurt us more than you think. Keep that always in mind. But do not be soft about things. We like reinforcement and total conviction and determination from you both as our parents.

- We are still learning on a daily basis, so do not stop guiding us. Just do it from your heart and with the right tone of voice. Don't let us imitate your mistakes, but help us develop your assertiveness. If we fall, guide us back on track with a gentle, positive, but firm action. Don't leave us fallen down. This is when we most need your support.

- Do not let us down. Swallow your pride, please! You should both know we are really trying. You have the experience, which we still lack and we acknowledge this, but let us save face. Once again, accept us as we are and according to what we can achieve and be.

- Yes, you can squeeze our necks, but just don't choke us. You are our mentors and our support, but you need to understand that you are just that. It is our life, not yours. Kindly understand that. Again, we want both of you to understand that, as teenagers, our friends are more important and crucial to us than you as our parents. Please do not ask us to choose and explain, just try to understand and respect this. This will change with time, but for now that is the way it is.

- Above all, we teenagers require you both to be our mentors while holding our hands in harmony. We need you to be our role models and good examples. As children, we learned what we were exposed to. You are definitely part of our success or failure so far, so please provide us always with a good example and correct us if we go sideways.

- There is a very old and wise saying: "If you grow up with wolves, you will grow up howling." Therefore, your example is very important to us as children and teenagers. We are being formed as we grow, and our behaviors can turn into habits and into our future way of being, so please provide us with a good example.

- Do not ask us to do what you cannot do or are not willing to do yourself. Do not yell at us if you do not want us to yell back. Do not answer rudely if you also expect the same respect from us. Do not swear or use bad words in our conversations. Please respect us, if you expect the same. Remember, life is a two-way street. You have taught us that—just do not forget this. Keep it always in mind when you are with us. Do not ask us to comply with something if you yourself broke that promise. Do not ask us to come back early if you arrive late several times a week. Do not expect us to love you and respect you both if we do not receive the same treatment from you.

## Main Sources:

- Joanne Stern (Ph.D.), "5 things every teen wants their parents to know," website of the magazine Psychology Today, Sept 14, 2011. For more information, visit:

  psychologytoday.comparenting-is-contact-sport/201109/5-things-every-teen-wants-their-parent-know

- Liz Hale (Ph.D.), Jan 30, 2008, on her own website: drlizhale.com She has written extensively about marriage, parenting, children, and overall family interactions. For her, proper communication and self-esteem are key.

- University of Illinois at: extension.illinois.edu

- Megan Vivo, "10 things teens wish their parents knew" published by the Aspen Education Group (2009):

  aspeneducation.crchealth.com

- • An article published by Child, Youth and Family (a service of the Ministry of Social Development) on their website:

cyf.govt.nz

## Reversed Values and Breast-feeding

Recently I found a very interesting article (Netlore Archive: Text of "politically incorrect" prayer delivered by Pastor Joe Wright before the Kansas House of Representatives on January 23, 1996) that talked about a speech at the Kansas State Legislature by Pastor Joe Wright concerning prayer. There is even a YouTube video, which is interesting to watch:

YouTube.com/watch?v=F-

Even though I absolutely respect every religion, I am not someone who goes to church every Sunday and prays every day. Therefore, I do not read much on religious matters, but, in my research for this book, I did, and I was surprised by what Pastor Joe Wright had to say. Above all, I definitely agree in general with his speech. He started by saying, "Woe to those who call evil good," and that alone caught my attention.

He then argued that we have all lost our compass in life. The formerly precise, high-quality compass (which we all ought to possess as human beings) has been lost or replaced by a cheap one-dollar compass that is definitely not directing us on the logical and correct path in life.

Pastor Wright specifically said, "We have lost our spiritual equilibrium and reversed our values." This is a simple, truthful, and deep thought. There will be catastrophic results if we do not get our old compass back.

The main part of his speech was simply brilliant and deserves to be quoted at length:

We confess:

We have ridiculed the absolute truth of Your Word and called it pluralism.
We have worshipped other gods and called it multiculturalism.
We have endorsed perversion and called it alternative lifestyle.
We have exploited the poor and called it the lottery.
We have rewarded laziness and called it welfare.
We have killed our unborn and called it choice.
We have shot abortionists and called it justifiable.
We have neglected to discipline our children and called it building self-esteem.
We have abused power and called it politics.
We have coveted our neighbor's possessions and called it ambition.
We have polluted the air with profanity and pornography and called it freedom of expression.
We have ridiculed the time-honoured values of our forefathers and called it enlightenment.

I truly take my hat off to Pastor Wright for having repeated such painful truths, which are difficult for many to acknowledge and accept. However, with absolute respect, I feel Pastor Wright fell somewhat short. I would add the following few points:

- We have augmented our insensitivity to lie and to cheat. But even worse, we seem not to care, and sometimes it appears we feel proud of it. Some even say, "That's life, get used to it."

- We have devalued the true meaning of trust and honesty, but we say, "Deal with it."

- We have reduced our efforts in helping the needy, but some people say, "To each his own."

- We are exploiting and destroying our planet. But we call it "progress and development."

- We abuse our children and the elderly. But we say, "I am sorry" or "I did not mean it."

- We constantly make the same mistakes, repeat the same lies, betray ourselves and others, while trying to justify our actions with all sort of excuses, but we say, "I am just human."

- We eat unhealthily and damage our bodies and minds with alcohol and drugs, but we say, "Why not?" or "I have the right", or "Who cares", or "Because I feel sad."

- We keep making the same or bigger mistakes in life and do not listen to the experienced words of our elders, but we say, "It is my life", or "I need to learn by making my own mistakes", or "That happened to you, but it will not happen to me", or "It will not happen again."

- We disgrace ourselves in public through lack of politeness and rude attitudes, but we say, "Who cares?"

When I was little, I often used to hear (as we also do today) that all extremes are wrong and bad. Unfortunately, it is very difficult to reach a proper balance in whatever people do, especially as a group. To successfully achieve the right balance in any activity, method, or tradition is a real challenge, but excess in any activity tends to bring unwanted results. We humans are a species of extreme activities, tastes, and preferences. We do not know when or how to stop or when to just let go. New and extreme things are not always better. We need to be wise in our choices. We fail to see the proper balance and the invisible line that says, "Enough", or "Stop."

A good example is breast-feeding. There is no doubt that breast-feeding is the best thing there is for a baby. Yes, and especially during the first six months and even up to a year, as recommended by The American Academy of Pediatrics.

Among having many immunization benefits, breast milk protects the baby against diarrhea and respiratory tract infections. Breast milk is so important that researchers say it is the only food the baby really needs for the first six months of life, although there is some debate about this.

Breast milk contains amazingly valuable antibodies that assist the baby to keep allergies and diseases at bay. We all know that breast milk is full of vitamins, minerals, required fats, carbohydrates, and the perfect balance of proteins. Breast-feeding also protects mothers by reducing their risk of breast cancer, ovarian cancer, uterine cancer, and endometrial cancer. There is no doubt that breast milk is best for a baby's well-being and growth.

But the question remains, for how long should women breast-feed their babies? The most common answer from researchers is: As long as you and your baby feel comfortable. But here is when the concepts of reversed values and exaggerations or extremes kick in. A growing number of mothers think that, by breast-feeding their children beyond three years of age, they are doing their children a favour when, in reality, some psychological issues start to develop that may even be manifested in the future. Issues ranging from giving in to peer pressure to insecurity can affect children who breast-feed beyond three years of age.

In Okanagan Sunday (October 4, 2014), Steve MacNaull reported in an article entitled "Breast still best" that "[the World Health Organization recommends babies be 'breastfed exclusively for the first six months of their life'." However, some local mothers in Kelowna in the Okanagan Valley, BC, seem to "know better" than the researchers of the World Health Organization. With the article, there is a photo of three mothers breastfeeding their children in public and fighting for their right to do so. One is breastfeeding two children at a time, one of whom is three-and-a-half years old. The article then states that another mom in the picture said she had a five-and-a-half-year-old who was still nursing at the time.

According to the great majority in society, and many mothers themselves, to nurse your children beyond three years of age is wrong and selfish. In fact, we have an example, which was widely criticized, of a Time magazine cover published May 10, 2012. It shows an attractive lady nursing a boy who, according to Time, "looks old enough to be attending nursery school." It is really a bit uncomfortable to see this image and others taken of her and her children. Kate Pickert, a staff writer for Time, authored the cover article, "Why attachment parenting drives some mothers to extremes—and how Dr. Bill Sears became their guru." Dr. Sears is a pediatrician who is an author and co-author of several parenting books.

An important and debated question arises: Is there a benefit in nursing a child beyond the age of one? In reaction to the Time cover photo, Dr. Ellie Cannon wrote on May 19, 2012: "That's just selfish and wrong: How the image of a mother breast-feeding a toddler reignited a health controversy." She starts the article by saying: "Revolting! Just wrong! Surely that's child abuse!" Dr. Cannon says that there is very little evidence of any health benefit of nursing beyond the age of one and that, as a doctor, she believes there is possibly even harm in breastfeeding older children. In fact, she even wrote:

> Breast-feeding until a child goes to school is fulfilling a mother's needs, not a child's. It is self-indulgent and possibly narcissistic. Children are at the centre of our world, but it does not mean we need to be at the centre of theirs.

In addition, according to Dr. Cannon and many developmental psychologists:

> Extreme breast-feeding dampens the children's stage of natural exploring of the world around them, while limiting the children's development and serves only to indulge the mother. It gives her attention and purpose.

Personally, I have seen mothers breast-feeding their children many times in public, and the trend is growing. These types of mothers are selfish and push the boundaries of the logic, the reasoning, and the true well-being of their children to the extreme. To breast-feed a child under two years of age (my personal preference is one year maximum) can be good, sweet, nurturing, cuddly, emotionally bonding, etc. But beyond a certain age, it becomes creepy, selfish, and (according to many experts) detrimental to the child.

There is evidence that children are sexually aware and curious about body parts as early as three years of age. There are many grown-ups who still remember images of things that they saw or that happened at this early stage of life. Imagine remembering your mother's breast and you being latched onto it? Yikes, that is definitely creepy and perhaps even a bit traumatic for some.

There is an article in Time Magazine from August 01 of 2014, in Living - Motherhood, entitled "The Top 16 Breastfeeding Controversies." Two of the controversies caught my attention, and I cannot help but bring them to your attention and add my own personal perspective as a normal grown-up man.

The first has to do with breastfeeding an older child who is a little too old. A 30-year-old woman called Amanda Hurst was still breast-feeding her daughter, who was six years old at the time of the interview. In this same article, they mention the case of another woman who breast-fed her son even at eight years old. To my mind, this should definitely be considered child abuse.

Can you imagine being eight years old and instead of opening the fridge for the jug of milk, you go instead to your mother's breast for a drink of milk to quench your thirst? How sick and abusive is this? Without being a psychologist or pretending to understand the human brain thoroughly, I strongly believe that this might cause psychological problems later in life. That is perhaps why some children grow into adulthood with quite twisted minds.

I cannot help thinking about the Freudian theory in relation to the emotions aroused in a small boy. These emotions circle around his sexual desire for his mother while resenting his father. This complex of emotions can happen as early as the age of four, according to Freud, so imagine a child between the ages of four and eight still breast-feeding. To my mind, this should be considered absolute child abuse and have legal repercussions, because you are marking that child for the rest of his or her life.

The second example in the article is about breast-feeding in public, particularly with the breast exposed, even for just a few seconds. A lady in Ottawa was having coffee in Starbucks and saw another woman pulling out her breast to breast-feed her child. She complained to the barista that another woman was breast-feeding openly without a shield. The barista told her that he would take care of the situation.

Unfortunately, he then went and offered a free coffee to the mother breast-feeding her child, saying that he hoped this would mitigate and assuage her feelings.

Superficially, it seems like a nice gesture, but, really, what is a mother doing breast-feeding her child without a blanket (or other type of shield) in a public place like Starbucks, which we all know is always very busy? Worst of all is that in my view the barista went against Starbuck's policy of trying to make everybody feel welcome and have a pleasant experience. Instead of being neutral, he decided to make the woman who complained feel humiliated, while praising the mother who started everything by creating an unpleasant environment. It had nothing to do with the right of breast-feeding a child; it had to do with the time, place, and manner in which she did it, forcing everybody else to look away and feel uncomfortable in a place in which we should feel relaxed and at ease.

To my mind, Howard Schultz, Starbucks' owner, should fire that barista for taking sides and humiliating a customer who came to him for help and assistance. She trusted the barista, and he turned around and betrayed that trust. Starbucks should implement a serious and meticulous policy regarding breast-feeding. Perhaps even offer little blankets with a Starbucks logo to use, or else….

I think we should just add to a properly positioned sign the following: "No Shirt, No Shoes, No Shield = No Service." Voila, I guess we got it! The four S's Policy.

I absolutely agree that mothers should be able to breast-feed in public places, if they did not manage to do it privately at home for whatever reason that day. But please, be discreet. Look for a more private spot within a public setup and shield yourself and your child as much as possible. At least, pretend you are trying to do this, which will ease the way for many. It is your right to breastfeed—just do not impose it on others in a challenging manner. It is simply a courtesy to yourself, your child, and others.

## Realities of the Ten Commandments and of Being Human

As much as most people out there believe that religion should not be imposed on people, I personally believe that at least some religious thoughts, philosophies, and the commandments should be taught in society and some even enforced by law if need be, with serious consequences if not obeyed. I respect life in all its shapes and forms, I believe in good behaviors, and I believe in the survival and flourishing of the human species within a framework of good, positive behaviors. I also accept and respect any religion, as long as nobody tries to impose it upon me. In this chapter, I will only refer to seven out of the ten commandments as follows:

### You shall not kill

Humans commit murders every day. It happens in every corner of the world on a daily basis. Humans are always in some kind of war somewhere on this planet at any given time. Some examples, out of many, many more, include: Israel vs. Palestine, North Korea vs. South Korea, many African countries, Syria's civil war since 2011 and still to date (2016), and the continuing problems in the Middle East with Iraq, Afghanistan, and others.

In the African country of Angola, thousands of children in rural areas are left to die by the government through absolute inaction and lack of interest in their own people, by not providing clean water, medicines, and other government programs to aid the poor.

On July 20, 2015, in southeastern Turkey, a suicide bomber killed 31 people and injured over 100. A similar atrocity happened in Istanbul on June 28, 2016, when over 40 people lost their lives. Immediately thereafter, on July 15, 2016, there was a failed attempt to overthrow President Erdogan in which close to 300 people died and over 6,000 were arrested. On July 1, 2016, in Dhaka, Bangladesh, 28 people were killed in an attack by terrorists on a café. In Quebec City, a shooting at Grande Mosquée de Québec left six people dead and 18 wounded last January 29, 2017.

I could go on, but what would be the point? We risk going numb and forgetting at a faster rate than we already do. All of the above, and much more, happened because we are humans and tend to follow our most primitive instincts. Greed and political interests make us behave even worse. Just read about George W. Bush and his department of secret intelligence that, using false claims, invaded a country and killed hundreds of thousands of people in search of non-existent "weapons of mass destruction."

**You shall not commit adultery**

People have committed adultery for centuries and will continue to do so for centuries to come. We are humans with animal instincts that many cannot control. Humans are betrayed by their own instincts, their greed, and their false feelings of superiority and power. We tend to put our desires and instincts above our reasoning, and so most of us fail to act on the basis of logic and common sense. Whether we like it or not, that is how the majority of humans behave and it has been proven throughout history. Sad but true!

**You shall not steal**

People all over the world steal on a daily basis and, in fact, try hard to do it as long as they do not get caught. Some do it for need, for greed, or for twisted psychological reasons. People do not always think with a clear head on their shoulders. The excuse? Because we are humans. It is part of our DNA. Lack of remorse is rampant and, unfortunately, is taught to children through generations. Do it, just do not get caught! Right?

## You shall not lie

This is a joke, because everybody lies. White lies or not, but they are lies. We all know we will not end up in Hell for saying white lies, regardless of what many religions want us to believe. People do it all the time, and they get so used to it that many do not realize they are even lying. Men and women lie as a protective measure, sometimes due to external pressures, in order not to hurt others, for the sake of political correctness or simply for some odd and weird personal reasons. Lies come easily to most people. A very dismal but true fact of life.

## You shall not covet your neighbors' belongings

We all tend to do this throughout our lives. We simply cannot help ourselves. It is our true nature, but it can be overcome with conscious effort, time, and maturity. Humans tend to have a very weak sense of self-control. The desire for more and better things is bestowed on us as a malediction rather than as a gift. Let's face it; do you really need that new curved LED 60" TV? "Yes" is usually the answer! Another sad fact of life!

## You shall not be vengeful

Luckily, not everybody is vengeful, but the majority do tend to seek revenge, both as personal compensation and as a deserved retribution. Due to a lack of deep rational and logical thought, people are pushed to commit vengeful acts, thinking this might make them feel better and level the playing field. This is sad and primitive. We need to leave those feelings behind and forget revenge. The truth is we should never forget, but we should let go! Humans in general cannot control their needs, instincts, and overall desire for self-satisfaction and immediate gratification. We tend to practice the theory or tradition of "an eye for an eye," and as Gandhi once wrote: "That would make the world blind!"

**You shall not betray**

Betrayal is such a devastating act that it deserves a classification of its own. It is practiced without remorse by millions of people, governments, and companies around the world at any given time. A traitor, in my eyes, is the lowest kind of human being walking on planet earth, almost on a level with substandard humans such as pedophiles and mass murderers.

There is nothing worse than a traitor, somebody you trusted and who stabbed you in the back without remorse and, what is even worse, sometimes with feelings of satisfaction and accomplishment.

Note:

What about our own human traits and their relation to the Ten Commandments?

I trust the reader has noticed that, in all the previously

mentioned situations, I always referred to "humans." Well, that is sometimes the perfect excuse for many people, but it is shameful to use being human as a scapegoat or to justify who we are or our weakness as a species. It is superficial and lame and should never be accepted as an excuse. Why? The answer is very simple: because we have brains and the ability to reason.

With the proper education, guidance, support, and self-control, we can learn to direct our behaviors and desires properly and overcome our weaknesses. It is like when a priest or a coach sexually abuses a child and says: "I am very sorry. I repent. I tried to control my urges but I couldn't. I am ill. I am sick and I need help." Why not look for help before traumatizing children for the rest of their lives?  The same applies to men who rape and kill women. If proven guilty without a shred of a doubt, they should have their pride cut off or sent with a one-way ticket to Siberia in the middle of winter for hard labour for the rest of their lives with the rest of the world's rapists and pedophiles. Let them rape each other over there, if that is what they want to do. Unfortunately, they often get off lightly, which is an insult to the victims, their families, their community, and society itself.

These "sick" people should know better, because they all have a mother, sister, daughter, or simply a female friend they appreciate and respect. Let's face it. Not all such perpetrators are sick; some just have an urge that needs immediate fulfilling. How low and unspeakable can that be?

Yes, some perpetrators do need help from doctors, psychiatrists, psychologists, medical institutions, or even from the town's voodoo-priest. Others are literally in a state beyond repair. Would lethal injection or seclusion not be a better solution instead of supporting and maintaining them in prison with our tax dollars? Unless we are in the United States, where prisons are a private and lucrative businesses.

I had a friend who used to say: "Proper retribution will always come to those who learn to control themselves, but punishment will follow those who failed to control themselves, and then use lame excuses for having performed their hideous acts if caught." When I was younger, I really did not pay enough attention to philosophers like Mahatma Gandhi. We studied them at school, but my full attention was not necessarily there. The same applies to many other influential leaders and authors. But I was lucky that my parents, my school system, and my friends taught me the proper way to act within our society. They always tried very hard to keep us on the right lane of the road. So, I took proper behavior for granted because it was a normal thing in the society I was brought up in. I was too busy studying, practicing sports, romancing my girlfriend, and working, too focused on my own goals and dreams to concern myself with what others might be doing.

We all grow up, and we all learn, observe, and realize that others do not necessarily follow our decent and rational standards. Luckily, they are still a minority. There are always a few rotten apples on every tree. It happens everywhere, though we need to admit that, in some societies, we have to wonder what is going wrong and why things have gone so awry and moved so far away from the core of real and important human values.

I have been very lucky, because I was born and brought up

and have made my life in North America. I have had the good fortune to live in Mexico (where I was born), the United States (where I had the chance to study and work), and in Canada (where I now proudly live and work). That was pure luck at the beginning (my family background) but a lot of work, effort and sacrifice later in life, when I had the chance to choose to study abroad and then to choose Canada as a place to live the rest of my days. I cannot even imagine what I might have been like if I had been born in a less fortunate country in Africa, the Middle East, or Asia. With exceptions, North America is still safe, with a good degree of controlled and monitored freedom, and you can still bring your dreams to fruition here with a positive attitude.

When Pastor Joe Wright gave his prayer in the Kansas State Legislature in January, 1996, he was not reinventing the wheel. Instead, he was doing us a favour by reminding us, from a different angle and in his own words, what Mahatma Gandhi wanted us to understand many years before. He wanted to remind us of what happens when people lose their equilibrium, their sense of reality, and their perception of values. They literally reverse many values that for centuries have been kept precious and intact, until recently.

## Mahatma Gandhi's Seven Social Sins and My Interpretation

Let us briefly analyze some of Mahatma Gandhi's "Seven Social Sins," which he published on October 22, 1925, in a newspaper called Young India in his country of origin, India. Many other authors (such as Dr. Stephen R. Covey in his book Principle Centered Leadership) have cited this list of seven social sins for various important reasons. These seven social sins are certainly at the core of the problems of every modern society. We need to list them, understand them, and interpret them in a positive spirit and with a proactive attitude. The list goes like this:

## Wealth without work

People throughout history have wanted to get as much as possible with the least amount of work. Although that sounds logical and smart, in almost every single working activity performed by humans, it is neither. We have to put time and effort into things to get adequate results and proper compensation. In fact, when things come easily with little or no work, they tend to go away as easily ("easy comes, easy goes.") But if we treasure our compensation due to the hard work and sacrifice we put into earning it, then I guarantee we will take better care of it and our accomplishments and achievements.

This principle applies to moral, spiritual, and material things as well as to money. If you win money in a casino in Las Vegas, you are likely to spend it more easily and more quickly than if you had earned it with sweat, sacrifice, and hard work over a long time and with serious effort.

A good example can be seen in our modern world in the government's manipulation of soldiers sent to other countries to fight wars for certain economic interests, wars that the soldiers would not be involved in otherwise. Another example is the manipulation of the financial markets by elite financiers for the benefit of their own pockets, causing economic crashes and the loss of people's savings, crucifying 99 per cent of the investors in their path. A third example is when people make a profit on the backs of others (e.g. the mining industry in Africa and some Asian countries) or through the exploitation of child labour such as in Bangladesh and some Latin American countries.

## Pleasure without conscience

Humans throughout history have been failing profoundly in this sin. Nothing has really changed. Just look at what our youth is doing now. A good example is "Girls Gone Wild." If you have not heard about this or seen it, just Google it. Young girls do not realize they are being exploited and will most likely regret it in the future.

Teenage girls in the United Sates get drunk and flaunt their breasts in a very sexual way. All this is taped and sold for profit without any real cost to the so-called producer. If you Google this, please sit down first, because it will literally flip you over in disgust or desire if you have not seen it or heard about it before. Imagine if it was your daughter doing this?

Pleasure above conscience is increasingly driving our behavior and, unfortunately, at all ages. Small children are being taught to expect immediate gratification without first earning the right. The pleasure of eating huge amounts of unhealthy food is good example. Another example is when men walk in the street without a T-shirt showing off a big, fat, sweaty belly on a hot sunny day. Other people do not really care how hot these men may feel, and nobody needs to see their love handles, bulky pregnant-style stomachs, sweaty nipples, or, even worse, endure the pain of a smelly and stinky body odor.

Pleasure without conscience is rampant, and it is an immature and selfish attitude in society. Unfortunately, it is growing exponentially in younger generations, while leaving behind the true meaning of patience and responsibility.

## Science without humanity

Throughout human history, different civilizations have studied and experimented on human victims, regardless of the suffering imposed on them, as long as a discovery is made or a theory confirmed. A notorious example is the experiments that Doctor Josef Mengele practiced on his victims during World War II. He conducted countless genetic research studies on human subjects while completely disregarding their suffering, health, and safety. He literally tortured thousands of people to gain "knowledge."

Today, we are becoming victims of our own technocracy by manipulating DNA and trying to bring to life species that disappeared hundreds of years ago. But isn't that the way humans invent and discover new possibilities? There is a very fine line between progress and inhumanity in various areas of science.

## Knowledge without character

Stephen R. Covey wrote the following in his book, Principle Centered Leadership:

> As dangerous as a little knowledge is, even more dangerous is much knowledge without a strong, principled character. Purely intellectual development without commensurate internal character development

makes as much sense as putting a high-powered sports car in the hands of a teenager who is high on drugs. Yet all too often in the academic world, that's exactly what we do by not focusing on the character development of young people.

It is evident that, as a society, we need commonly accepted ethical standards, values, and principles to assist in the creation and strengthening of a positive character in every individual within our society. Without ethical standards, values, and principles, people's characters and attitudes can be nefarious, that is, contrary to divine law and with negative impacts on our world. Consider the brutal regime of Idi Amin Dada in Uganda during his government from 1971 to 1979 that left behind negative memories in millions of people.

## Politics without principles and commerce without morality

These two items in Gandhi's list go hand in hand. Morality is to values as principles are to ideals. The meaning of morals, ethics, and principles definitely overlap. While morals are the individual principles of what is right and what is wrong (which every politician has, or lacks), the structure of ethics deals directly with those principles.

What I am about to write may seem like a bold statement, but a friend of mine once told me (and I agree with him): People do not do the right thing because it does not seem to pay enough. We constantly see people who are uneducated and unprincipled making tons of money. In our society, it seems that money is all that counts to be considered successful and a role model for others.

Ethics and morality should hold hands with politics and commerce. Unfortunately, they usually do not. Morality defines the personal character of an individual, while ethics are more related to the social codes and behaviors of a particular society. In 99 per cent of countries, politics are distinguished by their lack of both ethics and morality in many of the public servants' daily activities. Corruption and the indiscriminate use of excessive power distort the basic principles and values with which every country needs to be managed and run on a daily basis. Unfortunately, it is often not that obvious, so the average citizen cannot perceive what is really going on until it has happened and it is too late.

Good examples are those lookalike "ghost cities" built in mainland China, which are almost identical replicas of Manhattan and Paris. Billions of dollars were spent to build these cities, but nobody is living in them. Just Google "Ghost Cities in China," and you will find all sorts of information about them. Why were they built when nobody is really living in them? If the first city did not work, why did they build the second and third? Who is making money out of these ventures? Where are the principles and morality of the politics behind these megaprojects? Local Chinese do not care about North American and European architecture, so why replicate them? The phenomenon certainly raises many questions with few sincere and honest answers.

It seems that international commerce is only based on pure profit, regardless of where the products come from and who are being exploited. A good example is Bangladesh, where the great majority of people work for foreign companies that exploit their labour for the benefit of their businesses and the benefit of people in other countries. With time and effort, we hope the condition of the labour market in these poor countries will improve. We can only trust that at least the exploitation of child labour in these markets will disappear with time, but we have to take a stand and participate as members of the international groups striving for equality through fair salaries and opportunities. We need to get out of our comfort zone, sincerely care about these matters, and try our best to do something about them.


## Worship without sacrifice

This is also referred to as religion without sacrifice by other authors. A great many religious people are active in church but do not do the real religious "walking," that is, they maintain a religious façade socially but do not act accordingly. They pray and promise but do not deliver. Only a minority of religious people are really devoted in soul and spirit in their daily actions. Many people continually break one or more of the Ten Commandments. Similar things take place in every religious group around the world. As Steven R. Covey in an MBA project on management using Gandhi's principles (mkgandhi.org/mgmnt.htm) says, "These people are neither God-centered nor principle-centered." So, what are they? Selfishly-or hypocritically-centered?

When religious people are willing to sacrifice their egos, pride, and personal needs, then they are real worshippers and devotees. Unfortunately, many people only want to feed their spiritual needs and feelings without surrendering and forfeiting their positions and the power it brings with it. People cannot truly worship without personal sacrifice. I had a builder once who was working for me in the construction of a house. He was a very religious man and heavily involved in his local church, but his business lacked principles. I caught him cutting corners and lying and cheating on the costs and quality of work involved in building and had to let him go. Some people like him go to church, pray, and promise good behaviors, but they are incapable of doing the right thing by being professional, honest, and hardworking. Needless to say, he is not a builder anymore and ended up looking for another job. Regardless, I truly wish him well.

I recently read in Spanish some of the most famous quotes of Gandhi that clearly show how our modern society has reversed established values and is surfing on a "new set of values," as if these are the ones to follow and teach our children. Regretfully, they are utterly wrong. There are six quotes that caught my attention, and after my interpretation and translation, are as follows:

1. "Help me to speak the truth in front of the strong ones and not to say lies to gain me the applause of the weak." Sadly, many politicians build up their careers by providing inaccurate or misleading information to voters. Apparently, that is how England voted in their referendum to leave the European Union in June of 2016 (referred to as Brexit). These politicians need the people's acknowledgment, applause, and, above all, their current and future votes, so they promise things they cannot fulfill and tend to exaggerate or even lie to gain the voters' support. We all know this, but do we do anything about it? We need to do our research before voting or believing everything somebody says to gain our trust.

2. "If you give me fortune, do not take away my reasoning; if you give me success, do not take away my humility." Regretfully, there are many young people who inherit

properties and money from their parents but do not really know how to handle their new position in society. Some tend to pretend they earned the money themselves. They forget who they were and how they started. They act with a feeling of preeminence over others. It is usually an attitude of inflated superiority due to lack of self-confidence and respect. No wonder the term *nouveau riche* is being used so much. Sadly, they turn into very unhappy people, but they have that fictitious sense of power that seems to be more important to them than being down-to-earth, friendly human beings.

3. "If you give me humility, do not take away my dignity." It is not unusual for the average person to be a great pretender in life. Sometimes it is good to be like that to buy yourself a chance to climb up the first few steps of the ladder, but if you continue, it will come back to haunt you. We need to constantly have our feet set firmly on the ground. People are losing their self-respect and self-esteem and adopting an attitude of "I do not care" with an absolute lack of self-control. Their dignity goes out the window and, unfortunately, they do not really care. They turn into arrogant individuals, which is sad, because I am sure these people are not, and never will be, truly happy!

4. "Teach me how to love others as I love myself." This is similar to the previous point about more and more people forcing and twisting their values and not loving or taking care of themselves as much as they should, causing a similarly distorted, careless, irresponsible attitude, with correspondingly bad behaviors toward others. But there will always be people who love themselves above all others and do only what they want with no regard for others.

5. "Do not allow me to be proud if I achieve success nor feel desperate if I fail." On this point, I believe you need to feel proud of yourself when you achieve something but not let that attitude or feeling govern your life. Try always to be down to earth in your attitudes and behaviors. Everybody feels frustrated and desperate when facing failure. We would not be human otherwise. It is part of our DNA, but you need to learn from your failures and strive harder, with courage and a positive attitude, to achieve success next time. Remember, never, but never, give up! Again, if there is an iron will, there is definitely a path to success and glory. Attitude and self-confidence are everything in life!

6. "If I offend somebody, please give me the courage to ask for forgiveness, and if others offend me, please give me the courage to forgive." This is, for me, the most difficult challenge. I always try my best to ask for understanding if I do something wrong. Why? Because it is the right and civilized thing to do. But I find it very difficult to forgive somebody who knowingly and intentionally perpetrated something wrong. If it was just a mistake, I can easily let go and forgive. But not when it was premeditated. That I will never forgive. I simply do not always have the ability to do so. But I put it out of my daily thoughts and in a small drawer inside my hypothalamus with a sticker on it that says, "Alert!" Yes, I might be a bit wrong here, but hey, that is just me, and even so, I strive daily to achieve happiness and do not think about it.

## CONCLUSIONS

After my research and overall personal experience throughout many years in various countries as a student and then as a professional, I truly feel comfortable and convinced about what I have observed and studied, and with what has been written and expressed throughout this book. I know there are people who will not agree with many of my opinions and some who may even be disturbed by my points of view. That is the beauty of being independent, with our own minds, reasoning, and perspectives. Cherish yours with respect and courtesy to others, as I tried my best to do here in this book. We all need to be open, understanding, tolerant, and accepting, but there are, and always will be, certain limits or boundaries we will not accept. There are things we will not be willing to agree about.

In life, the truth always finds its way to freedom, but it is sometimes painful and hard to accept. If we are people of integrity and are honest with ourselves and our principles, then we need to learn to accept the truth regardless of how uncomfortable it can be. Above all, we need to do something about it. We should always remain active throughout our daily lives and strive to improve our status and well-being. It is our duty and responsibility as members of society to take care of what we have and protect it the best way we can. Never take things for granted. Never! That should be considered an eternal sin. It is easy to shrug our shoulders and say, "I am happy with who I am, and who cares anyway? There is really nothing I can do."

Hello! There is a lot anybody can do, but you need to want to do it for yourself first, and then for your loved ones!

Two Key questions remain:

1.    Are you being honest, fulfilled, and happy in your life?
2.    If you had the strength, stamina, and perseverance to change and improve your life and surroundings, would you remain indifferent or indolent?

If the answer to either of the above questions is "No," then I truly believe you have the civic and moral duty to do something about it! Why? Because it is the right thing to do and when there is a will, there is a way! Only we have the answers to the above questions and the ability to change. If we put our minds and souls into it, we will no doubt succeed. And yes, sometimes we need to sacrifice personally to achieve our goals. If there is no pain, there is no gain, and that's life!

Learn to set up specific goals and work hard to achieve them. We need to live with self-respect and self-control. Pride, honor, health, and happiness must be sought constantly. Proper objectives, targets, and goals in life are good to have and to follow until achieved.

Albert Einstein once wrote, "If you want to live a happy life, tie it to a goal, not to people or things."

Best wishes!

# APPENDIX 1

## LEGAL ADVICE ....

# PUSHOR MITCHELL
### ——LLP——
### LAWYERS & TRADE-MARK AGENTS

**Our File:** PKS/57991.016

*Parveen Shergill's Direct Line: (250) 869-1220*
*Amanda's Direct Line: (250) 869-1173*

**BY E-MAIL,**
**original to follow by mail**

April 25, 2016

**CARRERAS INTERIORS LTD.**
P.O. Box # 25203
Kelowna, BC V1W 3Y7
carreras@shaw.ca

**Attention: Rafael Augusto Carreras**

Dear Mr. Carreras:

**RE:      Legal Opinion Regarding An Excerpt In Your Upcoming Book**

Further to our previous discussion in which you asked that I review certain portions of your upcoming book which includes comments about Rob Ford (the "Excerpt") and advise as to whether your comments could expose you to legal liability, namely in terms of possible defamation, I write to advise with respect to same.

Please note that my opinion, set out below, is based on Canadian law only. My advice relates solely to the excerpt you provided me by e-mail, dated April 13, 2016. I confirm that I have not reviewed any other portions of your book. Lastly, as per your instructions, I confirm that I did not engage in any fact checking.

**OVERVIEW OF DEFAMATION LAW**

The terms defamation, libel and slander can often be confusing. Defamation is a "communication" about a person that hurts the person's reputation. When the communication is written, or has a permanent record, it is called "libel". When the communication does not have a permanent record, it is called "slander". Slander usually involves spoken defamation; however it can also include hand gestures or something similar. Since your concern relates to written material, we are concerned with libel and the general law of defamation.

To establish a defamation claim, three elements must be proven:

1.  the words complained of must be defamatory, in the sense that the words tend to lower the reputation of the other person in the community;

---

301-1665 Ellis Street
Kelowna, B.C. Canada V1Y 2B3

E-mail: shergill@pushormitchell.com
www.pushormitchell.com

Telephone: (250) 762-2108
Fax: (250) 762-5219

---

CARRERAS INTERIORS LTD.
Attention: Rafael Augusto Carrera
April 25, 2016                                                                              Page 2

2. the words are defamatory of the person claiming defamation; and
3. the words have been published to a third party.

A group of persons cannot be defamed as a class. The government also has no legal basis to bring legal proceedings for defamation.

If the three elements of defamation outlined above are established, a defamation claim can be made. However, there are multiple defences that could apply. The main defences are as follows:

1. justification (in other words, the comments are true or justified);
2. fair comment (specific rules apply to this category); and
3. privilege (that an established ground of privilege protects the communication).

## ANALYSIS

It is settled law that no action will lie for defaming the character of a dead person. The defamatory words must be made against the person claiming the defamation. Therefore, Rob Ford's family and friends cannot bring an action against you for your comments in your book, even if your words are determined to be defamatory.

Further, you took the step of fact-checking to ensure that any statements of fact about Rob Ford in the Excerpt are true. For facts that are true, the defence of "justification" would apply. The other statements in the Excerpt about Rob Ford are merely your opinion and would be protected as "fair comment". Fair comment on issues of public interest is not libel.

There is one paragraph, reproduced below (see underlining), where I believe there may be an incorrect statement of fact, or at minimum an exaggeration:

> ... Well, our ex-mayor Rob Ford was caught smoking crack and driving under the influence. He was caught in videos and guess what? _Nothing happened to him. He was not arrested and put in jail like any other citizen. He literally got away with murder_ and that is an insult and a slap in the face to all Canadians and a horrible example to the younger generation, our children and their future...

I would suggest that you review the above, simply because it is good practice to avoid excessive exaggerations or misstatement of facts.

CARRERAS INTERIORS LTD.
Attention: Rafael Augusto Carrera
April 25, 2016                                                    Page 3

## CONCLUSION

As indicated above, your comments about Rob Ford are not actionable because he is dead and he cannot make a claim in defamation. Even if this was not the case, you would be able to rely on the defence of "justification" or "fair comment".

Yours truly,

**PUSHOR MITCHELL LLP**

Per:

**PARVEEN K. SHERGILL**

/ard

## APPENDIX 2

Some selected personalities throughout history are considered under the following three categories: Positive World Leaders, Famous and Infamous Military Leaders, and Worst "Leaders" (Dictators and Genocide Perpetrators).

All three categories are presented by historical progression.

## Positive World Leaders

### Muhammad (Abu al-Qasim)
570-632
Arabian merchant, then revered preacher:
~stated he was the prophet and messenger of God
~preached that "God is only one" and demanded "complete surrender"
~gathered an army of 10,000 Muslims and marched on the city of Mecca.

### Confucius (Kong Qiu)
551-479 BC
Chinese politician, teacher and philosopher, father of Confucianism:
~strong advocate of family values, loyalty, and respect for elders
~"Do not do to others what you do not want done to yourself."

### Cleopatra VII Philopator (Cleopatra)
69-30 BC
Queen of ancient Egypt and last ruler of the Macedonian dynasty:
~her family ruled Egypt for over 100 years
~had ups and downs but was very influential as Egyptian ruler

*and in Rome through Julius Caesar and Marc Antony.*

## Johann Gutenberg
1398-1468
German blacksmith, goldsmith, printer and publisher:
*~invented the first mechanical moving parts for printing*
*~improved casting methods and efficiencies.*

## Queen Isabella I (Isabela de Castilla)
1451-1504
Spanish Queen and great leader, married to Ferdinand II de Aragon:
*~reorganized the government and reduced internal debt and crime rates in the country*
*~she financed the expeditions of Christopher Columbus.*

## Leonardo da Vinci
1452-1519
Italian mathematician, engineer, painter, inventor, sculptor, architect, writer, geologist, and cartographer:
*~designed flying machines, an armored tank, diving suit, a self-propelled machine, and many other inventions.*

## Michelangelo di Lodovico Buonarroti Simoni (Michelangelo)
1475-1564
Architect, poet, painter, engineer and sculptor:
*~sculptures and paintings are considered unmatched*
*~known for works like the statue of David, the Pieta, and the Genesis frescos in the Sistine Chapel.*

## Queen Elizabeth I (Elizabeth of England or The Virgin Queen)
1533-1603
Queen of England and Ireland:
*~daughter of Henry VIII and Anne Boleyn*
*~helped the English Renaissance theatre to flourish*

*~helped ensure that England remained Protestant*
*~a very charismatic personality throughout her rein.*

### Galileo Galilei
1564-1642
Italian mathematician, astronomer, and engineer:
*~main contribution was the Theory of Heliocentrism*
*~key leader of the scientific revolution of the time*
*~defended his theories against the Roman Inquisition.*

### Isaac Newton
1642-1726
English physicist and natural philosopher:
*~established the laws of motion and gravity*
*~developed prism theory of white light changing into different colors.*

### Peter the Great
1672-1725
Ruler of the Russian Empire:
*~ led a cultural revolution based on Enlightenment values of modern science-oriented systems.*

### Catherine the Great
1729-1796
Longest-ruling female leader of Russia:
*~born in Prussia and wife of Peter III*
*~ruled during the golden age of the Russian Empire*
*~protected the Russian nobility from the military.*

### Simon José Antonio de la Santisima Trinidad Bolivar y Palacios Ponte y Blanco (Simon Bolivar)
1783-1830
Venezuelan soldier and statesman who fought Spaniards for the freedom and independence of today's Panamá, Venezuela, Colombia, Ecuador, Perú and Bolivia:

~wrote the "Letter of Jamaica" in which Latin American ties with the Spanish monarchy were severed from Chile and Argentina all the way to Mexico
~known by many as "El Libertador" (The Liberator).

## Abraham Lincoln
1809-1865
American president who signed the Emancipation Proclamation:
~opposed the Mexican-American war
~abolished slavery and promoted fairness and equality.

## Henry Ford
1863-1947
Industrialist who founded the Ford Motor Company:
~pioneered mass-production of affordable cars in the 20th century
~developed a franchise system for automobile dealers.

## Alexander Graham Bell
1847-1922
Scientist, inventor, and engineer born in Scotland:
~awarded the first US patent for the invention of the telephone.

## Thomas Alva Edison
1847-1931
American businessman and inventor of the phonograph, light bulb, motion pictures, and many other technologies:
~inventor of principles of mass production, with 1093 patents in his name
~revolutionized the recording, mass communication, motion picture, electric, and utilities industries.

## Mohandas Karamchand Gandhi (Mahatma Gandhi)
1869-1948
Led India to liberation from the British Empire:

~known for his honesty, nonviolence, and truthfulness
~devoted to ending famine and advocating religious harmony
and civil rights
~considered "The Father of the Nation" in India.

## Winston Churchill
1875-1965
Prime minister of the United Kingdom:
~his strong will inspired British resistance until the defeat of
Nazi Germany during World War II.

## Khalil Gibran
1883-1931
World-renowned Lebanese-American poet and writer
~author of The Prophet, published in over 50 languages
~offered dogma-free universal spiritualism
~exhorted people to be non-judgmental
~admired by leaders around the world.

## Albert Einstein
1879-1955
German theoretical physicist and philosopher of science:
~originator of the general theory of relativity (Mass-energy
equivalence formula: $E=mc^2$)

## Franklin D. Roosevelt
1882-1945
32nd US president and outstanding political leader:
~won four consecutive presidential elections
~his program, the New Deal Coalition, defined American
liberalism and Democratic Party policies for the middle third of
the 20th century.

## Golda Meir
1898-1978
Fourth prime minister of Israel:

*~born in Russia from Jewish background, emigrated to the US
and then to Jerusalem in 1924.*
*~appointed Israel's ambassador to the Soviet Union*
*~formerly Minister of Labour and Foreign Minister*
*~elected Israel's prime minister in 1969, world's fourth woman
to hold such an office.*

**Indira Gandhi**
1917-1984
Second-longest-serving prime minister of India:
*~the only woman prime minister of this country*
*~fought to centralize power and known for being ruthless,
warring with Pakistan, and creating Bangladesh*
*~major contributor to India's current constitution.*

**Nelson Mandela**
1918- 2013
South African leader of anti-apartheid movement and first
president after apartheid:
*~tackled institutionalized racism, inequality, and poverty in
search of reconciliation.*

**Maria Eva Duarte de Peron (Evita)**
1919-1952
Argentina's first lady, married to President Juan Peron:
*~women's rights activist*
*~advocated for the poor and for quality health care for all.*

**Margaret Thatcher**
1925-2013
Leader of British Conservative party and United Kingdom's
first female prime minister:
*~introduced political and economic reforms and pulled Great
Britain out of recession*
*~privatized state-owned companies.*

## Martin Luther King Jr.
1929-1968
American activist and civil rights leader:
~*promoted civil rights for African-Americans through nonviolent civil disobedience*

## Mikhail Gorbachev
Born 1931
Russian general secretary of the Soviet Union Communist Party:
~*last Soviet leader before the formal dissolution of the Soviet Union.*

## Martha Helen Stewart (Martha Stewart)
Born 1941
American businesswoman, writer, publisher, and merchandiser, successful in broadcasting:
~*exposed her world with Martha Stewart Living magazine and TV show*
~*example of women entrepreneurship.*

## Sheikh Hasina Wazed
Born 1947
Prime minister of Bangladesh, born in Pakistan:
~*main contributor to Bangladesh independence*
~*advocate of democracy and freedom*
~*one of the most powerful women on earth (per Forbes list).*

## Albert Arnold Gore (known as Al Gore)
Born 1948
45th vice-president of the US (under President Bill Clinton):
~*philanthropist and politician, Harvard University graduate, environmental activist, and Nobel Peace Prize winner*
~*professor and speaker advocating climate protection worldwide.*

## Benazir Bhutto
1953-2017
Prime minister of Pakistan for two terms:
~promoted initiatives for Pakistan's economy through deregulation and greater flexibility in labour markets

## Oprah Winfrey
Born 1954
American media giant first recruited by a Chicago TV station:
~created The Oprah Winfrey show and the Oprah Winfrey network
~followed and admired worldwide.

## Angela Merkel
Born 1954
First female chancellor of Germany:
~formed a coalition government and was president of the European Council
~de facto leader of the European Union.

## Diana Spencer (Princess Diana of Wales)
1961-1997
English Princess of the British royal family and worldwide social figure:
~married Charles, Prince of Wales, and had two sons
~one of the first to support AIDS victims and abolition of land mines
~devoted to charities and goodwill around the world.

## Most Famous and Infamous Military Leaders

## Alexander the Great
356-323 BC
Ruler of ancient Greek kingdom of Macedonia:

*~tutored by Aristotle to be an ideal leader*
*~conquered the Persian empire, founded numerous cities*
*~considered by many as the greatest general and strategist that ever lived.*

## Julius Caesar
100-44 BC
Roman statesman and general:
*~built the unrivaled Roman Empire*
*~known to many as the best military general and commander in history.*

## William the Conqueror
1028-1087
First Norman ruler of England:
*~invaded England in 1066 and was crowned king.*

## Genghis Khan (the Great Khan)
1162-1227
Ruthless, relentless founder of the Mongol empire:
*~promoted religious tolerance*
*~conquered most of Eurasia (central Europe to the Sea of Japan).*

## Kublai Khan
1215-1294
Mongolian ruler over Korea and Mongolia, assumed role of Emperor of China
*~established the Yuan Dynasty.*

## Joan of Arc
1412-1431
Known as The Maid of Orleans, led French army in the Hundred Years' War against England
*~supported King Charles VII until his coronation*
*~captured by English and burned at the stake*
*~declared a martyr by Pope Callixtus III.*

## George Washington
1732-1799
First president of the United States:
~military leader of American Revolution, defeated the British
~ensured financial and economic strength of the new nation
~supervised the foundation of a great country.

## Napoleon Bonaparte
1769-1821
French military leader and politician:
~ended the French Revolution and created the Napoleonic Legal Code
~built a free, democratic republic and organized an excellent civil administration.

## Che Guevara
1928-1967
Argentine Marxist and revolutionary:
~fought the capitalist exploitation of Latin America by the US
~joined forces with Cuba and the Russians and commanded guerrilla-style movements.

## Worst Leaders (Dictators and Genocide Perpetrators)

## Hernán Cortés de Monroy y Pizarro
1485-1547
Spanish adventurer, conquistador, traitor, thief, sadist and cold-blooded killer:
~overthrew the Aztec empire
~massacred native Americans through betrayal, mass murder, chicken pox and measles
~ brought the spirit of the Spanish Inquisition with him to America.

## Ismail Enver
1881-1922
Leader of Turkish Ottoman Empire:
~ *instigator of the Armenian genocide*
*~motto: "All seeking to enrich those who do not work should be destroyed."*

## Leopold II of Belgium
1835-1909
Second king of Belgium:
*~used public force in Congo for his own gain by exploiting ivory and rubber*
*~enslaved, mutilated, and killed local people when quotas were not met.*

## Adolf Hitler
1889-1945
Chancellor and dictator of Germany
~ *dedicated to ethnic cleansing*
*~committed genocide of over 17 million people (including 5.5 million Jews).*

## Joseph Stalin
1878-1953
Leader of the Soviet Union for over 25 years:
*~during his control, Russia developed nuclear weapons shortly after the US*
*~befriended Mao Zedong and Kim Il-sung during the Cold War with the Western world*
*~a famous quote: "Death solves all problems—no man, no problem."*

## Josip Broz Tito
1892-1980
President of Yugoslavia:
*~established the Kingdom of Yugoslavia and joined the Communist party*

*~suppressed nationalism and promoted "Brotherhood and Unity," but Yugoslavia ultimately disintegrated anyway.*

## Mao Zedong
1893-1976
Chinese Communist revolutionary and ruthless dictator
*~anti-imperialist Chinese nationalist*
*~founder of the Communist Party of China*
*~agrarian policies led to the worst famine in human history.*

## Pol Pot
1925-1998
Cambodian Communist revolutionary who led the Khmer Rouge:
*~served as prime minister of Democratic Kampuchea*
*~absolute dictator who forced agrarian exploitation.*

## Idi Amin Dada
1925-2003
Ugandan ruler and president:
*~a criminal during his brutal nine-year regime*
*~destroyed Uganda's economy and consistently violated human rights.*

## Ta Mok
1926-2006
Khmer Rouge commander and Cambodian military chief:
*~created strong resistance against the French and Japanese*
*~leader of the national army of Democratic Kampuchea which earned him the title of "The Butcher"*
*~accused of war crimes against humanity.*

## Fidel Castro
Born 1926
Cuban president
*~created a leftist, anti-imperialist regime*
*~forged tight relations with the Soviet Union*

~secured Cuba's independence from the US
~abuser of many human rights and absolute dictator.

## Saddam Hussein
1937-2006
Ruler and president of Iraq, known as "The Butcher of Baghdad":
~put on trial for crimes against humanity
~found guilty, sentenced to death, and executed by hanging.

## Jean Kambanda
Born 1955
Prime minister of Rwanda:
~known as the only head of state that has pleaded guilty to genocide
~sentenced to life in prison by the International Criminal Tribunal of Rwanda for aiding and abetting genocide.

## Bashar al-Assad
Born 1965
President of Syria, graduated from medical school and later became physician:
~directly implicated in Syrian Civil War and crimes against humanity by the United Nations
~has pushed his own people to look for refugee status all around the world, with tens of thousands dying in the process
~provoked the destruction of ancient archeological sites.

## APPENDIX 3

Everyone has the right to aspire and achieve a better life, regardless of physical, mental, psychological, or any other type of disability. Some people, including those with disabilities, have had the courage and stamina to follow their dreams and even go against current or established traditions to achieve greatness in their specific fields. I humbly believe that when you try hard and play smart, anything can be done. However, we need to understand what we really want and where we are standing at a given time in our lives. We need to fully understand and accept our limitations and strengths, and we need to focus and be realistic about our situation (overall social and natural surroundings).

It is imperative to understand the depth and strength of our desires and always listen to our gut feelings. We must discover and understand what we really want and, when we do, try and live happy lives from that moment on. Above all, we must to take a large step forward, with an improved attitude, and dare big. We need to try harder and, if we slip and fail, get back on our feet, learn our lesson, and try again with better knowledge, keener strategy, stronger will, and a more focused and positive attitude.

The purpose of Appendix 3 is to give a few examples of amazing people who I personally believe have struggled in life with some disadvantages or obstacles compared to "average" people. I dare to put the word average in quotes, because the people contained in this appendix have been harder-working, more dedicated, risk-taking, adaptable, and skillful than the average person. Against all sorts of difficult odds, they have dared to try and achieve greatness along with the respect and admiration of the world that surrounds them. These wonderful people are strong, focused, resilient human beings who have sincerely dignified humankind.

The following people I truly admire for their accomplishments and for achieving success by overcoming, in some cases, almost overwhelming barriers, from physical obstacles to very difficult social conditions. They made outstanding achievements and went way beyond the call of duty, with relentless effort and sacrifice, to attain triumph in the way of international recognition and success. Some of them overcame fear and anxiety. At the beginning, and in the majority of cases, these first came along with a low self-esteem, which later was transformed into a sense of security and a strong self-esteem. I encourage readers to visit their websites.

## Roman Abramovich

Born in Russia, Abramovich's parents died when he was just four years old, so he was raised by family members. He used to sell toys from his apartment to support himself. He got involved in some controversial and disputed oil export deals and then took over the oil company called Sibneft in 1995. At 48 years old, he is considered to be the fifth richest person in Russia, with an estimated net worth of over 9.4 billion USD. He is also the owner of the Chelsea Football Club in the English Premier League. He is currently in the process of buying almost an entire city block in New York, where he wants to build his mansion.

biography.com/people/roman-arkadyevich-abramovich-13501148

therichest.com/celebnetworth/celebrity-business/men/roman-abramovich-net-worth/

---

## Jennifer Bricker

Jennifer was born in Romania and came into this world without her lower limbs—no legs. For unspecified reasons, her parents appeared to have been forced to abandoned her, but a couple from the United States (Gerald and Sharon Bricker) later adopted her and took her home to Oblong, Illinois. The Brickers had three sons of their own and decided to bring Jennifer up with the same discipline and principles. They encouraged her to try and do what she wanted. She chose gymnastics as one of her favorite sports and excelled in trampoline and tumbling. Jennifer was so dedicated and distinguished in the sport that she ended up winning state titles and even competed in the Junior Olympics. While she was growing up, Jennifer idolized a famous gymnast from the United States called Dominique Moceanu, who won an Olympic medal in the 1996 Summer Olympics Games in Atlanta, Georgia. Jennifer did not know that her hero was her own estranged sister from Romania. They ended up meeting and now have a close relationship. Jennifer Bricker presently works at Universal Studios in Hollywood as an aerial gymnast and performer.

dailymail.co.uk/news/article-2157021/Dominique-Moceanus-secret-sister-given-parents-born-legs.html

lifenews.com/2014/09/03/mother-was-forced-to-abandon-her-daughter-with-no-legs-now-shes-a-gymnast/

---

## Andrew Carnegie

Carnegie emigrated from Scotland to the United States with his parents at age 12 in 1847. They had very few pennies to rub together, so he had to immediately start working in a textile factory 12 hours a day. He then worked at a telegraph company, where he developed his professional skills and strong ambitions that helped him to achieve success in life. Hard work, focus, and risk-taking helped him to excel in anything he tried.

For Carnegie, opportunities were abundant. He added hard work, strong will, and the right attitude to take advantage of these opportunities. Carnegie once said:

> Man may be born in poverty, but he does not have to go through life in poverty. He may be illiterate, but he does not have to remain so. But no amount of opportunity will benefit the man who neglects or refuses to take possession of his own mind power and use it for his own personal advancement.

Years later, he incorporated Pittsburgh's Carnegie Steel Company, which he ended up selling to J.P. Morgan for over 12 billion dollars in today's money. Carnegie also founded Carnegie Hall in New York.

americaslibrary.gov/aa/carnegie/aa_carnegie_phil_1.html

biography.com/people/andrew-carnegie-9238756

## Jessica Cox

This amazing lady was born with no arms, but her relentless

spirit did not stop her from being the first licensed armless pilot in the world. She is also an avid Taekwondo black belt with an impressive strength of heart. She is a motivational speaker who has a degree in psychology from the University of Arizona.

rightfooted.com/

en.wikipedia.org/wiki/Jessica_Cox

## Celine Dion

Born in Canada from a French-Canadian background, Celine Dion was part of a family of 14 and struggled throughout her earlier years. A devoted and immensely gifted singer, Celine won five Grammy awards. She has record sales of over 200 million copies worldwide. As a successful entrepreneur and artist, she has accumulated an estimated 630 million+ USD with the help of her late manager and husband Mr. Rene Angelil. She sings mainly in French and English, but sometimes also in Italian, Spanish, Latin, Japanese, German, and even in Mandarin Chinese.

celinedion.com/ca/home

celineinvegas.com/

celebritynetworth.com/richest-celebrities/singers/celine-dion-net-worth/

## Mia Hamm

Mia Hamm is a retired professional soccer player who scored more goals internationally than any other player in the history of soccer (male or female). Hamm mainly played as a forward for the United States women's national soccer team. She was also a founding member of the Washington Freedom (American professional soccer club based in the Washington, DC). She has been a real inspiration to athletes of both sexes due to her relentless strength, stamina, and, above all, conviction. According to various sources she was born with a clubfoot. After several operations, she spent many years in casts while allowing her foot to heal. She then trained exhaustively, which allowed her to improve and dominate women's soccer. She was ultimately chosen as one of FIFA's best players by Pelé himself (the famous Brazilian soccer player).

miafoundation.org/

biography.com/people/mia-hamm-16472547

## Patrick Henry Hughes

Patrick Henry Hughes, from Louisville, Kentucky, was born with no eyes due to a disease known as anophthalmia, an extremely rare disorder strongly related to genetic abnormalities. He was also born with hip dysplasia and has been unable to stretch his arms and legs. His father introduced him to the piano when he was only nine months old, and he has been playing piano (and other instruments) ever since.

patrickhenryhughes.com/

en.wikipedia.org/wiki/Patrick_Henry_Hughes

## Shahid Khan

One of the richest men in the United States, Shahid immigrated to the US from Pakistan. He started by washing dishes, but he currently owns the Jacksonville Jaguars of the National Football League (NFL) and an automobile parts manufacturing facility in Urbana, Illinois, called Flex-N-Gate, plus other companies. It is calculated that his net worth is over 4.5 billion USD. From a Muslim middle class family in Pakistan, he went to the USA and studied at the University of Illinois, where he graduated with a Bachelor of Science degree in industrial engineering. From washing dishes for a meagre wage, he climbed his way up by means of vision, hunger, focused dreams, and a strong work ethic. Shahid Khan is a professional to be admired and acknowledged for his entrepreneurial achievements. For more information, refer to:

jaguars.com/team/management/shad-khan.html

jacksonville.com/sports/football/jaguars/2011-12-03/story/shahid-khan-has-true-rags-riches-american-story

## Stephen King

King is an amazing writer with a fascinating and wild imagination. The iconic thriller Carrie was his first book. It was rejected about 30 times, so he ultimately gave up and threw it in the trash, where his wife picked it out and encouraged him to submit it again. This time, it was accepted, published, and turned out to be his first successful book of many to come. With an amazing, prolific mind, King has written suspense, thrillers, horror, supernatural, fantasy, and other genres.

stephenking.com/

biography.com/people/stephen-king-9365136

## Jan Koum

Jan Koum is the founder of WhatsApp. At one time, he was living on food stamps on a social support program in Mountain View, California. He was born in Kiev, Ukraine, from a Jewish background. He graduated in computer engineering and became an Internet entrepreneur with an app that is now used all over the world. He sold his company, which he started from scratch, for 19 billion dollars to Facebook. At just 38 years old, his personal net worth is over 7 billion USD.

His partner Brian Acton made a cool 3.8 billion USD in that sale for his 20 per cent shares. Brian applied to Twitter and Facebook for a job years earlier, and both companies turned him down. Facebook would have spent a lot less money if they had hired him instead. Go figure!

mashable.com/2014/02/20/whatsapp-jan-koum-career/

business.financialpost.com/fp-tech-desk/how-whatsapp-co-founder-jan-koum-went-from-food-stamps-to-a-us19b-deal-with-facebook?__lsa=56a1-5721

## Todd Love

Todd Love is a Marine corporal in his early 20s who lost both legs and an arm in an Afghanistan explosion. He is a war hero and an amazing individual who knows no fear and has no barriers to stop him in anything he decides to do or venture in. He has bigger soul, spirit, and "cojones" than over 99 per cent of earth's population, no doubt!

He is a very active and daring individual who practices skydiving, snow skiing, water skiing, surfing, participate in marathons, practice gymnastics, ride a horse, play piano, etc., He is also known to have struggle a crocodile.

dailymail.co.uk/news/article-1375803/Hundreds-turn-Marine-Corporal-Todd-Love.html#ixzz2KGLdoQII

dailymail.co.uk/news/article-1375803/Hundreds-turn-Marine-Corporal-Todd-Love.html

## Jack Ma

Ma has become China's richest man, with an estimated 25 billion USD by December, 2014. He was born in Hangzhou, Zhejiang Province, China. He did his entire undergraduate and graduate studies in China and later visited the United States to better understand Internet marketing. He then returned to his hometown of Hangzhou where, with 17 friends and his wife, he started a company called Alibaba, that in a short time grew exponentially to surpass, by far, companies like E-Bay in the United States.

forbes.com/sites/parmyolson/2014/09/30/how-jerry-yang-made-the-most-lucrative-bet-in-tech-history/

cnbc.com/id/102173940

## Liz Murray

Born in the Bronx, New York, Liz lost her parents to drug addiction and AIDS. At age 15, she had to take care of herself and her sister. She turned her life around by taking advantage of what was given to her in the way of scholarships. She never gave up and, with her relentless spirit and desire to succeed in life, was accepted by Harvard University, despite being homeless earlier in life. She is the founder and director of Manifest Living, which is a motivational company that focuses on empowering and motivating those looking to change their lives for the better. She is a well-known speaker focused on enabling and allowing adults to achieve what they want in life.

theglobeandmail.com/life/liz-murray-shares-her-tale-of-life-from-homeless-to-harvard/article1314532/

washingtonspeakers.com/speakers/speaker.cfm?SpeakerId=3821

## Francois Pinault

Francois Pinault is a French businessman with a keen eye for collecting art. He was teased so much at school for being poor that he dropped out and started working at a very early age just to survive. Eventually he founded a company called Pinault-Printemps-Redoute (PPR), which managed to get ownership of international brand names such as Yves Saint Laurent, Gucci, Stella McCartney, and others. His net worth is estimated to be over 11 billion USD. He is considered to be the 67th richest person in the world by Forbes magazine. Not bad for a school dropout!

kering.com/en/group/biography/francois-henri_pinault

zonebourse.com/barons-bourse/Francois-Pinault-10/biographie/

## Sidney Poitier

According to an article on the BBC, after his first audition, the casting director asked Poitier, "Why don't you stop wasting people's time and go out and become a dishwasher or something?" But Poitier had other plans and, with a lot of pride, effort, and sacrifice, went ahead to win an Oscar years later and be considered one Hollywood's best actors.

biography.com/people/sidney-poitier-9443345

cbsnews.com/pictures/celebs-who-went-from-failures-to-success-stories/7/

## Nando Parrado

On October 13,1972, Uruguayan Air Force Flight 571 crashed into the South American Andes mountain range. Nando was one of the 16 survivors who recovered from the gruesome experience that almost cost him his life. He overcame his trauma and is now known as a successful speaker who wrote a bestseller called Miracle in the Andes. He has written and given speeches about unlocking one's own potential and excellence not just in the workplace but in everyday life.

parrado.com/

en.wikipedia.org/wiki/Nando_Parrado

## J.K. Rowling

This bestselling author was very poor before she wrote her Harry Potter novels. She depended on welfare to support herself and her child. She is now a very successful woman and one of the richest in the world. Ms. Rowling is a woman with absolute focus, proud of what she does and confident of herself and her potential. The Potter series of books gained worldwide attention and positioning. They have won multiple awards and have sold more than 400 million copies worldwide. Her estimated net worth is over 1 billion USD.

biography.com/people/jk-rowling-40998

businessinsider.com/jk-rowling-harry-potter-play-2015-6

## Li Ka-shing

Li Ka-shing's family fled mainland China for Hong Kong, where they tried to make a living. His father died when Li Ka-shing was barely 15 years of age, so Li had no choice but to go to work to support his family.

Eventually he managed to start his own company called Cheung Kong Industries, which was involved in the manufacturing of plastic parts. He then switched into real estate and has become the richest man in Asia, with an estimated net worth of over 31 billion USD. He is considered to be a quite generous philanthropist, who has donated over 1 billion USD. He entered the Vancouver real estate market and bought precious land where others did not dare to invest. He built modern skyscraper condominiums, and it is said that he more than tripled his investment in the False Creek and Yaletown areas.

stmichaelshospital.com/knowledgeinstitute/

businessinsider.com/the-life-of-li-ka-shing-2015-3?op=1

lksf.org/

## Stephen Spielberg

This celebrated director is a true visionary, entrepreneur, and risk taker. Spielberg was rejected by the University of Southern California School of Theater, Film, and Television three times. He eventually attended school at another location, only to drop out and become a director before finishing school. Thirty-five years after starting his degree, Spielberg returned to school in 2002 to finally complete his work and earn his BA. He started out by directing programs such as Rod Serling's Night Gallery and the famous TV series, Columbo. He has directed some of the most famous and successful films in Hollywood. Among the most important are Raiders of the Lost Ark, E.T. (Extra Terrestrial), and Indiana Jones and the Temple of Doom. He also directed The Color Purple. He then continued with the rest of the Indiana Jones movies (The Last Crusade and the Kingdom of the Crystal Skull). Among his most famous films are the Jurassic Park series and Schindler's List. Others include Deep Impact, Poltergeist, Men in Black, Twister, The Mask of Zorro, Amistad, etc.

nytimes.com/movies/person/112325/Steven-Spielberg/biography

biography.com/people/steven-spielberg-9490621


## Miles Stojkoski

Miles Stojkoski was born in 1965 in the Republic of Macedonia. He was always into sports until he had a motorcycle accident that severed his spinal cord, rendering him a paraplegic, which has impaired all movement of his lower extremities. Since then, he has had to surmount extremely difficult physical, emotional, and psychological barriers, but he has succeeded and has placed himself on the map of relentless and admirable people with a strong desire of living fully while setting an example for others with disabilities. He is currently a long-distance marathoner.

milestojkoski.com

en.wikipedia.org/wiki/Mile_Stojkoski

## Nick James Vujicic

This Serbian-Australian motivational speaker was born with a syndrome called Tetra-Amelia Syndrome. This is an autosomal recessive congenital disorder, a very rare condition in which a newborn has no legs or arms. Only a few families worldwide have ever reported this syndrome. Vujicic is the author of books called Unstoppable and The Incredible Power of Faith in Action.

jotrachel-christian.blogspot.ca/2011/03/nicholas-james-vujicic-man-of-hope.html

en.wikipedia.org/wiki/Nick_Vujicic

## Liu Wei

Liu Wei is a disabled Chinese pianist who lost both arms at the age of 10 while playing hide and seek, having accidentally touched high-voltage wires. He was unconscious for 45 days, and when he woke up, his life had completely changed forever. At age 23, he was introduced to the world after winning the program called China's Got Talent by playing piano. He is a real inspiration for his strong will and unique spirit.

china.org.cn/video/2012-02/14/content_24630732.htm

en.wikipedia.org/wiki/Liu_Wei_(pianist)

## Oprah Winfrey

Born into a poor family in Mississippi, Oprah has always had strong working values with a positive and altruistic attitude. She moved to Chicago after earning a scholarship at Tennessee State University. She worked for a time with a talk show and years later started what would become The Oprah Winfrey Show. From nothing, she grew up to be above and beyond the frontiers of fame, respect, and wealth. She is a role model who has influenced societies around the world.

Oprah is admired by all her fans for her hard work, ethics, and dedication to improve people's ways of living, morals, self-esteem, and overall well-being. She is so well known and highly regarded in her country, that many people in the United States want her to be a contender for the presidency of their country after President Donald Trump's term is over in 2020.

imdb.com/name/nm0001856/bio
oprah.com/index.html

**APPENDIX 4**

## Brief Biography of the Author

Born and raised in Mexico City (D.F.) from 1958 to 1987, Rafael Carreras studied for his undergraduate degree in Economics (Mexico City) followed by a Master of Business Administration (MBA) in a joint program between Notre Dame University (USA) and the London Graduate School of Business (England).

His professional career started as a professor in economics and finance in the Mexican banking system. He immigrated to Canada in 1987, where he concentrated on the creation and promotion of businesses under the 'turnkey operation' concept. He assisted the Ministry of Economic Development at the time and created a database for businesses in the service industry for the BC provincial government.

In conjunction with government and banking programs, he worked to assist foreign business investors and local entrepreneurs establish and run a successful business. He assisted his various clients throughout their business start-up stage in trying to achieve their break-even point in the shortest and most efficient time possible, while trying to minimize their risks and expand their potential.

Carreras has acquired extensive professional experience in North America (Mexico, United States and Canada) and has travelled considerably for business and research throughout Europe, Asia and the American continent. As a researcher and writer, he is detailed and always tries to apply a logical and critical thinking to his overall framework and presentation.

<u>As an Author</u>:

His passion for writing is fuelled by the desire to open people's eyes to what is happening around them. He trusts this will improve their lifestyle and bring harmony to their lives. Throughout his "Runaway Trilogy", an important goal is to bring awareness regarding the delicate situation Planet Earth is going through. He wants to share his experience and points of view for others to learn and benefit from the way he perceives this world and its progressive changes. As an author, he does not try to change people's views. Backed by real life experience and scientific evidence, his main goal is to create awareness of the situations our societies and surroundings are undergoing. It is up to the readers to make an informed decision and act wisely. Motivated by trust and hard work, the author hopes his readers see their reality in a different light, and perhaps, cause them to protect their society, environment, and ecosystem above and beyond the search for money and power.

Carreras does his best to experience life from a realistic, responsible, and pragmatic perspective. This trilogy has been written with a down-to-earth and rational approach for anyone to understand and apply to improve their lifestyle if they choose to do so. All his groundwork, structure and conclusions are based on existing research platforms of well-known authors, scientists, book and magazine publications, newspapers, and the web. All this is backed by extensive travel experience and systematic evaluation. He is observant and detailed-oriented, trying always to uncover the truth, with a humble and respectful approach in spirit and to the best of his abilities.

# INDEX